The Political
Uses of Symbols

LONGMAN PROFESSIONAL STUDIES IN POLITICAL COMMUNICATION AND POLICY

Editorial Advisor: Jarol B. Manheim

Robert E. Drechsel   *News Making in the Trial Courts*

Charles D. Elder and Roger W. Cobb   *The Political Uses of Symbols*

Myles Martel   *Political Campaign Debates: Images, Strategies, and Tactics*

Brian Weinstein   *The Civic Tongue: Political Consequences of Language Choices*

Forthcoming:

Doris A. Graber   *Processing the News: How People Tame the Information Tide*

The Political Uses of Symbols

Charles D. Elder
Wayne State University

Roger W. Cobb
Brown University

New York & London

The Political Uses of Symbols

Longman Inc., 1560 Broadway, New York, N.Y. 10036
Associated companies, branches, and representatives
throughout the world.

Developmental Editor: Irving E. Rockwood
Editorial and Design Supervisor: Joan Matthews
Production Supervisor: Ferne Y. Kawahara
Manufacturing Supervisor: Marion Hess

Table 1.3 is reprinted from Louis Harris. *The Harris
Survey*. New York: The Tribune Company Syndicate,
Inc. October 22, 1981. By permission.

Table 1.4 is based on material from Jack Citrin,
"Comment: The Political Relevance of Trust in
Government," *American Political Science Review*,
vol. 68, 1974, and Bruce Campbell, *The American
Electorate*, New York: Holt, Rinehart and Winston, 1979.
By permission.

Table 5.1 is reprinted from Martin Plissner and Warren
Mitofsky, "Political Elites," *Public Opinion*,
October/November 1981, p. 49. Copyright 1981 by the
American Enterprise Institute. By permission of the
copyright holder.

Library of Congress Cataloging in Publication Data

Elder, Charles D.
    The political uses of symbols.

    (Longman professional studies in political
communication and policy)
    Bibliography: p.
    Includes index.
    1. Communication in politics. 2. Signs and symbols.
I. Cobb, Roger W. II. Title. III. Series.
JA74.E39 1983   320'.0141   82–12722
ISBN 0-582-28392-2
ISBN 0-582-28393-0 (pbk.)

Manufactured in the United States of America

To Allison and Andy,
with the hope that they will find politics as intriguing as we;

and to

the transportation system of America,
without which this project would have never been completed.

Contents

Figures and Tables

FIGURES

TABLES

Foreword

In this book, Charles Elder and Roger Cobb review and extend recent theory on the role and importance of symbols as a basis for political activity. Readers familiar with the work of such scholars as Lasswell, Sapir, and Edelman will find *The Political Uses of Symbols* to be sympathetic in its point of view with these earlier efforts, but more constructively taxonomic and more rigorously empirical in its argument. As a result, the book constitutes both a solid introduction to the concepts of symbolic interaction in politics and a significant, indeed, the next logical, step forward for the literature.

Beginning from several extended examples, the authors systematically explore the relationships between symbols and a variety of psychological and sociological aspects of the political process. Included in this analysis are affect, cognition, political culture and cultural change, mobilization, conflict definition (and relational definition generally), and social aggregation and differentiation, to name only a few. The organization and thoroughness of Elder and Cobb's argument and its grounding in the several relevant areas of social science literature give to this book a fundamental soundness and utility. The authors' emphasis on empirical reasoning and evidence, and their ability to develop and build upon a synthesis of early and more contemporary work, impart to *The Political Uses of Symbols* a sense of forward movement that merits the attention of all students of politics.

The books in this series are intended to illuminate the institutional and theoretical foundations of communication as political phenomena. In their treatment of symbols as the currency of political activity, its primary medium of exchange, Professors Elder and Cobb clearly contribute to the achievement of this goal.

Jarol B. Manheim

Preface

Much of politics revolves around symbols. Yet save for the pioneering work of Murray Edelman, relatively little systematic attention has been given to explicating the role that symbols play in the political process. Through this book, we hope to contribute to a fuller understanding of that role. In the course of the book, we attempt to develop a perspective that not only illuminates the social and individual functions of political symbols, but also serves to show how the study of political symbols can contribute to our understanding of the basic dynamics that sustain a political system and structure its concerns. In developing our arguments, we have drawn upon and sought to integrate a wide variety of social science research. In doing so, we have sought to demonstrate how the study of political symbols can inform, as well as be informed by, systematic empirical inquiry.

Our study begins with a survey of some of the ways political symbols are used. While acknowledging the potential for abuse inherent in the political uses of symbols, we suggest that it is also important to recognize the positive and necessary functions they serve. To understand these functions, we argue that it is necessary to inquire into the nature of popular involvement in the political process and into how people, individually and collectively, relate to political symbols. Such inquiry suggests that symbols not only provide a vital link between the individual and the larger social order but also serve to structure the politics of a community. It also suggests that popular vulnerability to manipulation through symbols is limited by a number of factors, to include the problems of credible symbol usage and the constraints imposed by the political culture.

Throughout the book, we made extensive use of contemporary examples to illustrate our arguments. We also make extensive use of data from national polls conducted by major survey research organizations. We would like to acknowledge the Center for Political Studies/Survey Research Center at the University of Michigan, in particular, for the data they have made available.

As our thinking about the political uses of symbols has evolved, we have profited much from the insights and criticisms of others. Like most of our contemporaries, we owe a profound intellectual debt to Murray Edelman, a man we scarcely know, but whose work has contributed much to our understanding of politics. We are also indebted to Professors Marc Ross, Jennie Keith, and Jarol Manheim, both for their encouragement of the project and for their detailed criticisms of earlier drafts of the manuscript. We are also grateful to Irving Rockwood for his encouragement and helpful suggestions.

Like several other projects that we have collaborated on in the past, this book is the product of a totally joint effort. We planned, wrote, and rewrote the manuscript together and jointly bear responsibility for any errors it may contain. In our previous work together, we have listed our names alphabetically. Here, we continue that practice but use first names instead of last. In this case, as in our previous work, the ordering of authors' names is totally arbitrary.

We would like to thank Chris Dobrovich for her assistance, good humor, and skill in helping to prepare the final manuscript. We also would like to thank Professor Eric Nordlinger and Gail Gresser for the support they provided to help us complete the manuscript. Finally, we would like to thank Elizabeth Elder, whose patience, support, and encouragement were essential ingredients in the completion of this project.

Charles D. Elder
Roger W. Cobb

The Political
Uses of Symbols

1

Symbolic Basis of Politics

The important role that symbols play in political life was recognized years ago by Lasswell et al., (1965), Arnold (1962), and others (Sapir, 1934; Merriam, 1964; Boulding, 1961; Lasswell and Kaplan, 1950). Only recently, however, has the weight of these early insights come to be widely appreciated. This resurgence of interest has been sparked largely by the provocative work of Murray Edelman (1964, 1971, and 1975). Perhaps more than any other theorist, Edelman has succeeded in showing the pervasive and profound importance of symbols in politics. His work has not only stimulated further study of the use of symbols (e.g., Kautsky, 1965; Nimmo, 1974) but has also served to illuminate a number of major concerns of contemporary political science; e.g., public opinion, political behavior, and public policy.

Through the study of the symbolic aspects of politics, one gains insight into both the logic of collective action and the dynamics of political behavior. Symbols serve to link the individual to the larger political order and to syncronize the diverse motivations of different individuals, making collective action possible. Because of this, symbols are vital to the operations of the political system. In the chapters that follow, we will explore the important functions that symbols perform and the peculiar properties that allow them to serve these functions. The perspective that we offer suggests that politics is best understood as neither a rational nor an irrational process. Rather, it is more appropriately regarded are *arational.*

Rationality implies that political actions and evaluations are the product of consistent preferences, logical analysis, and abundant information. Irrationality, on the other hand, presupposes that political actions and reactions are based on emotional impulses and blind prejudices that defy logic and that are insensitive to fact. Elements of both are found in politics, but political actions and reactions are seldom the product of unitary preferences or stable prejudices, systematic analysis or pure impulse, abundant information or blind faith. Instead, they arise from a loosely structured process of interpreting fragmentary information and ambiguous cues in the light of prior expectations and changing, uncertain, or conflicting personal preferences. To illustrate what we mean, consider the following episodes from contemporary American politics.

THREE CASES OF SYMBOLIC POLITICS

Race Relations and Equality of Opportunity

The U.S. Supreme Court decision on school desegregation in 1954 marked the beginning of a new era in the struggle of black Americans for their civil rights. The decision not only affirmed the basic "rightness" of their cause but heightened the expectation of equal treatment and set in motion forces that were to elevate race relations to a prominent position on the agenda of American politics. The issues involved aroused passions and sparked conflicts that have yet to be fully and satisfactorily resolved. The recognition of one demand seemed to precipitate another, as black Americans grew ever more insistent on the full benefits of citizenship and full participation in the social and economic life of the polity.

Although the civil rights movement encountered severe resistance, by the early 1960s a majority of Americans had come to endorse many of its goals, despite strong reservations about the movement itself. At the urging of President Kennedy and the subsequent prodding of President Johnson, Congress passed legislation in 1964 and in 1965 that was heralded as a historic turning point in American race relations. Despite this legislation, black demands persisted; and America became accustomed to the fear of "long hot summers." Rather than resolving grievances, positive governmental responses seemed to accentuate for many blacks the gap between promise and reality. While blacks made substantial gains in social and economic well-being, their gains were outpaced by improvement in the standards of living enjoyed by whites. In absolute terms, the disparity between blacks and whites in material well-being actually widened (Watts and Free, 1973).

Although a majority of Americans continued to embrace the goal of integration and to accept most of the changes that had occurred, a growing number of people became disenchanted with the tactics being used and resentful of the pace of change. By 1968, a sizable majority (65%) had come to see civil rights leaders as unreasonable in their demands for change (Dawson, 1973, p. 42). A majority (54%) felt that government was pushing integration too fast, a sentiment expressed by only 30% of the population in 1964 (Skolnick, 1969, p. 144). Lemon (1970) reports that by the end of the decade, a near majority of middle Americans (whites with annual incomes between $5000 and $15,000) had come to see blacks as getting preferential treatment at their expense. Although it is impossible to square this view with the facts, many middle Americans were convinced that blacks now had a better chance to get ahead than they did; and they resented it (Lemon, 1970, pp. 66–67). This growing resentment found expression in 1968 in the candidacies of George Wallace (Pettigrew, 1971, pp. 231–251) and Richard Nixon (Lubell, 1971, p. 60).

The election of 1968 was probably "as sharply polarized along racial lines as at any time during American history" (Converse et al., 1969, p. 1085). The Survey Research Center estimates that some 97% of black voters in the nation cast their ballots for Humphrey, while less than 35% of white voters did so (Converse et al., 1969, p. 1085). With the election of Richard Nixon, the federal government retreated to a policy of "benign neglect." However, blacks continued to press their demands for a fuller share of American life, relying heavily on the courts and administrative agencies to consolidate and to extend their previous victories. Racial issues indexed by such symbols as "school busing," "open housing," and "affirmative action" became stable fare in American politics, even as the civil rights movement began to fragment and to slip from national prominence. Racial polarization became a persistent feature of American presidential politics with Democratic candidates receiving an overwhelming majority of black support and Republicans, a consistent majority of white support in every Presidential election from 1968 to 1980. During this same time, however, racial intolerance and white opposition to the principles of black integration into the mainstream of American life steadily diminished (Erikson et al., 1980, pp. 38–42).

It is apparent that throughout this continuing controversy, blacks and whites have tended to have different perceptions of the realities and of the promise of American life. Particularly after the major national efforts of the mid-1960s, many whites came to see past injustices as largely rectified. Thus, despite growing sympathy for the "legitimate" aspirations of black Americans, many whites have become increasingly resentful of further black demands. "While most Americans favor equal rights and opportunity, they overwhelmingly reject the use of conventional affirmative action and preferential treatment to achieve them" (Lipset and Schneider, 1977, PART IV, p. 1). With the removal of legal barriers to black participation in American politics and in the economic and social life of the community, most considered the promise of equality and opportunity to be redeemed. For a disproportionate number of blacks, however, poverty, unemployment, and deprivation have continued to make a mockery of that promise. Despite more than a quarter-century of attention and concern, the gap between whites and blacks in material achievement remains. "Equality" and "discrimination" are the watchwords of the controversy, but it is not simply a matter of promoting one and purging the other. It is a question of what these symbols mean. We will explore this question in subsequent chapters. The point we would

note here is that such questions are not matters of rationality or of irrationality but of social construction and adaptation, an arational process
that goes to the heart of politics.

Welfare Reform and Guaranteed Annual Income

In a nationally televised speech on August 8, 1969, President Nixon proposed sweeping reforms of the nation's welfare system. He called for the
enactment of a Family Assistance Plan (FAP) to replace many of the existing, heavily criticized welfare programs. He suggested that his plan
would break the "cycle of welfare dependency" and restore a semblance
of family stability to the "working poor." The plan called for federal cash
supplements to families whose earnings fell below the poverty line, provided that the head of household would accept job training or a job.

   The plan was, in effect, a modest version of a "negative income tax"
or a "guaranteed annual income," although this was explicitly denied by
Nixon in his presentation of his program. Such schemes had been endorsed by both liberal and conservative social and economic theorists.
The original proposal would have guaranteed an income floor of $1600 a
year for a family of four. This figure was subsequently raised to $2400. It
was estimated that well over a million persons, mostly white and largely
Southern, would be added to the welfare rolls by this plan at an additional cost to the federal government of around $4 billion a year (Lubell,
1973, p. 94). In presenting the plan, President Nixon emphasized its
work-incentive features, suggesting that it was really "workfare" not
"welfare." Although the immediate effect would be to increase federal
welfare spending, he held forth the plan's potential to lift families out of
poverty into "self-sufficiency."

   As Congress took up the proposal in late 1969, a national survey by
Harris found 78% of those polled in favor of the Nixon welfare program
(Lamb, 1974, p. 187). The plan encountered considerable opposition in
Congress, but Nixon continued to push for its passage. It was the lead
item in a package of legislative proposals set forth in his 1971 State of the
Union Address that called for a "New American Revolution." Congressional opposition continued to come from those who felt the program was
either too modest or too radical. As Congress delayed, the President
quietly abandoned FAP.

   1972 was, of course, an election year. One of the issues attracting the
greatest attention during the campaigns of that year was welfare reform.
Interestingly, the focus of concern was not FAP, but one of several proposals offered for welfare reform by Senator George McGovern. In an
almost offhanded way, he had suggested a guaranteed annual income of
$1000 per person as part of a negative income tax scheme. The idea was
new only in that it offered a simplified way of administering a guaranteed
income floor. Instead of an elaborate bureaucracy to determine and

police eligibility, families and individuals would receive $1000 per person. The money going to people with incomes above the minimum level would be recovered through their normal income tax payments. Although little notice was given to McGovern's suggestion when it was first made, it attracted considerable publicity when attacked by Hubert Humphrey during the June California primary campaign for the Democratic presidential nomination. Just as Humphrey had ridiculed the McGovern plan as costly and unfair, Nixon capitalized on the issue during the fall campaign. The McGovern proposal was portrayed as unworkable, "un-American," and offensive to traditional conceptions of distributive justice.

"He wants to take our money and give it to the colored who won't work," "Where's he going to get all of those thousand dollar bills?" (Lubell, 1973, p. 93), and "What would Howard Hughes need a thousand dollars for?" (Lamb, 1974, p. 189) were typical of the contemptuous reactions of many to McGovern's plan. Despite the similarity between McGovern's proposal and Nixon's warmly received FAP, many people simply could not understand "giving everyone $1000 whether he needs it or not" (Lamb, 1974, p. 189). The Nixon campaign played upon these concerns and exploited this confusion. "The amount of attention the issue received suggested that, if the 1972 voters were voting against any specific policy, they were against McGovern's proposal for welfare reform" (Lamb, 1974, p. 189). It was simply not the kind of proposal Americans expect of a man of "Presidential caliber."

The McGovern plan would have guaranteed $4000 a year for a family of four, compared with only $1600 for a family of four (subsequently revised upward to $2400) under the Nixon proposal, and it lacked explicit work incentives. However, it is difficult to believe that the vastly differing public responses to the two proposals can be explained in terms of these differences. "Actually, on no issue were the two candidates closer in their expressed views. It had been Nixon, in fact, who first proposed that the 'working poor'—families whose earnings fell below the poverty line—be given cash supplements" (Lubell, 1973, pp. 93–94).

Public opinion polls taken during this period did not show that Americans had suddenly become averse to helping the poor or even that they had become more niggardly. "More than 7 out of 10 . . . were at least in favor of maintaining the present level of spending on welfare" (Watts and Free, 1973, p. 173), and the alternative that evoked the widest public support for aiding the poor was a federally guaranteed family income (Watts and Free, 1973, pp. 173–174). Moreover, "if a guaranteed income plan were to be adopted, slightly more than one-half (51%) of the public thought that the amount the government should assure a family of four should be at least $100 a week or $5200 per year . . ." (Watts and Free, 1973, p. 175).

Thus, we are stuck with an apparent anomaly. Two candidates, both of whom can be regarded as proponents of innovative yet cognate policies, are popularly perceived as poles apart. One is greeted with ridicule and contempt, while the other is applauded. Clearly, it would seem that a "rose by any other name" does not smell so sweet. How an idea is presented and by whom makes a difference. By invoking a frame of reference emphasizing positive symbols and traditional values, Nixon's "presidential" proposal wins acclaim. Lacking that frame of reference and the imprimatur of presidential authority, McGovern's plan becomes an albatross around his neck. That people rely on familiar cues and the status of the communicator to evaluate the merits of an idea may not be rational; but given that they often have limited information and little reason to search for more, it is not exactly irrational either. This arational mode of coping undoubtedly has its costs. However, it does not necessarily preclude innovation. It does require that innovation be framed in symbols that reflect sensitivity to popular values and beliefs. How this is done and why it is important are matters that we will consider more fully in the chapters that follow.

Presidential Popularity and Kennedy Charisma

As with most Presidents, popular approval of Jimmy Carter's performance began to decline almost from the time he took office. During his first year, he managed to maintain majority approval; but by the middle of 1978, his popular approval ratings as recorded by Gallup had dipped to less than 40%, with more people disapproving than approving of the job he was doing. Although his popularity was to rebound somewhat in the fall of 1978 following his success in bringing about the Camp David Agreement between Egypt and Israel, disenchantment with his leadership continued to grow.

Although it was known that Carter planned to seek a second term, speculation began to surface among his fellow Democrats about alternative candidates for the Presidency in 1980. Some held out the hope that Vice President Mondale would seek the nomination, but it was generally conceded that Mondale would not challenge the President. Since no one expected that the President would simply step aside, speculation centered on Senator Edward (Ted) Kennedy, carrier of the Kennedy legacy and leading spokesman for the liberal wing of the Democratic Party. However, Kennedy denied any interest in challenging President Carter. He repeatedly indicated that he expected Carter to be renominated and that he intended to support him.

Carter's fortunes steadily waned during the early months of 1979; and by July, Gallup found that twice as many people disapproved as approved of the way he was handling his job. Pressure mounted for Kennedy to challenge the President for the 1980 Democratic nomination. Polls consistently showed him to be preferred by a substantial margin over Carter among both Democratic Party identifiers and independents.

They also showed Kennedy to be the strongest candidate that the Democrats could field against likely Republican Party nominees. Although Kennedy continued to disavow any intentions of seeking the nomination, draft-Kennedy movements led by disgruntled Democrats began to spring up around the country. Kennedy disassociated himself from these efforts; but he did not repudiate them forcefully, feeding suspicions that he might run. With Carter's popular standing hovering at historic lows and with more than 20 draft-Kennedy committees pleading for him to rescue the Democratic Party from sure electoral disaster, Kennedy indicated that he was reconsidering his position. By the end of September, it was clear that he intended to run.

In mid-October, three weeks prior to Kennedy's formal entry into the race, Gallup found Kennedy the overwhelming choice among Democrats as their party's nominee for President. He led Carter by a 60–30 percent margin. Following the formal announcement of his candidacy, Kennedy's lead among Democrats slipped 11 points; but he still held a commanding 55–36 percent margin. His lead among independents was more modest but still impressive at 50–37 percent. (*Gallup Opinion Index*, January, 1980, p. 9). Although the race seemed a mismatch, Carter and his staff seemed to revel in Kennedy's challenge and remained confident that they would, in the words of the President, "whip his ass."

Particularly in light of the expectations fostered by the mystique that had grown up around Kennedy and his family name, his campaign got off to a lackluster start. By the time he announced his candidacy, some 66 campaign committees throughout the nation were working for his nomination. However, he lacked the well-organized and centrally coordinated campaign organization that Carter had built in 1976 and had firmed up during his years in office. As a candidate, Kennedy seemed uncertain in purpose and lacking in enthusiasm. Moreover, he continued to be haunted by the spector of Chappaquiddick—that small Massachusetts island where, more than a decade earlier, he had driven his car off a bridge late one night carrying a female campanion, Mary Jo Kopechne, to her death. The circumstances of that incident were never explained to the satisfaction of many, and it left a residue of doubt about his "character" in the minds of a substantial segment of the electorate (see *Newsweek*, January 14, 1981, pp. 38–39).

Carter, for his part, assumed a Presidential stance, vowing that he would not campaign actively until the "hostage crisis" created by the November 4th seizure of the American Embassy in Iran was resolved. Instead, he would stay in the White House to attend to his duties during the crisis. The crisis itself was precipitated by the President's decision to allow the recently deposed Shah of Iran to enter the United States for medical treatment. The militants who had seized the Embassy were demanding the return of the Shah as ransom for the 50 Americans held captive there.

On December 4, the eve of Carter's formal announcement of his candidacy, Kennedy, weary from a long day of campaigning, was asked in a television interview about the American government's obligation to the Shah for his years of friendship toward this country. Kennedy responded by condemning the Shah for "one of the most violent regimes in the history of mankind" and for stealing "umpteen billion dollars" (*Newsweek*, December 14, 1979, p. 46). The comments were hailed in Iran but roundly condemned by much of the American press and by many political leaders who found them to be ill-timed, ill-advised, and a disservice to the country and to the President. At the President's behest, the Carter people held their tongues, letting others do their bidding.

Kennedy's mid-November 19-point lead among Democrats evaporated, and by the second week in December, Gallup found Carter leading Kennedy by 46% to 42%—a 23-point shift in as many days. Among independents, the shift in preferences for the Democratic nomination was even more dramatic. Carter moved from a 37–50 percent deficit to a 56 to 31 percent lead—a 38-point shift (*Gallup Opinion Index*, January, 1980, p. 9). Simultaneously, popular approval of Carter's performance in office soared from 38% to 61%. By early January, his approval rating had leveled off at about 55%, where it was to remain for the next two months before decaying back to pre-December levels (*Gallup Opinion Index*, October–November, 1980, p. 13).

Playing on what one staff member called the "patriotic factor" and on his superior campaign organization, Carter destroyed any remnants of Kennedy's image of invincibility in January's Iowa caucuses, handing him a 2 to 1 defeat, Kennedy's first in eighteen years of politics (*Newsweek*, February 4, 1980, pp. 43–44). Indeed, as an early Carter staff memo had observed, "Nothing [takes] the shine off charisma faster than the image of a loser" (*Newsweek*, October 29, 1979, pp. 33–34). Carter went on to win 24 of 34 Presidential primaries, dominating the early ones and suffering major defeats only after it seemed clear that he had the nomination sewed up. Kennedy's late resurgence was fueled by Carter's declining popular standing, but it was also perhaps facilitated by the fact that Kennedy was now less a viable candidate than a relatively safe way of registering discontent.

The fluctuations in popular approval of Carter's performance in office and the shifting fortunes of Carter and of Kennedy in their contest for the 1980 Democratic presidential nomination are unusual only in the vividness of the patterns they reveal. Almost every contemporary President has experienced sharp shifts in his popular standing (Mueller, 1973). Dramatic reversals have become commonplace in American electoral politics, not only at the presidential level but in other highly visible races as well. What accounts for these gyrations in the public's assessments of candidates and officeholders? Are people simply fickle or are incumbents and candidates so erratic in their behavior as to account for these changes? While people can be fickle and political actors, erratic, more than this is involved. Changing events and circumstances call forth different expectations of persons in prominent positions. These expectations define the various roles that people assign to political actors depending on the situation and the positions those actors occupy. Carter and Kennedy did not change that much, but what they represented did. As a noncandidate, Kennedy could represent all that Carter was not. As such, he symbolized the diverse discontents with Carter's leadership. As an active candidate, however, he represented a specific alternative with flaws and blemishes of his own. Similarly, as the hapless and seemingly irresolute man in the nation's highest office, Carter provided a convenient focal point for the discontents of a nation undergoing severe economic strains and countless other social changes. However, with the Iranian crisis, he became the embattled President defending the nation's honor and protecting its interests against a foreign assault. As Kennedy was to learn to his chagrin, one may criticize the man but one is expected to rally around the President. The logic of all this may defy rationality, but it is an integral part of the logic of politics. To understand that logic better, it is necessary to appreciate the peculiar role that symbols play in political communication.

POLITICS AS COMMUNICATION

Bell has argued that "politics is talk" and suggested that Lasswell's famous definition of politics, "who gets what, when, why, and how," ought to be reformulated accordingly (1975, pp. 10–11). While we are not inclined to go as far as Bell, we concur that whatever else may be involved, communication is central to politics. Certainly, the questions of who communicates what to whom, how, and with what effects go to the crux of the political process. Almost all of us are involved to some extent in this process, although most of us seldom play a prominent role. For the most part, we are consumers, the major political actors being the primary communicators and the mass media serving as the primary channels of political communications.

Symbols are the currency of this communication process. They represent the focal objects of political attitudes and opinions and serve to define the procedural and substantive concerns of government. These symbols are an important part of the political heritage and traditions that define the political culture of a community. To understand what is communicated to whom, it is necessary to inquire into the symbols that characterize this political culture. Of interest is not only the nature of the symbols themselves but also the way they are used and how people relate to them.

When the symbols of politics are evoked, what is communicated is not strictly a function of the intent of the communicator nor of the manifest content of the message. The meaning of the message is heavily colored by the significance to the receiver of the symbols involved and his or her own interpretation of their meaning. The same symbols may communicate different things to different people. What is perceived by some may be substantially at odds with what is perceived by others. This heterogeneity of interpretation is likely to go unrecognized, however, because all are reacting to the same objective stimuli and tend to assume that the meaning they find there is intrinsic to the symbols involved and thus common to all.

If what is communicated by political symbols is not intrinsic to the symbols themselves nor invariant across individuals, the question is not so much "what do symbols mean?" as "how do they mean?" The latter question is critical if we are to understand what is communicated to whom and to anticipate the likely effects of that communication. To address this question, it is appropriate to begin by looking at the nature of political involvement and some of the political uses of symbols.

THE NATURE OF POLITICAL INVOLVEMENT

Although few actively participate in the ongoing political process (Verba and Nie, 1972, pp. 25–94), almost everyone is involved in politics to the extent of monitoring what Edelman has called "the passing parade of abstract symbols" (1964, p. 5). For most people, this monitoring is a rather casual process, seldom occasioning further involvement. It is not, however, a totally passive form of behavior. At a minimum, it involves actively assessing continuities and changes in one's political environment from the flow of symbolic stimuli from the political arena. The vigilance with which one monitors political communications will vary, of course, with the significance one attaches to the symbols involved.

Politics is only one of a variety of concerns competing for people's attention, and it is not usually given high priority. Day-to-day concerns of jobs, family, and friends tend to dominate most people's attention (Sears and Whitney, 1973, p. 6). Because politics is not generally a prominent concern, people tend to dismiss a great deal of political communication as noise, i.e., "politics as usual," and assume that it can be safely ignored. More intense concern will be prompted only when signals are received that violate prior expectations. Since most people find politics remote from their daily lives, their expectations are not very exacting and are more likely to be reinforced than challenged by the communications they receive.

The tendency to find one's expectations confirmed by political communications is aided by certain psychological dynamics which influence the receipt of political information and color the interpretations given to it. Perhaps foremost among these is a "constancy principle": people tend to perceive and to interpret political stimuli in such a way as to make it consistent with their existing predispositions. As political stimuli are frequently ambiguous, people normally do not have to strain very hard to find confirmation of preexisting views. Sears and Whitney have identified three additional biases in the way people tend to process political information. The first is the "consistency bias." It refers to the tendency of people to agree with those they like and to disagree with those they dislike. The second is the so-called "positivity bias." It refers to the general inclination of people to perceive things in a positive rather than in a negative way. Most people, it seems, tend to accentuate the positive. Finally, there is the "agreement bias," which leads people to agree more often than they disagree with all types of political communication, regardless of its content. All these psychological tendencies contribute to relatively stable and largely uncritical assessments of politics and the political system.

While the "positivity bias" has the effect of muting negative evaluations and of encouraging supportive sentiments, the dominant effect of these psychological dynamics taken together is to reinforce individuals' current predilections, be they positive or negative. These dynamics also serve to bring individual opinions into line with the prevailing climate of public opinion. If prior inclinations are essentially negative and accord with general community sentiment, they are likely to persist even in the face of evidence to the contrary. Thus, Kahn and his colleagues in a study of how people's own experiences with public bureaucracies affect their assessments of those bureaucracies find that

> most Americans do not let their experiences affect their stereotypes; it is apparently much easier to decide that their experiences represent an exception to the rule. People who have had bad experiences, however, are likely to bring their general perceptions into line with their encounters. Those who report unfair treatment, for instance, tend to think that everyone else is getting unfair treatment too. (1975, p. 71)

Because of this tendency for predilections to be self-confirming, alienation and mistrust can feed on themselves as surely as allegiance can foster support. Because the American political culture has historically encouraged an ambivalent attitude toward authority, suspicion of power, and a mistrust of "politics" (Lamb, 1974, pp. 150–154), these dynamics are of substantial importance in understanding contemporary patterns of distrust and political disaffection. Dramatic violations of positive expectations that confirm latent suspicions can lead not only to frustration but also to altered expectations and heightened cynicism (Gilmour and Lamb, 1975). It is not surprising, then, that the high levels of trust in government exhibited by the American public in the late 1950s and early 1960s, having been shaken by an unpopular war in Vietnam, evidence of official deceit (e.g., the Pentagon papers), and the Watergate scandal, have given way to a pervasive distrust that resists abatement (see Table 1.1).

TABLE 1.1   Trends in Trust in Government, 1958–1978.

Question: How much of the time do you think you can trust the government in Washington to do what is right?

	1958	1964	1966	1968	1970	1972	1973	1974	1976	1978
Always or most of the time:	76%	78%	68%	63%	55%	46%	34%	37%	34%	30%
Only some of the time:	24	22	32	37	45	54	66	63	66	70
	100%	100%	100%	100%	100%	100%	100%	100%	100%	100%

SOURCE: SRC/CPS Election Studies.

The Channels of Communication

The monitoring of politics for most people is a mediated process. Typically, it involves reliance on the mass media, especially television (Strouse, 1975, pp. 56–60). It may also involve friends and associates who are regarded as trustworthy and who are assumed to be more vigilant in their monitoring of the political process. The latter have been called "opinion leaders." Their information also tends to be gleaned from the media, but they serve as a secondary filter through which political communications may flow to others (Katz and Lazarsfeld, 1955).

The mass media are thus the most direct link that most people have to politics. The type of surveillance the media provide is typically geared to the interests and concerns of its audience. Of necessity, especially to the electronic media, this means that vast amounts of political phenomena must be summarized, condensed, and simplified—leaving only vague outlines and symbolic representations of complex political events (see Graber, 1980, pp. 57–85). The deluge of facile images conveyed by television, lacking context and detail, constitutes a primary form of political exposure for most. For many, it is the only source. For those who are more attentive, a multiplicity of media serve as sources; more depth of coverage is found in the printed media and through organizational activity. This more intense exposure, however, tends to be governed by a principle of selectivity that is both motivational and structural in nature (Sears and Whitney, 1973, p. 8).

Motivational selectivity arises from the fact that most people have access to more information than they have the time or the inclination to consider. So they pick and choose, focusing on those things they care about most. People are selective with respect not only to the type of things they pay attention to but also to the sources upon which they rely. Those sources are typically ones that offer views congenial to their own. Structural selectivity arises because the sources and types of information available to people are often constrained by situational factors over which they have little control. Many people, for example, have ready access to only one daily newspaper. Much of what they know and understand about contemporary politics may depend heavily upon what that paper chooses to report and how (see Tichenor et al., 1980). Both types of selectivity tend to have the effect of reinforcing existing biases.

The images that emerge both from direct exposure to the media and through the "two-step flow" from the media to "opinion leaders" to individuals are framed in terms of familiar political symbols. The images created by these symbols can communicate both threat and reassurance, although most are likely to be found merely entertaining and lacking in substantive significance. This, in and of itself, can be mildly reassuring.

Support for the System

Insofar as the meanings gleaned from the passing array of political images are consonant with prior positive conceptions of how the political system is supposed to work, they tend to redound to the support of the system, reinforcing dispositions to perceive the system as legitimate. By the same token, ambiguity or incongruence can prompt withdrawal of support and ultimately undermine the legitimacy of the system. This process relates to what Easton calls "specific support" (1975, pp. 435–458). It is support that is contingent upon assessments of the system's performance in comparison to one's performance expectations.

The problems involved in sustaining specific support are multidimensional, relating to matters of procedure as well as substance, to nonmaterial as well as material costs and benefits. They involve, among other things, the need for continuity in the uses of political symbols (Merelman, 1966). The absence of such continuity can generate mistrust in government and prompt disaffection. If such a situation is not rectified, it can lead to widespread estrangement not only from the symbols but also from basic institutions and political values, therein creating a crisis of legitimacy (Miller, 1974).

The effects of Watergate on popular perceptions of the Presidency would seem to support this. That scandal emerged in 1972 and ultimately drove Richard Nixon from office in 1974. The Presidency is for many the focal symbol of government. The power and majesty of the office is such that it is widely perceived to ennoble the person who holds it. People expect their President to observe the highest standards of integrity and probity. Confronted with strong evidence to the contrary, often only grudgingly accepted, many people became disillusioned not only with the incumbent but with the entire political process. As shown in Table 1.1,

TABLE 1.2   Perceptions of Honesty in Government, 1958–1978.

Question: Do you think that quite a few of the people running the government are a little crooked, not very many are, or do you think hardly any of them are crooked at all?

	1958	1964	1968	1970	1972	1973	1974	1976	1978
Not very many or hardly any:	74%	70%	74%	67%	62%	47%	53%	56%	58%
Quite a few:	26	30	26	33	38	53	47	44	42
	100%	100%	100%	100%	100%	100%	100%	100%	100%

SOURCE: SRC/CPS Election Studies.

this disillusionment was reflected in the sharp drop in trust in government that occurred in 1973. It was seen even more vividly in the sharp increase that occurred that same year in the number of people who were inclined to think that the people running the government were frequently dishonest (see Table 1.2).

When political offices, which within the American culture are conceived as "public trusts," are commonly perceived to be populated by "crooks," confidence in public institutions is bound to be affected. It is not surprising then to find the correlation between patterns of trust and perceived honesty to be a robust .77 (partial r, $p < .05$), even when the generally downward secular trend in both indicators is controlled. The adverse consequences of this kind of discontinuity are also suggested by the changes in popular confidence in major social and political institutions as reported by Harris (see Table 1.3).

Whether the problems occasioned by the discontinuities in the use of symbols of the Presidency can be compensated for and corrected in the

TABLE 1.3   Popular Confidence in People Running Key Institutions, 1966–1978.

	% Expressing "Great Deal of Confidence"					
Institution	*1966*	*1972*	*1973*	*1978*	*1979*	*1981*
Medicine	73	48	57	42	30	37
Higher Education	61	33	44	41	33	34
Major Companies	55	27	29	22	18	16
Press	29	18	30	23	28	16
Military	61	35	40	29	29	28
U.S. Supreme Court	50	28	33	29	28	29
Federal Executive Branch	41	27	19	14	17	24
Congress	42	21	30	10	18	16

SOURCE: Harris Louis. *The Harris Survey*. New York: The Tribune Company Syndicate, Inc. October 22, 1981.

short term is uncertain. Popular responses to the early efforts of both the Carter and Reagan Administrations, as well as the surge of support Carter received in the wake of the seizure of the American Embassy in Tehran, suggest that the symbols of the Presidency have great resilience. They seemingly tend to engage latent predispositions that are essentially positive and readily reinforced by almost any gesture or action that symbolizes effective leadership. However, in the absence of such gestures and actions, doubts surface quickly.

It is important, of course, to recognize that the legitimacy of the system is not contingent solely upon the momentary reckonings that characterize specific support. A stable system is characterized by a more or less unconditional reservoir of legitimacy that serves to cushion transitory fluctuations in specific support. Easton refers to this as "diffuse support" (1965, pp. 273–274). It arises from a relatively stable set of predispositions that are manifested in the form of emotive attachments and sentimental identifications with the symbols of the political system. Although the continual failure of the system to generate specific support can lead to the erosion of diffuse support, momentary fluctuations in specific support are not likely to have much effect on the overall legitimacy of the system. Evidence for both of these propositions is provided in a study by Sigel and Hoskin (1977). They find a modest linkage between support for the system and satisfaction with current governmental performance but a more impressive reservoir of supportive sentiment that is not immediately tied to evaluations of current performance.

It is also important not to mistake the casual or ritualistic negativism encouraged by the American political culture and common to partisan politics for a fundamental sense of estrangement (Citrin, 1974, pp. 985–

TABLE 1.4   Support for the American Form of Government.

	1972	1976
I. Pride in Government		
Proud of many things about our form of government	86%	80%
Can't find much to be proud of	14	20
	100%	100%
II. Need to Change our Form of Government		
Keep as is	59%	47%
Some change needed	26	28
Big change needed	15	25
	100%	100%

SOURCE: Citrin, 1974; Campbell, 1979.

988). Such negativism may exist without significantly affecting the system's fundamental legitimacy. This is reflected in Table 1.4, which suggests that despite the growth in distrust and disaffection noted earlier, Americans have remained remarkably steadfast in their allegiance to their political system. Nonetheless, the impact of the decline in specific support is evidenced by post-Watergate increases in both the number of people who take little pride in "our form of government" and those who feel that major changes are needed.

Acquiescence and Arousal

In its normal operations, the political system provides a surfeit of political communications that are symbolically reassuring to the public. This reassurance promotes acquiescence and sustains a low level of involvement by reinforcing perceptions that the normal order of things is being maintained. Within this environment, the more substantive transactions of politics—transactions that tend to be the province of the relatively few politically well-organized segments of society—proceed largely unattended by the public at large. This serves to sustain the status quo, preserving existing patterns of privilege and the prevailing biases of the system.

Discontinuities do, of course, occur as events and changing circumstances give rise to new demands on the political system. These demands are frequently couched in terms of familiar symbols in order to legitimize the demands and to solidify support. The new application of familiar symbols is likely to be unsettling to many and perceived as threatening by some. It can prompt anxieties that feed upon themselves unless assuaged. Anxieties aroused in the public can generally be assuaged by a dramatic symbolic gesture that serves to restore popular confidence in the political order and that gives assurance that the problem is well in hand. The relative ease which this can be done has led Edelman to argue that symbolic demands are more readily satiated than substantive ones (1964, pp. 22–43). This proposition seems to be borne out by the difference we noted earlier in black and in white perceptions of the gains resulting from the civil rights legislation of the 1960s. A dramatic gesture reinforced by the normal flow of reassuring symbolic images usually is sufficient to satisfy the general public, although it may leave the original claimants with little in the way of tangible benefits.

Demands or expectations that go unanswered breed discontent that can prompt activism, as well as alienation. Such discontent is most likely to be given political expression when it is predicated on social comparisons that result in feelings of "fraternal relative deprivation" or "status anxiety."

Relative deprivation is the perception that a person is not getting his fair share in comparison to others. Insofar as a person experiences it as a problem peculiar to himself, he may feel frustrated but is likely to consider the fault to be his own. However, when a person perceives his relative deprivation as a problem common to others like himself or sees it as arising from the status he shares with others, he is likely to fault the social and political order. Such persons are said to be experiencing "fraternal relative deprivation" and are prone to political mobilization. Pettigrew (1971) found that feelings of fraternal relative deprivation were prevalent among segments of both the black and the white communities in the late 1960s. These feelings prompted black unrest and expressions of white bigotry. Shingles (1981) found that such feelings help to account for higher levels of political participation among blacks than among whites at comparable levels of socioeconomic status.

Status anxiety refers to a similar phenomenon. It involves perceptions that the status one enjoys and shares with others is threatened or is under assault (Lipset and Raab, 1979). The status in question is not simply a matter of material well-being but is also a matter of the prestige accorded one's values, beliefs, and life-style. The different responses to the Nixon and to the McGovern welfare reform plans noted earlier are suggestive of such status anxiety. Whereas Nixon took pains to portray his proposal in symbolic terms affirming traditional middle-class values; to many, McGovern's sketchy plan seemed to represent a direct challenge to those values.

If either of these types of feeling is widespread and intense, it is likely to serve as a basis for arousing segments of the population that are normally only marginally involved in the political process. Symbols are critical in communicating the frustration underlying the two phenomena. Symbols serve as a rallying point for the mobilization of support for demands and provide a catalyst for the organization of a political movement. The solidarity of a mobilized group will depend heavily upon the extent to which unifying symbols capture the fears, anxieties, and frustrations of its adherents. The themes involved may be preserving or innovative. In either case, they must, if the movement is to be successful, serve to give affirmation to a common group identity, life-style, or set of values. In recent years, the Equal Rights Amendment (ERA) seemingly has served just this function for both proponents and opponents of "women's rights" and "sexual equality" (see Boles, 1979; Conover, Coombs, and Gray, 1980).

The mobilization of previously inactive segments of the populace tends to disrupt normal patterns of political communication. Since it injects new and unfamiliar images into the drama of politics, it is likely to be a source of anxieties for those otherwise not involved. This will be expressed through aroused popular interest and a heightened vigilance with which politics is monitored.

If the symbols evoked by the movement and the application of those symbols are familiar ones, the movement is likely to benefit from the interests aroused through increased popular support. For example, the so-called "tax revolt" that surfaced in California and led to the 1978 success of "Proposition 13" in that state undoubtedly benefited from the familiar symbols of "governmental waste and extravagance" and "high taxes." When the symbols used are new or alien in their application, the movement is likely to be widely perceived as a threat. The concern piqued by the movement for "gay rights" in Dade County, Florida, and other areas of the country in the late 1970s provides a striking case in point. Although the "civil rights" symbols evoked were familiar, their application to homosexuals, widely regarded as not only deviant but as a threat to traditional "family" values, was not. In any case, the movement can expect to encounter opposition that will seek to exploit familiar symbols in an effort to discredit it and to undermine its support. Particularly if the movement is widely perceived as threatening, countermobilization is likely to occur and efforts to discredit the original demands are likely to be successful. Such was the fate of "gay rights" in Dade County.

The arguments we have made are amply illustrated by the history of the civil rights movement in the United States (Skolnick, 1969, pp: 97–130). Previously suppressed demands surfaced under the guise of familiar legitimacy symbols to be greeted by both embarrassed sympathy and open hostility. Mobilization and countermobilization occurred around these unsettling demands, prodding political leaders to respond with dramatic symbolic gestures to assuage the anxieties and passions that had been aroused. These gestures ranged from formal assurances of black voting rights and access to public accommodations at the federal level to open encouragement of defiance of the law in some local jurisdictions. Parallel illustrations can be found in the contemporary drive by women for fuller socio-economic opportunities. In fact, the dynamics we have described surround almost every major political issue and are constantly being played out in the day-to-day operations of the polity.

LEADERSHIP ROLES AND PUBLIC POLICY

Just as symbols serve to structure popular involvement in politics, they are crucial to the functions of political leadership and policymaking. Symbols undergird authority by legitimizing the distribution of power. In general, the more remote power is and the greater its scope, "the greater the need and the greater the possibility of using symbols to suggest and justify authority" (Mitchell, 1962, p. 127). As Merriam observed, symbols contribute to the efficiency of power:

> It is the way of power to surround itself with an array of things to be believed and admired, *credenda* and *miranda*. No power could stand it if it relied upon violence alone, for force is not strong enough to maintain itself against the accidents of rivalry and discontent (1964, p. 109)

Leadership

The symbolism that supports power arises not only from the trappings of position but also from the gestures and the behavior of officeholders. While myths and rituals serve to sanctify political power within any system, the legitimacy of its exercise is contingent upon positive assessments of role performance. Leadership roles are defined by the expectations others hold of the occupants in such positions. Thus, as Edelman observes, to understand leadership, one must look to the followers and the expectations they hold (1964, pp. 74–75). These expectations are shaped by myth and colored by past experience. They need not be internally consistent nor realistic in order to persist; in fact, they are frequently neither. Nonetheless, through the symbolic gestures they monitor, people find confirmation of their expectations, or failing this, they grow restive.

As Anton observed, we are "taught to believe that there is 'someone' in charge of the government and that there must be a reason for every governmental act" (1967, p. 38). Moreover, we are eager to find evidence to support such beliefs and readily accept any evidence that they are true. Thus, we are inclined to perceive the occupants of prominent political positions as endowed with extraordinary qualities. They tend to be seen as nearly omnipotent, highly moralistic, and benevolent. Cronin characterizes this type of myth as it relates to the American Presidency as follows: "If and only if the right man is placed in the White House, all will be well, and somehow, whoever is in the White House is the best person for the job—at least for a year or so" (1980, p. 84).

To sustain these myths, and through them the *credenda* of power, leaders must engage in actions that symbolize for followers responsible coping behavior. People expect leaders to cope with problematic situations.

> Because it is apparently intolerable for men to admit the key role of accident, of ignorance, and of unplanned processes in their affairs, the leader serves a vital function by personifying and reifying the process. As an individual, he can be praised or blamed and given "responsibility" in the way that processes cannot. (Edelman, 1964, p. 78)

Unless a leader provides reassurance of his ability to cope through the appropriate symbolic gestures with respect to commonly perceived problems, he will lose the confidence of his followers and destroy his credibility as a leader. Dramatic fluctuations in Presidential popularity can be understood largely in these terms. As George Gallup has observed:

> Any sharp drop in popularity is likely to come from the President's inaction in the face of an important event. Inaction hurts a President more than anything else. A President can take some action, even a wrong one, and not lose his popularity . . . . People tend to judge a man by his goals, by what he's trying to do, and not necessarily by what he accomplishes or how well he succeeds. (Quoted in Edelman, 1964, p. 78)

The action required need be neither logically consistent nor consonant with previous actions. What is important is that the leader appear to be in control and to have the right intentions. Consider the 1961 Bay of Pigs disaster. Shortly after he had taken office, President John Kennedy authorized the invasion of Cuba by American-supported Cuban refugees. The invasion proved an embarrassing fiasco. When it was all over, a chastened President took full blame for the whole sorry mess. The sanctioning of the invasion had been one of the first major acts of a new President still enjoying the glow of popularity typically accorded newly elected officials. Gallup reports that popular approval jumped from 73% in the period preceding the invasion to 83% immediately after Kennedy's declaration of responsibility (*Gallup Opinion Index*, October–November, 1980, p. 27).

By shouldering the blame for the ill-conceived Bay of Pigs operation, Kennedy reinforced the myth that he was in complete control of the situation and undaunted by failure. Leadership for the polity was therefore secure and need not be the cause for further concern. Similar popularity benefits, albeit more modest ones, accrued to President Carter when he acknowledged responsibility for the ill-fated attempt of April 1980 to rescue the Americans held hostage in Iran. A notable counterexample is provided by the steady erosion of popular support for President Richard Nixon in the face of the Watergate disclosures. He wavered and hedged, leaving the impression of being unwilling to own up to his responsibility. It is doubtful that Watergate would have been more than a momentary embarrassment had he publicly assumed early and complete responsibility for the incident and summarily fired a prominent member or two of his campaign organization for allowing it to happen.

Popular assessments of leadership performance tend to rest as much upon matters of style as of substance. Since most people are not very vigilant in their monitoring of the political process and lack detailed information, they rely on symbolic cues in making their assessments. Failure to provide the appropriate cues when they are needed is perhaps the most damning mistake a leader can make.

The settings that typically surround the exercise of authority are contrived to inspire awe and reverence. The vestments of leadership suggest special and extraordinary qualities to which deference is due. Elaborate rituals, such as those found in the courtroom, and special titles used even in casual conversation (e.g., "Mr. President" or "Governor") convey a sense of rightness, solemnity, and order that promotes public confidence and respect. These are the *miranda* of power that accrue to a person merely by virtue of the office he holds. As the Carter-Kennedy contest for the 1980 Democratic nomination attests, they can be a potent asset in silencing criticism and commanding support. Especially during periods of uncertainty and external challenge, people are inclined not only to defer to the judgments of those vested with the *miranda* of power but also to insist that others do likewise.

By dramatizing and personalizing the actions of government, the mass media both promote and confirm the myths of leadership. The routine work for innumerable people is often presented with ceremonial flourish as the work of a single individual, the one who is presumed to be the "someone" in charge. Thus, we have the "President's program" or the "governor's budget." These impressions are enhanced by frequent portrayals of feverish activity and long hours. All this serves to create among the public "symbolic satisfaction built upon the idea that affairs of state are being dealt with, that responsibility is being exercised, and that rationality prevails" (Anton, 1967, p. 39).

Given all this, it is not difficult to appreciate the unique advantage typically enjoyed by incumbents seeking reelection or the peculiar deference that is accorded almost all prominent officials. These benefits, however, are not without disadvantage. Role incumbents can become captives of these same myths and rituals that fortify their legitimacy and can be blinded to the realities of their own dispensability and the fallibility of their policies (Nimmo and Coombs, 1980; Cronin, 1980).

In addition to justifying the distribution of power and legitimizing its exercise, political symbols serve to assuage the problems of transferring power from one set of authorities to another. Elections, for example, are not only mechanisms of collective choice but important symbolic rituals. As Ginsberg and Weissberg (1978) have shown, elections serve as vehicles for mobilizing popular support for both the regime and its leaders. Even among voters whose candidates lose, there is evidence of increased support. Elaborate rites of passage, such as inaugural ceremonies, are established to ordain new power holders and to give testimony to the vitality and the continuity of the social order. These rites impress upon the power holder and the constituent alike the gravity of the responsibilities being conveyed and provide vital assurance that these responsibilities will be respected.

One would err in assuming that the symbolism associated with power creates a facade of no consequence. Nor should it necessarily be viewed as part of some pernicious ploy to manipulate the unwary masses. Without such symbolism, the majesty of governmental authority would be destroyed and the reality of power would be diluted to the point of resting on little more than physical coercion—a situation that no government can likely long endure.

Public Policy

Public policy making tends to be a highly stylized and ritualized process. It is replete with symbolism that conveys reassurance and serves to rationalize the product, whatever it may be. The process represents a very peculiar form of problem solving in that its significance lies as much in the drama that attends it as in its actual output. It is the *making* of policy rather than its execution that the public is most sensitive to. In fact, satisfaction can accrue from the process even if the process fails for one reason or another to produce actual policy outputs. Whatever is produced tends to give symbolic testimony to "responsibility" being fulfilled.

Anton describes this drama in characterizing state budgetary politics. He finds highly stylized behavior in the form of moves and countermoves played around the symbols of "economy," "service," and "competence." He notes that the actual outcomes may seldom correspond to the symbols by which they are justified but suggests that they are nonetheless important; "they reassure actors and their audiences that powerful figures are engaged in important activities, in a significant context" (1967, p. 43).

That policy as a symbolic gesture is sufficient to assuage anxieties and to reassure the public that a problem has been resolved is seen in the old bromide that commonly greets almost any problematic situation: "There ought to be a law." Implicit in this reaction is a tendency to perceive officially sanctioned and appropriately processed statements about a problem as a solution to the problem. All that is required is an official act of prescription or prohibition and the problem will go away. By the same token and for the same reason, showcasing and tokenism can be used to provide even more compelling evidence that remedial action has been taken.

To a large extent, this form of "problem solving" through symbolic action explains the growing disparity between black and white perceptions in the late 1960s recounted earlier. With the Civil Rights Acts of 1964 and 1965, many whites came to see the "legitimate" grievances of black Americans as largely answered; to expect more was unreasonable. For blacks, these legislative gestures merely heightened their expectations and affirmed the legitimacy of their claims. As the gap between the promise of progress and actual progress continued and even grew, so did black frustration and impatience.

That a timely act may be more important than its consequences is supported by the fact that the act frequently receives little in the way of follow-up attention. This is illustrated by Nadel's description of the politics of consumer protection:

> The attentive public follows the controversy through Congress and may exert pressure on behalf of the regulatory measure, but once the policy is out of the legislative mill, it generally is also out of the public eye . . . . Having witnessed the successful course of legislative action through Congress, citizens assume that the administrative agency will in fact implement that legislation in accord with their perception of legislative intent. (1971, p. 47)

Thus, problems are presumed to be solved by fiat; and the citizen seldom has occasion to inquire further into the matter. This presumption is fortified by commonly held, symbolically laden images of the administrative process and of governmental regulation. Lowi's extended critique of the myths involved show them to be both pervasive and fallacious (1969, pp. 1–30). Where the public often perceives a clear and unambiguous mandate, there is considerable latitude for self-definition of function. Where the public assumes its interest is being protected, the specific interests of a few may be what is promoted. This is not, however, to be understood as a malicious plot. As Nadel argues:

> The administrative system as a whole is a symbol to citizens of government faithfully protecting their interests. The citizenry may believe a policy is being implemented in a certain way when in fact it is being implemented in an entirely different fashion . . . . This symbolism may proceed without any conscious attempt by the administrators to manipulate the public. Inaction by an agency due to lethargy or inertia may proceed alongside feverish activity within Congress on issues directly related to the agency's responsibilities. The more general case occurs in the absence of any publicity when the public assumes that the government is taking care of some particular problem, when no one is actually responsible. (1971, p. 48)

Oftentimes, not even the semblance of definitive action is required to provide symbolic reassurance that a problem is being taken care of; mere consideration of the problem in an auspicious setting will suffice. Thus, with great flourish, special commissions, task forces, and study groups are appointed to conduct "comprehensive" investigations and to provide policy recommendations. The reports of these groups are ceremoniously heralded and received with elaborate ritual, often only to be forgotten or ignored. Although nothing of substance may have changed, the expectation of action has been satisfied. Nadel notes this important symbolic function of official attention in his analysis of the proceedings of administrative agencies:

> Just as the very existence of a consumer protection agency nurtures the belief that something is being accomplished for consumers, so too can hearings create the belief that something will be done once the agency knows of the problem . . . . Thus, witness after witness brought forth matters not within the legal jurisdiction of the commission. They spoke as though they believed that by airing the problem before a government agency, some progress has been made toward alleviating it. (1971, p. 62)

Truman identifies the same phenomenon in Congressional hearings. Public hearings may have little direct effect upon legislation but still serve as a "quasi-ritualistic means of adjusting group conflict and relieving disturbances through a safety valve . . . . Open hearings satisfy the forms of the democratic 'rules of the game' even when they [do] not immediately grant the benefits of real access" (1951, pp. 372–373).

Public policy is, then, not simply a response to popular demands and public anxieties. Policymakers, frequently in alliance with organized interests, are actively engaged in initiating policy demands and manipulating how those demands are perceived. In other words, they create as well as respond to policy demands. The situations that provoke public anxiety and heighten expectations of official action are generally sufficiently ambiguous or ill-understood that they afford policymakers great latitude in defining the substance of the problem. Consider the problems of crime, inflation, poverty, or almost any other major matter of public concern. In each case, it is fairly easy to describe the conditions that prompt concern, but the source of the problem, what can be done about it, and who is responsible for doing it are both uncertain and matters of dispute. While there may be public clamor for something to be done, precisely what is being demanded is largely determined by how policymakers choose to interpret the situation that occasions those demands. In this sense, public officials play a significant role in shaping popularly generated demands.

To promote favored policies, the policymakers may define situations so as to evoke public anxiety and elicit support for their preferred course of action. In doing this, they may play upon real or imagined threats of an external enemy or exploit stereotypic images which they may or may not share with the public. The myth of a worldwide communist conspiracy that has dominated foreign policy making for decades and its attendant "national security" imperatives provide a notable example of this phenomenon. Dramatic events and crises often serve to focus public attention and to galvanize support. Both, however, are also matters of interpretation and definition. Events and circumstances do not speak for themselves. Whether they constitute a policy problem, or a particularly urgent one, depends on the meaning attributed to them. Policymakers play a central role in this definitional process, interpreting events to suit their own purposes and predilections. Thus, an ambiguous incident in the Gulf of Tonkin involving United States naval vessels and North Vietnamese patrol boats in 1965 became an excuse for a dramatic escalation of American involvement in the Vietnam War; the 1974 seizure of the *Mayaguez*, a United State merchant ship, in or near the disputed territorial waters of Cambodia became an opportunity forcefully to affirm "national will" by sending in the Marines, even though it turned out they attacked the wrong place and the crew was being released anyway; and an internal struggle among contending factions in El Salvador in 1981 became a convenient place to "draw the line" against "communist interventions" in Latin America, calling for sharp increases in military aid and the sending in of military advisers.

Because of their unique position in the symbolic order of things, public policymakers can often create the "problems" they wish to address and "solve" problems by simply declaring them solved. After years of frustrating American involvement in the Vietnam War with this country seemingly mired in an interminable conflict for reasons that were unclear, then-Senator George Aiken suggested the solution was simple: all that needed to be done was to declare ourselves the winners and bring our troops home. As it turned out, his prescription was not far off the mark in terms of the resolution of the problem. The American policy of withdrawal was called "Vietnamization." The Vietnamese were left to fight their own battles, and the more or less unilateral termination of American involvement became "peace with honor." Essentially similar policies, then, can be cast as real alternatives. Withdrawal is rejected in favor of "Vietnamization," and defeat becomes victory. Similarly, having vowed to stay in the White House until the Iranian crisis was resolved and following an abortive effort to rescue the Americans held captive there, President Carter began his active campaign for renomination in 1980. He said that the situation had "stabilized," even though objectively it was impossible to see that anything had really changed.

The different public responses to the guaranteed annual income proposals of Nixon and of McGovern recounted earlier in this chapter are testimony to the power of symbolic manipulation. The difference was as much in the way the programs were presented as in their content. As Lamb notes:

> It would seem that President Nixon won public acquiescence for his proposal by couching it in terms that appealed to values held dear by the middle class; and those values include a desire, which may be only vaguely articulated, that the lower strata of American society should be assured an equality of economic opportunity. Senator McGovern's presentation of a guaranteed income proposal stimulated fear, rather than sympathy. To many, he seemed determined to reward the poor for their lack of success. (1974, p. 190)

Lest all this sound more manipulative than it necessarily is, it must be noted that the dynamics we have described are not so much the products of Machiavellian motivations on the part of policymakers as they are the imperatives inherent in collective decision making in a large-scale society. People expect their leaders to be alert to perilous situations and to be sensitive to the needs of the community. Although people must rely to a significant extent on their leaders in these matters, those leaders must give evidence of being in command and of acting responsibly if they are to sustain their credibility. Because modern communications capability makes information about events and problems widely and almost instantaneously available to the public, the options of delaying or of ignoring a particular problem are circumstantially limited. Moreover, the options available to policymakers at any time are constrained by the range of symbols that are commonly perceived as appropriate for manipulation through the political process. Policymakers are successful only to the extent that they take care not to offend the symbolic sensitivities of the populace. This is a lesson that Senator McGovern seemed to ignore at his peril.

Policymakers are further constrained by the ambivalence with which people naturally tend to embrace the symbols of power, an ambivalence strongly reinforced by the American cultural tradition. Popular suspicions are easily aroused by anything that smacks of an "abuse of power" or suggests a violation of the "public trust." Insofar as this ambivalence serves to ensure a modicum of vigilance, it is an important restraint on the actions of decision makers, as was clearly shown in Watergate.

This is not to deny that policymakers have substantial discretion. Rather it is simply to note that they do not have complete latitude. As James has observed with respect to poverty programs, the range of policies that are likely to prove viable is circumscribed by culturally ingrained myths and images (1972, pp. 21–44). These myths and images frequently play a more telling role than hard realities do. Thus, fear of "big government," the specter of "socialism," and the sanctity of "free enterprise" remain potent policy constraints even in the face of demands for expanded public services, more rational economic planning, and greater accountability from a private corporate structure of enormous scale. Such constraints have hampered the ability of the American government to recognize, let alone cope with, such problem as the energy crisis. They also help to account for the comparatively underdeveloped social welfare system in the United States.

Thus, while popular myths and images can constrain the latitude of policymakers and temper the opportunity for abuses of power, they can also impede reform and stifle social change. Because they are highly resistant to change and tend to be immune to even firsthand experience, they can be a major obstacle to effective social policy. The power and durability of such myths and images is strikingly illustrated by the study of America's experiences with governmental bureaucracies by Kahn and his associates. They find that while most Americans consistently describe their own encounters with bureaucrats as positive (80% feeling that they are treated fairly), only 42% think that government agencies treat most people fairly. They attribute this anomaly largely to the overwhelmingly negative image that most people have of "bureaucracy" and of "bureaucrats." They write:

> Americans, then, have tackled the great bureaucratic beast and found it not such a dragon after all. But stereotypes live long and die hard, and the image of the insolent bureaucrat and his inefficient organization survives in spite of people's experiences, not because of them. (1975, p. 70)

That images tend to take precedence over experience helps to explain a variety of otherwise perplexing anomalies in the patterns of popular concerns. For example, Watts and Free report that concern with crime is nearly as prevalent in areas with low crime rates (i.e., rural areas) as it is in areas where there is a high incidence of crime (i.e., cities) (1973, pp. 115–116). Consider also the example of the aerospace engineer, reported by Lamb (1974, p. 110), who "continues to believe that welfare recipients are bums, while waiting in line for his welfare check." That symbolic images are not necessarily the product of experience or necessarily affected by experience is a tribute to their peculiar potency. For good or for ill, they tend to persist, shaping individuals' concerns and influencing the direction of public policy.

SUMMARY AND PREVIEW

We have argued that symbols play a critical role in the political process. To support this contention, we considered the nature of individual involvement viewed from the perspective of political communication. Here we found that symbols provide a vital link between the individual and the larger social order and that they are crucial to the processes of legitimacy. To illustrate further the significance of the symbolic aspects of politics, we surveyed some of the ways political symbols are used. It was suggested that such symbols are vital to political leadership and undergird the policy process. Throughout, we have emphasized that the potentiality for abuse inherent in symbolic manipulation should not obscure the positive and necessary social function of symbols.

In the next chapter, we begin a more formal and rigorous treatment of the dynamics of the symbolic processes which we have described to this point with a broad brush. In Chapter 2, we attempt to make more explicit the individual-level assumptions upon which our symbolic perspective rests. Consideration is given to the nature of an individual's orientations toward symbols and to how these orientations are acquired. The ways people use and respond to symbols and the factors that bear upon their credible application are considered in Chapter 3. The constraints imposed by the political culture upon both the meaning and the use of symbols provide the focal concern of Chapter 4. These constraints are illustrated by reference to elements of the American political culture. In Chapter 5, the social functions of political symbols are discussed and several symbolically based principles of social aggregation are identified. These principles, we suggest, play a critical role in structuring patterns of conflict and consensus within a political system. In Chapter 6, we summarize the perspective emerging from our analysis and suggest its possible implications for the study of politics.

2

Symbolic Attachments

Symbols are essential to the processes of social organization and communication. As Firth has observed, "Man does not live by symbols alone, but man orders and interprets his reality by his symbols, and even reconstructs it" (1973, p. 20). To approach the study of politics from a symbolic perspective is to recognize the peculiar problems of synchronizing diverse motivations, expectations, and values so as to make collective action possible. Symbols provide the vehicle through which this is done. To understand how, it is necessary to inquire into the nature of symbols and how people relate to them.

In the previous chapter, we attempted to illustrate the crucial and pervasive role that symbols play in the political process. Decision makers actively engage in the manipulation of symbols and rationalize their actions through them. People respond to these symbolic stimuli, finding in them sources of both anxiety and reassurance (see Edelman, 1964, 1971). The use of symbols is commonly recognized and frequently noted in the popular press and in social commentaries. Nonetheless, the symbolic aspects of political life have not been the subject of much in the way of systematic inquiry.

Part of the problem that has retarded the study of political symbolism lies in a variety of conceptual and theoretical ambiguities surrounding the notion "symbol" itself. What is a symbol? Where do they come from? What do they mean and why? All these seemingly simple questions remain problematic. We will address these questions and raise additional ones in the arguments that follow.

WHAT IS A SYMBOL?

A symbol is any object used by human beings to index meanings that are not inherent in, nor discernible from, the object itself. Literally anything can be a symbol: a word or a phrase, a gesture or an event, a person, a place, or a thing. An object becomes a symbol when people endow it with meaning, value, or significance. As White states:

> A symbol may be defined as a thing the value or meaning of which is bestowed upon it by those who use it. . . . The meaning or value is in no instance derived from or determined by properties intrinsic in its physical form. . . . Symbols "have their signification," to use John Locke's phrase, "from the arbitrary imposition of men." (1949, p. 25)

A symbol, then, is a human invention and arises from the process of attributing meaning to an object. For an individual, a symbol has no meaning beyond that which he or she gives to it; and an object is a symbol only for those who impute meaning to it. One can imagine symbols that are constructed for purely personal purposes and that have no meaning and thus are not symbols for anyone other than the solitary individual who uses them. However, our concern is with social, or what Mead has called "significant," symbols (1934, pp. 71–72). These are objects to which different individuals both singly and collectively attribute meaning. It is this process of different individuals' attributing meaning to the same objects that makes social communication possible. It is, in essence, what language is all about.

The most rudimentary symbols are the names, labels, or signs we use to designate physical objects and concrete operations. Here, the relationship between the object used as the symbol and that which is being symbolized is established simply by stipulative definition. Such symbols merely serve as pointers and are purely denotative. They are notational conventions and have no meaning beyond the immediate objects or specific operations to which they point. Following Sapir (1934), they may be called "referential symbols."

How the conventions upon which referential symbols rest are established and become socially accepted is an important and intriguing question, but the symbols themselves are of limited interest. We are primarily concerned with objects which people imbue with meaning that transcends any concrete entity or operation that they may serve to reference. The symbol "Watergate," for example, is of interest not as a designator of an apartment complex located in Washington, D.C., but as a commonly recognized index of the meanings people associate with the political events that followed from the 1972 break-in at the Democratic Party headquarters located there. Such meanings are not a matter of stipulative definition but of social construction. They emerge from an ongoing process of social interaction and communication. Used in this way, the symbol "Watergate" has no precise and directly observable referent. It is what Sapir has called a "condensational symbol." Such symbols serve to summarize and to condense experiences, feelings, and beliefs.

Because socially significant symbols arise and are sustained through a

system of social interaction, they are appropriately regarded as characteristic elements of a culture. As Firth observes, "Criteria selected for classification of symbols may come from the natural world, but 'symbol' is a
cultural not a natural category" (1973, p. 56). We are interested in that
range of significant symbols that may be called "political"; i.e., those
symbols of relevance to the exercise of political authority and to the management of social conflict. While such symbols abound, every social system at any point in time will be characterized by a finite number of such
symbols. Because they are simultaneously elements of the culture and objects of individual meaning, these symbols provide a linkage between the
individual and the larger social and political order. They mediate the relationship between the individual and social reality, structuring people's
perceptions and allowing them to find meaning in events beyond their
own immediate experience. By the same token, symbols serve to constrain people's vision and make them vulnerable to manipulation.

WHERE DO SYMBOLS COME FROM?

In one sense, the question of where symbols come from is a vacuous one.
Since any event, phrase, situation, or gesture is potentially a symbol,
there is no dearth of possible candidates for symbolic status. The real
question is how an object becomes socially recognized and acquires
meanings that are not discernible from its physical form or immediate
function. The answer to the question of where symbols come from is
simply "people invent them, acquire them by learning, adapt them, use
them for their own purposes" (Firth, 1973, p. 427). Because symbols are
individual and social creations, it is impossible to predict what will become a symbol. However, it is possible to anticipate the circumstances or
the type of situation which will lead to the creation of a symbol.

New symbols are created when people find available symbols inadequate to capture or give expression to their experiences, feelings, or
beliefs. This is likely to occur in the face of dramatic events or major
changes in the natural, social, or political environment. In such circumstances, a symbol may emerge more or less spontaneously from the facts of
the situation. Simply because it referenced the location of events that re-
sulted in a major political scandal, "Watergate" came to symbolize not
only those events but also the misuse of political power. Similarly, the
dramatic events of the near–nuclear disaster at the Three Mile Island
power plant in Pennsylvania in 1979 made "Three Mile Island" an obvious candidate to symbolize the dangers involved in the use of nuclear
power.

Symbols may also emerge as a consequence of their deliberate
advocacy by political leaders or issue entrepreneurs. Presidents, for
example, are frequently eager to rally support for their programs and to dis-

tinguish themselves from their predecessors. To do so, they often attempt to cloak their programs in new symbols. Thus, Woodrow Wilson offered the American people a "New Freedom"; Franklin Roosevelt, a "New Deal"; Lyndon Johnson, a "Great Society"; and Ronald Reagan, a "New Beginning." Of course, for every label successfully transformed into a significant symbol through such advocacy, there are undoubtedly scores of would-be symbols that never make it. In 1971, Richard Nixon invited Congress and the nation to join in a "New American Revolution." It, like the "New Foundation" offered in 1978 by Jimmy Carter, found few takers. As these examples make clear, a prominent advocate can facilitate the emergence of a symbol but has, at best, limited control over the processes through which an object acquires widespread symbolic standing. Nonetheless, in any dynamic society, new symbols are constantly being generated.

The imperatives that occasion the creation of a symbol are at least threefold. The first of these is the human need for psychic economy—the need to summarize, capsulize, and index knowledge and experience. New symbols are therefore likely to be created when people find themselves in novel situations or confronted with unfamiliar circumstances—circumstances which for them are without clear parallel. Thus, with the American economy experiencing a peculiar combination of problems that seemed to defy standard economic characterizations in the mid-1970s, the term "stagflation" surfaced and was widely accepted as a symbol of these woes. Similarly, as the Reagan Administration embarked on a novel set of economic policies in the early 1980s, the whole experiment was quickly dubbed "Reaganomics."

A second impetus for the creation of symbols arises from the needs of communication. Efficient communication requires that experience, knowledge, and feelings be summarized and condensed in readily recallable form. Symbols provide common reference points for categorizing shared information, values, or anxieties. New symbols are thus created to facilitate the recall of shared experiences and to communicate these experiences to others. Such communication is, of course, likely to encounter what has been called the "difficulty of symbolic transfer—of ensuring that the object created or selected by one person as a symbol is identified by other persons as having the same meaning" (Firth, 1973, p. 40). Perhaps for this reason, symbols frequently involve the use of analogies, metaphors, and the transposition of older symbolic forms. For example, in 1979, when allegations surfaced suggesting that several Democratic congressmen had accepted large sums of money and other favors from South Korean lobbyists, numerous observers were quick to see parallels between the unfolding scandal and "Watergate." Despite protests from prominent Democrats that the analogy was not apt, the whole affair became widely known as "Korea-gate."

Of course, in the process of communication, some slippage in the meaning of a symbol is inevitable. A communicator may anticipate such slippage and intentionally seek to exploit the ambiguities involved. This is precisely what many Democratic leaders felt various Republicans and media people were trying to do in labeling the Korean affair "Koreagate." Presumably, Republicans stood to gain from a Democratic equivalent to "Watergate"; and the media, from another sensational scandal.

The third factor stimulating the creation of new symbols is the need to distinguish among people and to establish or to affirm social identities. Thus, new symbols are likely to be created when people find that they and others like them are disadvantaged by prevailing social conceptions and group distinctions. Similarly, new symbols are likely to be generated when an advantaged group finds itself challenged or its status threatened. Symbols generated for such purposes frequently employ stereotypes and play upon conceptions of an enemy.

A particularly striking example of the creation of new symbols to alter existing social distinctions and establish new identities is found in the substitution of the word "black" for "Negro" as a racial distinction. Finding the word "Negro" burdened with historical connotations that were negative and degrading, black activists during the 1960s and 1970s, especially the more militant ones, rejected that label and proudly proclaimed themselves "black." Aided and abetted by the mass media, the symbol "black" rapidly became a standard term of self-reference for members of that race. By promoting a new sense of group consciousness and solidarity, it facilitated political mobilization and stimulated greater political participation among blacks (Verba and Nie, pp. 157–160).

Another contemporary example of the use of symbols to establish politically important distinctions among groups is provided by the continuing controversy between "environmentalists" and proponents of "economic development." As self-proclaimed advocates of the "public interest" doing battle against rapacious "corporate greed," environmental groups successfully promoted policies of pollution control and environmental protection during the 1970s. However, more recently, they have found themselves on the defensive and their clout diminished. An important factor in this shift has been the emergence of the symbol "environmental extremists" that has been pinned on them by Ronald Reagan and other prominent proponents of economic growth and natural resource development. In effect, the new label makes environmentalists presumptive enemies of "economic progress," "prosperity," and "energy independence." It substantially redefines the terms of debate and therein alters the biases of the conflict.

For all the reasons we have cited, new political symbols are constantly being generated. As Merelman has observed, the normal operations of a polity almost assure the constant creation of new symbols and the erosion of old ones (1966, pp. 554–559). In seeking to elicit or to sustain support for themselves and for their policies, governmental decision makers can be expected to provide a fairly steady stream of would-be symbols. Their ability to generate new symbols is fortified not only by the legitimacy generally accorded the institutions of government but also by what Merelman calls "metasymbols"—symbols that serve to sanction the creation of new ones. Thus, a symbol such as "government of laws, not of men" almost assures the successful generation of new symbols by an institution such as the Supreme Court. Political campaigns and group conflicts are also the source of both spontaneously and intentionally generated symbols. As we have seen in the case of the environmentalists versus the developers, success or failure in group conflicts may hinge heavily on the symbols used to define the controversy. Disruptive environmental events and major social dislocations are also prime sources of new symbols. Such circumstances almost invariably defy old categorizations and give rise to gratifications or deprivations that find expression in new symbols.

WHAT DO SYMBOLS MEAN AND WHY?

The question of what symbols mean can be approached in a variety of ways. One alternative is to ask to what the symbol refers. As Firth observes, "the status of the relation between a symbol and that which it represents" (1973, p. 58) has remained a basic problem in the study of symbolism. Edelman addresses this problem using Sapir's distinction between "condensational" and "referential" symbols (Edelman, 1964, pp. 6–9). He suggests that some symbols will have ambiguous referents and will be heavily laden with emotive content (condensation symbols), while others will be emotively neutral and strictly denotative (referential symbols). It is important to recognize, however, that this distinction does not rest on any qualities intrinsic to the symbols themselves. Some are more ambiguous in their referents and evoke more emotive responses than others; but this results from the nature of the process through which they have acquired meaning, not from any quality inherent in the symbolic object itself. As Mitchell writes:

> Symbolism may be regarded as the attribution of meaning by a person or group to an object. . . . Symbolic objects derive their meanings from the actions and beliefs of persons, not from the objects themselves. Consequently, an object that possesses great or profound meaning for one person may be nothing more than a conventional item or practical instrument for another. Moreover, because symbols are attributed meaning, they act not only as resources, but as controls over the behavior of men, that is, those who attributed meaning to them. (1962, p. 123)

Thus, whether a symbol is condensational or referential or even a symbol at all varies from individual to individual and from situation to situation (e.g., see Edelman, 1964, p. 6). This, of course, tends to beg the question of the linkage between symbol and referent. Nonetheless,

> ...in studies of symbolism the tendency has been to emphasize the lack of "natural" links between symbol and thing symbolized— to view the symbolic attribution as a matter of cultural determination, as conventional, or even as "arbitrary." What is implied by such expressions is that the range of possible representations of something, particularly of an abstract quality, is so great that no exclusive choice of symbol is normally feasible by someone outside the system. The reason why a specific symbol then appears in use, seems to depend upon some form of cultural condition; at the worse, since cultural components in the relationship of symbol to object are often hard to identify, the choice is termed inexplicable. But in stressing the conventionality, the "arbitrary" character of the relationship...it is the complexity rather than the inexplicable nature of the link that is really being considered. (Firth, 1973, p. 60)

One can imagine that at their creation, most symbols have a fairly clear referent—that for their initial users they index common and fairly specific experiences or feelings peculiar to the particular context. As they are communicated to others and transported to different contexts, they are likely to be generalized and to encounter the problems of "symbolic transfer." In fact, the durability and the social utility of a symbol, particularly a political one, may depend on these very processes of generalization and transfer. The origins of specific symbols are, then, frequently remote either historically or physically from the experiences of the individuals who come to use them. Old symbols are detached from their initial referents and used in totally new contexts. Thus, as Hofstadter notes, "The issues of the twentieth century are still debated in the language of Jefferson's time and our histories of the Jefferson era are likewise influenced by twentieth century preconceptions that both Jefferson and his opponents might have found strange" (1958, p. ix).

Since a symbol is initially used as a vehicle for condensing and simplifying a variety of stimuli, it is likely to have some initial ambiguity. That ambiguity tends to be compounded over and over again the more the symbol is reused in different contexts. As a result of this process, many political symbols tend to invite the attribution of more or less idiosyncratic interpretations. Yet because the symbols are socially shared and culturally sustained, they prompt the presumption of a socially common meaning. "Part of our image of the world is the belief that this image is shared by other people like ourselves who also are part of our image of the world. In common daily intercourse, we all behave as if we possess roughly the same image of the world" (Boulding, 1961, p. 14).

Thus, in normal social discourse, we may find that we share a commitment to "democracy," that we abhor "violence" and value "freedom of expression." Yet we may never have occasion to realize that what these symbols mean to you may be quite different from what they mean to me. Where you see "violence," I may see "freedom of expression." Where you see the legitimate exercise of "social control," I may see "violence" and an infringement of "democratic rights." Should we become aware of these differences, we are more likely than not to interpret them as products of "communication failures" or inadequate knowledge of the "facts" of the situation on the part of one or the other of us. As a consequence, the differences in the meanings we attribute to the symbols tend to go unrecognized, and the myth of their common meaning is preserved. The real question in understanding the power of political symbols is not so much where symbols come from or what they initially mean. Rather, it is how they become the focal points of diverse meanings and commonly salient objects condensing and indexing different experiences, fears, apprehensions, hopes, and interests.

AN ANALYTIC FRAMEWORK FOR THE STUDY OF POLITICAL SYMBOLISM

In our exploration of some of the basic questions regarding the nature of symbolism, we have found that political symbols are commonly recognized objects to which people attach political significance. Because the meanings that people assign to symbols are conditioned by common social and cultural experiences, there may be substantial similarity in what they mean to different people. However, what the symbol means to a specific individual is ultimately determined by that individual and his or her own particular experiences. As a consequence, no symbol is likely to have precisely the same meaning for any two different people. Often the meanings different people attribute to a symbol are quite divergent. It is this social variability in meaning that explains the peculiar potency of symbols to arouse and to reassure persons of diverse backgrounds, interests, and concerns.

Classifying Objects Used as Political Symbols

New symbols are, of course, constantly being created. Nonetheless, at any time, the range of politically relevant symbols will be limited by the shared experiences and cultural heritage of the people who use them. It would be useful were we able to catalogue this universe of political symbols. The literature is suggestive of a variety of ways through which they might be classified. For example, Easton (1965), in developing the concepts of diffuse and of specific support, suggests three basic categories of objects of political orientation: (1) the political community, (2) the political regime, and (3) the authorities of government. As explained by Easton and Hess:

> Government refers to the occupants of those roles through which the day-to-day formulation and administration of binding decisions for a society are

undertaken. Regime is used to identify the slower changing formal and infor-
mal structure through which these decisions are taken and administered,
together with the rules of the game or codes of behavior that legitimate the
action of political authorities and specify what is expected of citizens or subjects. . . . The political community represents the members of a society looked
upon as a group of persons who seek to solve their problems in common
through shared political structures. (1962, p. 124)

A somewhat similar typology has been developed by Almond and
Verba (1963, pp. 14–15). They start their classification of objects of political orientation with the "general" political system. They further distinguish three broad classes of objects: (1) specific roles or structures, which
Easton refers to as the "regime," (2) incumbents of those roles, or what
Easton calls "authorities," and (3) particular public policies, decisions, or
enforcements of decisions.

Both of these schemes suggest the possibility of classifying the objects
used as political symbols in terms of the elementary, defining properties
of a political system. Moving from more inclusive and enduring elements to
more specific and transient ones, the resulting typology is loosely hierarchical in structure. Thus, those symbols associated with the political community are likely to be the objects of the broadest and most enduring
attachments. By the same token, those associated with particular authorities and particular policies are likely to be more exclusive and transient
objects of orientation. Taking inclusiveness and durability as our organizing principles, we would expand the range of more specific objects of
symbolic response to include nongovernmental political actors and policy
issues.

The typology of symbols we distill from this then includes (1) symbols
of the political community; (2) symbols associated with regime norms,
structures, and roles; and (3) situational symbols relating to (a) current
authorities, (b) nongovernmental political actors, and (c) policies and
policy issues. Examples of the symbolic objects that might be found in
each of these categories are shown in Table 2.1.

TABLE 2.1 A Typology of Political Symbols.

Type of Political Symbol	Example
Political Community	The Flag, America, the "Constitution"
Regime Norms, Structures, and Roles	The "Presidency," "Congress," "One Man, One Vote"
Situational Symbols	
(1) Current authorities	The "Reagan Administration," the "Burger Court"
(2) Nongovernmental political actors	Ralph Nader, NRA
(3) Policies and policy issues	"Right to Life," Gun Control

This scheme offers a fairly simple, straightforward, and comprehensive way to classify objects of political symbolism. It thus provides potentially useful criteria for sampling from the universe of political symbols. More to the point, it is potentially helpful in understanding variations in symbolic orientations across symbols, across time, and across individuals.

Dimensions of Symbolic Attachment

Having identified the types of objects that serve as political symbols, the problem now becomes one of characterizing the manner in which individuals relate to these symbols and give emotionally charged meaning to them. Geertz has stated the problem as follows: "There is a good deal of talk about emotions 'finding a symbolic outlet' or 'becoming attached to appropriate symbols'—but very little idea of how the trick is really done" (1964, p. 56). Lane offers some observations that provide insight into this puzzle:

> One source of their [symbols'] power is in the emotional charges or valences they carry, the very elements that make cognitions dissonant or consonant, and . . . another source of their power is their associative meanings, the very ambiguities that permit them, like Rorschach ink blots, to suggest to each person just what he wants to see in them. (1969, p. 316)

This suggests that an individual's orientation toward a symbol involves two basic components, one emotive and the other cognitive in nature. These two components have been identified by students of political behavior and cognitive psychology as the principal elements of a person's attitude toward any object (see Manheim, 1982, pp. 14–18). The emotive component is usually referred to as the affective component, or just "affect." It is also sometimes called "valence." It is defined by the direction and intensity of a person's feelings toward an object, i.e., whether the person views the object positively or negatively and to what degree. The cognitive component refers to the meaning a person associates with the object. It involves all that the person "knows" about the object or about what it stands for. By "knows," we do not mean knowledge in some objective sense but simply what the individual takes to be true. Such knowledge may be based on a sophisticated understanding of relevant facts and values, or it may be based on an uninformed opinion. It may amount to little more than some vague association of the object with persons or things with which the individual identifies. Thus, the cognitive component can vary substantially in richness and in clarity of substantive content. These two basic dimensions can be seen in Figure 2.1.

Both the affective and the cognitive components of a person's orientation toward a symbol contribute to the way he or she uses and reacts to that symbol. Starting with the affective component, we will con-

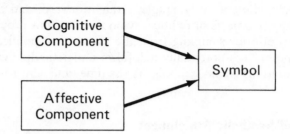

FIGURE 2.1   Components of a Symbolic Orientation.

sider both of these dimensions in some detail as we explore more fully how people relate to significant symbols and give meaning to them.

The Affective Dimension of Symbolic Orientations.   A person's affective orientation toward a symbol is simply the positive or the negative sentiment he or she associates with that symbol and the intensity of that sentiment. It may vary from strongly positive through neutrality to highly negative. Because of the peculiar character of symbols, however, a question arises as to what this affect is directed toward. Affect implies a summary assessment or evaluation of an object. But what is the object of this assessment? Is it the object being used as a symbol or is it what the symbol represents? Since by definition a symbol has no meaning beyond that which a person attributes to it, the affect must be directed at what it means or stands for. As we have seen, this meaning can vary from one person to another. Moreover, what a symbol means to a person can be quite diffuse and largely devoid of substantive context. Still, it is this meaning, not the symbol itself, that is the object of affect.

Because a symbol merely indexes the affect a person has for something else, whether or not the object that serves as the symbol engages that affect is contingent upon the way the object is used. If the object is used in a manner, situation, or context that is irrelevant to the symbolic meaning a person associates with it, it will not excite the affective sentiment that the object as a symbol carries for that individual. Consider, for example, the word "Washington." Used as a purely referential term, as in "Washington is south of Baltimore" or "Washington is the capital of the United States," it is not likely to prompt an emotive reaction. Used as a symbol of the federal government, as in "Washington wastes our money and ignores our problems," it is likely to engage strong affective sentiments. In Chapter 3, we will explore more fully the situational or contextual factors that bear upon the meaningful application of a symbol. Here we would simply note that the affect associated with a symbol presupposes that the symbol is used in a manner consonant with the meaning a person attributes to it.

Assuming credible usage, it is possible to characterize variations in affective orientations across symbols and among people by using the classificatory scheme we developed earlier. In that scheme, we distinguished three major types of objects of political symbolism based on their inclusiveness and durability: namely, community, regime, and situational symbols. Owing in part to the hierarchical structure the scheme implies, one would expect the intensity of symbolic affect to vary systematically across these categories. This is in keeping with the notion of "symbol weight" proposed by Merelman (1966, p. 556). He argues that different symbols tend to have different "weights" and that over time, and particular symbol tends to acquire a more or less stable role and weight. That weight is a function of the number of areas, problems, and contexts to which the symbol may be applied; the number of people among whom it is likely to evoke a response; and the intensity of that response.

Those objects that fall within the higher categories of our scheme will tend to possess greater symbol weight. For example, "freedom" will have greater weight than "deregulation." Logically, higher-order symbols have greater generality, and empirical evidence suggests that they are indeed the objects of widespread and intense affective sentiment (e.g., see Cobb and Elder, 1976). Moreover, there are both theoretical reasons (e.g., see Newcombe, Turner, and Converse, 1965, pp. 121–124) and empirical reasons (e.g., see Devine, 1972; Cobb and Elder, 1976) to believe that the categories of the scheme index stable patterns of affect toward political symbols.

In a stable polity, affective orientations toward higher-order symbols will normally be acquired earlier and be held longer than those directed toward lower-order ones. Children typically develop emotive attachments toward the flag and the institutions of government well before they are even aware of most situational symbols (Hess and Torney, 1967). These orientations tend to be among the most central and enduring a person will possess. Changes in these more basic sentiments are likely to precipitate changes in the affect associated with lower-order symbols. A person who becomes disillusioned with "voting" and "elections," for example, is unlikely to care much about "Common Cause," "Campaign reform," or the "Stockman ax." However, changes in the valence associated with lower-order symbols will typically not alter affective sentiments toward higher-order ones. A change in feelings toward "capital punishment" is not likely to influence one's commitment to the flag or to "democracy."

The higher a symbol falls in the hierarchy, the more uniform the affective orientations toward it are likely to be across persons and groups. We tend to respond more uniformly to a symbol such as "liberty" than to "ERA." Thus, there tends to be greater social differentiation with respect to lower-order symbols. Symbols such as "capital punishment," "deregulation," and "food stamps" typically prompt more diverse reactions than do symbols such as "free enterprise" and "national security."

Because they tend to command greater affect, higher-order symbols tend to dominate lower-order ones when the two conflict. A study by Westie (1965) serves to illustrate this. He found that most people in his sample responded positively to statements framed in terms of "equality," a major regime, if not community, symbol in American politics. However, when the dispositions seemingly implied by these general endorsements of "equality" were framed in specific terms with respect to "blacks," 20 to 40% of those who had endorsed "equality" denied these implications. When confronted with the contradiction (either through spontaneous realization or by the investigator), more than 80% resolved the conflict by altering their expressed dispositions to bring them into accord with their support for "equality."

It must be recognized that the objects in the scheme we have been using to characterize variations in symbolic affect will be specific to a political culture at a particular point in time. Over time, the focal objects of symbolism within any given category are subject to displacement and change. As Merelman shows (1966, p. 556), objects that are nominally of a lower order can, over time, be elevated to the status of higher-order symbols—a symbol that is initially a situational one can become a regime or even a community symbol. The apotheoses of historical authority figures such as Washington, Lincoln, and the two Roosevelts provide cases in point.

Prominent authority figures would seem to be particularly good candidates for such a transmutation of symbolic function. Studies have shown that an incumbent President or a mayor is commonly the focus of children's early orientations toward the political system (e.g., see Greenstein, 1965, pp. 27–54). In effect, such figures personify the political order. As children grow older, these sentiments may be transferred from prominent officials to more general symbols of the community and the regime (e.g., Statue of Liberty, Congress, Supreme Court, voting); and incumbents are distinguished from their roles (Hess and Torney, 1967, p. 34). But this transference may be partial and remain incomplete. This, of course, takes us back to the problem of the cognitive aspect of individuals' symbolic orientations.

The Cognitive Dimension of Symbolic Orientations. By definition, a symbol has no intrinsic meaning. Where then does its meaning come from? Clearly, it must come, in an immediate sense, from the individuals using and responding to the symbol. While a symbol references some aspect of reality external to the individual, precisely what is referenced is often unclear and varies from one person to another. When a person responds to a symbol, he is responding not simply to external reality but to his conception or interpretation of that reality. Thus, the meaning he gives to the symbol will be based on information and ideas he has stored away in his mind. To understand how symbols acquire meaning, we must inquire into the kinds of cognitive meanings that a person has available to assign to a

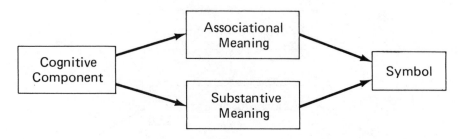

FIGURE 2.2   Cognitive Meanings Attributed to a Symbol.

symbol. As shown in Figure 2.2, two basic types of meaning may be distinguished: substantive and associational.

Substantive meaning is based on a person's internalized beliefs and values regarding the external world and the way it operates. These beliefs and values are a product of the person's socialization and life experiences. Depending upon how attentive and receptive he is to new information, these beliefs and values may be well informed and subject to continual modification and revision. However, new information seldom occasions major changes; and a person's values and beliefs tend to be fairly stable over time. Frequently, a person's values and beliefs will be neither well informed nor well organized. Nonetheless, it is this relatively stable set of values and beliefs that provides the repertoire of substantive meanings that the individual has available for attribution to a symbol. We will explore the nature and range of such substantive meanings more fully momentarily.

The second type of meaning that a person may assign to a symbol arises from his self-conception and the people and groups with whom he identifies. By self-conception we mean the way a person answers the question: Who am I? While there are undoubtedly many dimensions of self-definition, of interest here are those persons, groups, and social categories that people use as reference points to locate themselves in the social order. These include primarily groups such as family and friends, membership groups such as a professional association or a church, and general reference groups such as "veterans" or the "working class." A person's social identifications will include negative as well as positive reference groups; that is, his self-conception will be defined not only by those with whom he identifies but also by those he distinguishes himself from.

These social identifications provide a source of meanings that may be attached to a symbol. While these identifications influence and are influenced by one's more general values and beliefs, the cognitive meanings they predicate differ considerably from what we have called substantive meanings. The latter involve substantive interpretations of reality based on one's own beliefs and values. Associational meanings, on the other

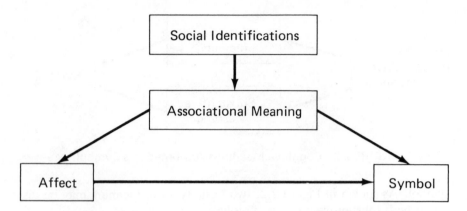

FIGURE 2.3   Associational Sources of Symbolic Attachment.

hand, are simply the positions a person associates with persons or groups he uses as points of reference. Insofar as he relies upon these identifications to give meaning to a symbol, he, in effect, suspends his own judgment and accepts or rejects the affective assessments of others simply on the basis of who they are. The relevant others are those persons and groups with whom he identifies in a positive or negative way. They include all the authority figures to whose judgments he is willing to defer and upon whom he depends for guidance in establishing what positions are associated with whom. These associations define the associational meanings that a person may assign to a symbol. This type of symbolic attachment is shown in Figure 2.3.

An example of the use of associational meaning is provided by the response of a Mormon woman living in Salt Lake City to a question about the "Equal Rights Amendment" (ERA). When asked if she were familiar with the "ERA," she responded that she was and viewed it negatively: "The prophet (Mormon Church president Spencer Kimball) is against it. What he says comes from revelation. You have to believe what he says" (*Newsweek*, July 13, 1981, p. 26).

The cognitive component of a person's orientation toward a political symbol will probably encompass both substantive and associational meanings. However, one or the other is likely to be predominant. With respect to most political symbols, especially lower-order ones, we suspect that most people rely heavily on social identifications to give cognitive meaning to their symbolic orientations. However, among those who are more attentive to and actively involved in politics, substantive meanings are likely to play a more prominent role. It is these meanings that give substance to politics and direction to public policy. Moreover, it is these meanings that ultimately define the limits of acceptable symbolic usage. For these reasons, it is appropriate to inquire further into the nature and range of these meanings.

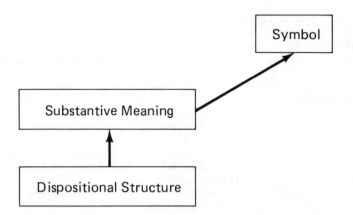

FIGURE 2.4 Basic Dispositions as a Source of Substantive Meaning.

The repertoire of substantive meanings that informs a person's symbolic orientations represents the store of "information" that he or she has acquired through experience and socialization. It involves all that the person "knows" about what is and what ought to be. We will refer to these beliefs and values, and the meanings they predicate, as the individual's "dispositional structure." It is this dispositional structure that defines a person's political world view and, as shown in Figure 2.4, gives substantive meanings to his or her symbolic orientations.

Although we are concerned with symbols of a distinctly political nature, to understand the substantive meanings these symbols may acquire requires that consideration be given to more general elements of an individual's dispositional structure. Our conception of that structure draws upon the insights and observations offered by a number of students of American politics, political behavior, and political psychology, most notably Rokeach (1960), Boulding (1956), and Lane (1962). It is also heavily influenced by the comparative work of Scott (1968), Pye (1962), and Banfield (1958). As here conceived, a person's dispositional structure rests upon a set of primitive assumptions regarding the world around him and the way it works—assumptions about the physical world, human nature, and the nature of society. These assumptions structure that person's conception of the empirical world. Although perhaps ultimately beyond proof, they are accepted as matters of "fact." We will therefore call them *empirical premises*.

These empirical premises predicate another set of ideas regarding what is important and the rules of conduct that should govern social life. Because these ideas are ultimately matters of preference or "value" rather than of "fact," we will call them *normative premises*. It is important to recognize, however, that these normative premises are typically taken as "givens" and accepted as "self-evident." While the distinction

TABLE 2.2   Symbol Linkage to Latent Dispositional Structure.

Latent Dispositional Structure	*Dimension*	*Examples of Symbols That Might Be Linked to Content Categories*
Empirical Premises:		
	I. Physical Nature	
	A. Abundance/ Scarcity	Foreign Aid
	B. Constancy	Breadbasket of America
	C. Malleability	Modern Technology
	II. Human Nature	
	A. Selfish/ Compassionate	Gas Rationing
	B. Weak/Strong	Pornography
	C. Trustworthy/ Deceitful	The American Taxpayer
	D. Fixed/Improvable	Rehabilitation
	III. Nature of Society	
	A. Individual/Society	Capital Punishment
	B. Social Borders	Women's Liberation
	C. Fragility	Law and Order
Normative Premises:		
	I. Social Obligation	Welfare
	II. Conceptions of Authority	Impeachment
	III. Distributive Justice	Reverse Discrimination
	IV. Personal Virtue	Work Ethic
	V. Life Values	Right to Life
Political Prescriptions:		
	I. Political Values	Liberty
	II. Scope of Politics	Government Regulation
	III. Decision Protocols	Unconstitutional
	IV. Standard of Political Conduct	Abscam
	V. Citizen's Role	Voting Rights

between "is" and "ought" is an analytically important one, it is often difficult to distinguish the two; and it is doubtful that they are generally experienced in distinct ways. What an individual "knows" to be right or wrong, true or false is probably more a matter of the degree of subjective certainty than of fact and value.

Associated with and to some extent derivative from a person's normative premises are a set of *prescriptions regarding politics and political behavior*. These structure his conceptions of government and provide the procedural and substantive criteria that he uses to guide his own political behavior and to evaluate the performance of the political system.

Individuals vary with respect to each of these components of a dispositional structure because of differences in biological makeup and life experiences. It is possible, however, to describe the general type of content that characterize each component.

Empirical premises. At the very foundations of an individual's dispositional structure is a set of empirical assumptions relating to the external world and the way it operates (e.g., see Rokeach, 1960; Scott, 1968). At least three subsets of assumptions are involved. The first has to do with the *nature of the physical world.* Here the individual must resolve for himself in some general way the following types of questions: (1) Is the physical world basically benign, one of bounty and abundance; or is it threatening, sparse, and hostile? (2) Is the physical environment one of constancy, stability, and predictability; or is it fickle and ominously uncertain? (3) Is the physical world basically malleable and subject to human intervention and control; or is it fixed and immutable?

The second subset of empirical assumptions deals with *human nature* itself. Issues to be resolved here include the following: (1) Are people basically selfish and self-regarding, or are they compassionate and other-regarding? (2) Are people inherently weak, irrational, and intemperate; or are they strong and dependable? (3) Are people trustworthy and honest, or are they deceitful and unreliable? (4) Is human nature fixed and unchangeable? Is it perfectable or at least improvable, or is it irretrievably flawed?

A final subset of questions that must be answered concerns the *nature of society* and social organization. They include the following: (1) Is primacy to be given to the individual or to society? Is the individual logically prior to society, or vice versa? (2) Are social borders fixed, natural, and immutable; or are they arbitrary, artificial, and subject to change? (3) Is society fragile and vulnerable, in constant threat of imminent collapse; or is it strong and resilient?

Normative premises. How the above questions are resolved influences the development of a set of normative premises regarding both the ends and the means of social behavior. These premises, like the empirical premises discussed above, are likely to be accepted at any point in time not as mere preferences or personal presumptions, but as enduring and self-evident truths. They tend to be experienced not simply as private standards and aspirations, but as generalized expectations and standards regarding what constitutes appropriate conduct.

The potential variability of normative premises is enormous, but again it is possible to identify some basic categories of content that may be linked to a symbol. These include the following: (1) *Premises regarding social obligation*: What are the responsibilities and duties of the individual to others and to society as a whole? What does the individual owe society, and how are these obligations to be fulfilled? (2) *Conceptions of authority*:

What is the basis of authority, and what are the limits of the legitimate exercise of power? (3) *Premises regarding distributive justice*: What constitutes fairness and equity, and how are these to be promoted? (4) *Conceptions of personal virtue*: What individual qualities are to be revered, admired, or encouraged? (5) *Life values*: What ends or goals are to be sought through individual and social activity, and what means are acceptable?

Political prescriptions.   Political prescriptions are also embedded in an individual's dispositional structure, although probably not as deeply or as firmly as most of the normative and the empirical premises. They tend to bear a clear relationship to the individual's normative premises, although they are not necessarily completely and logically consistent with those premises or derivative from them in any strict sense.

Again wide variation is possible, but the following are surely among the more important domains of content. (1) *Political values*: What values are to be protected or promoted through the political process, and what priorities should exist among them? (2) *Scope of politics*: What range of concerns are appropriately subject to governmental authority? Where are the boundaries between private concerns and public concerns? (3) *Decisional protocols*: What organizational procedures, institutions, and norms are appropriate to the management of social conflict and social decision making? (4) *Standards of political conduct*: What criteria are appropriate for evaluating the behavior of political leaders and the performance of governmental institutions? (5) *Conceptions of the citizen's role*: What rights and obligations accrue to an individual as a citizen? What constitutes responsible citizenship? What identities may a citizen legitimately assume?

The Cognitive Content Engaged by a Symbol.   Table 2.2 illustrates the domains of cognitive content in a person's dispositional structure that may be engaged by different symbols. It is important to recognize, however, that any given symbol may take on different meanings for different individuals owing not only to differences in latent dispositions within a content domain but also to differences in terms of what domain is engaged. Thus, for some, a symbol such as "Watergate" may engage dispositions simply involving political prescriptions regarding standards of political conduct or decisional protocols; for others, the dispositions engaged may involve more basic normative premises regarding conceptions of authority. For yet others, fundamental empirical assumptions about the fragility of the social order may be engaged. Similarly, a symbol such as the "energy crisis" may be linked to dispositional contents as diverse as primitive empirical premises regarding the abundance of the physical environment, normative premises regarding distributive justice, and political prescriptions regarding the scope of politics (e.g., see Schmitt and Grupp, 1976).

Not only is it possible for a particular symbol to engage different contents within and across domain for different individuals, it is also possible for a symbol to engage several content domains within the dispositional structure of a single individual. This would in fact be likely to occur among individuals with highly integrated or well-organized dispositional structures. However, even in the absence of a highly organized internal structure, multiple meanings are possible. Of course, it is possible for a symbol to fail to engage any content domain, in which case it remains for that individual virtually "meaningless" in a substantive sense. In such a case, the cognitive meaning attributed to the symbol will be almost purely associational, arising from positive or negative identifications with persons or groups for whom the symbol is substantively more meaningful.

The potency of a symbol in terms of arousing the attention of an individual probably tends to be greater, the greater the number of content domains engaged. However, symbols that are linked to more basic dimensions of an individual's dispositional structure are likely to have greater potency for arousal than those tied to less fundamental domains of content. Thus, symbols linked to empirical or to normative premises are likely to be more potent than those linked only to political prescriptions. This suggests that not only the meaning but also the potency of a symbol can vary across individuals because of differences in the content domains engaged.

The study of belief systems suggests the possibility of substantial variation in the way that the content within and across domains of individual dispositional structures is organized (e.g., see Converse, 1964; Rokeach, 1960; Stimson, 1974; Bem, 1970). For some, the contents within and across domains are highly integrated and interdependent. For others, specific contents may be compartmentalized, disjointed, and mutually inconsistent. Differences in terms of dispositional organization along these lines will have bearing not only on the complexity of meanings engaged by a symbol but also on the effect of new information and thus on the possibilities for change and growth in the face of changing circumstances.

A person's latent dispositional structure is the product of largely nonconscious learning and tends to remain largely unexamined. It represents a fundamental part of an individual's basic identity and provides his basic frame of reference for relating to the external world. It both affects and is affected by his self-conception and reference-group identifications. It also influences what sources of information are regarded as reliable and authoritative. Such information often serves to provide crucial guidance with regard to the linkage of specific symbols to cognitive content.

ESTABLISHING THE AFFECTIVE AND THE COGNITIVE LINKAGES TO A SYMBOL

There are a variety of ways through which a person's affective and cognitive ties to a symbol may develop. Some linkages may arise from the functional needs of the individual and are largely self-determined, although not necessarily in a conscious way. For example, in the early 1970s, as a consequence of simply following the news, many Americans became aware of a variety of environmental problems; and seeing these as threats to things they valued, they became strong supporters of "environmental protection." In contrast to such deliberative processes of linkage formation, affective and cognitive orientations toward a symbol may be acquired through the training one receives as part of his basic socialization. Here the linkages are more or less prescribed by external agents, rather than forged by the person in response to some specific need or situational imperative. We will distinguish between these two modes of linkage formation, referring to one as the active mode and the other as the passive mode. However, the distinction should not be overdrawn as the processes involved overlap and complement one another.

Active Linkage Formation: Functional Imperatives

In their classic study, *Opinions and Personality*, Smith, Bruner, and White (1964) identify three major functions that an individual's orientations toward an object may serve. They are "object appraisal," "social adjustment," and "externalization." These functions correspond to various needs or psychic imperatives that an individual may experience and seek to satisfy in relating to the external world. These functions help us understand how a person's orientations toward a symbol come about.

The first function, object appraisal, suggests that a person's symbolic orientations may be arrived at through an "objective" assessment of the objects or the situations that the symbol is presumed to reference. This assessment involves identifying the relevant "facts" from available referent information. These "facts" are then interpreted in light of the person's beliefs and values. This results in the substantive meaning or cognitive content that the individual assigns to the symbol. The affective component of the person's orientation toward the symbol follows more or less logically from this cognitive content. Both components are subject to change in the face of new information or changes in the person's basic values and beliefs. This pattern can be seen in Figure 2.5.

The emergence of "environmental protection" as a prominent symbol in the 1970s was probably attributable in large part to the dynamics of object appraisal. The experience of former Senator and environmental lobbyist Gaylord Nelson would seem to attest to this. He recounts how in the late 1960s he had difficulty finding a cosponsor for a bill to ban the use of

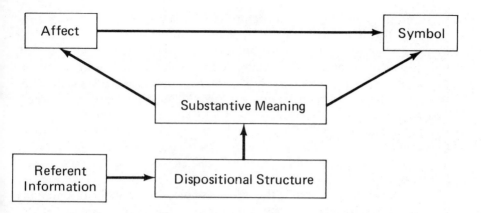

FIGURE 2.5   Substantive Sources of Symbolic Attachment.

DDT. He contacted about 30 members of the Senate and the House only to find that "half weren't sure what DDT was, and the other half were convinced it was a popular, foolproof pesticide" (*Detroit Free Press*, March 7, 1980, p. 8A). At the time, the latter were probably right about the popularity of DDT, at least among those who had heard of it. For many, it represented a triumph in human's efforts to control their environment. It was, after all, DDT that had brought both mosquitoes and the threat of malaria under control. However, when confronted with information about the enduring threat DDT posed to the environment, many Americans including most legislators, revised their opinions; and in the early 1970s, its use was banned by Congress.

One might suppose object appraisal to be the predominant way through which people relate to symbols. It is doubtful, however, that most people have either the interest or the inclination to engage regularly in the kind of calculus involved, especially with respect to most political symbols. Object appraisal is but one function that symbolic orientations may serve and not necessarily the most important one. While an accurate reckoning of reality may be important, uncertainties abound, informational costs are often high, and other things are important too—things such as social relations and peace of mind.

Social adjustment represents an alternative avenue through which a person's orientational linkages may be formed. Here cues provided by reference groups and authority figures are used as guides in formulating one's posture toward a symbol. By simply orienting oneself to a symbol in a manner that accords with others one considers important, one avoids the more taxing demands and potential risks of an independent appraisal. Moreover, in aligning one's views with those of significant others, one affirms identification with them and validates a claim to being like them.

The cognitive meanings attributed to a symbol as a consequence of social adjustment are likely to be primarily associational rather than substantive. The individual may attempt to reconstruct the substantive content others are perceived to attribute to the symbol, but this content may be largely irrelevant to the function that the symbol serves for the individual. It is affective agreement that is of primary importance. This is seen in the response of the Mormon woman to the "ERA" that we noted earlier. Her negative feelings toward the "ERA" were based less on the substantive arguments against it than the opposition of the Mormon Church. By opposing it, she affirmed her identity as a good Mormon and avoided any self-doubt and possible reproach that she might have experienced otherwise.

The social identifications that serve as guides to symbolic orientations may be either specific or diffuse in nature. One would expect that the more well defined the reference group, the clearer its cues and the greater its influence. However, even such amorphous aggregates as "Democrats" and "Republicans" can be significant points of reference and serve as guides to how "people like me" should feel toward various symbols. Erikson, Luttbeg, and Tedin (1980, p. 32) report, for example, that when asked about guaranteed jobs for people who wanted to work, 78 percent of the Democrats and 61 percent of the Republicans in a national sample supported the idea. However, when subsequently told that most Democrats favored the idea and Republicans generally opposed it, many of the respondents shifted their positions to those associated with their parties. When given the party cues, 81% of the Democrats supported guaranteed jobs, an increase of 3%, while Republican support declined nearly 20 percent to 42%. Presumably, those who shifted positions were previously unaware of where their party stood on the issue. Many of those whose positions were already in accord with the position of their party may have previously known their party's stance on the issue and may have adopted that position for the same reasons that led the switchers to change theirs; namely, social adjustment.

Externalization is yet another potential source of people's orientations toward political symbols. The affective and the cognitive linkages that serve this function are a product of psychic defense mechanisms that people use to assuage anxieties and to cope with personal problems they are reluctant to confront directly. The symbolic object serves as a convenient focus for affections or hostilities that may have little or nothing to do with the substantive content through which they are rationalized. Like orientations based on social adjustment, those arising from externalization may, in fact, be largely devoid of specific substantive meaning. Any meaning attributed to the symbol is likely to be of secondary importance to the affective sentiments it serves to focus.

Richard Reeves finds evidence of externalization in some of his encounters with zealous Christian conservatives. He writes:

Over the years, I have been surprised again and again by the anger of the folk of conservative Christianity. . . . Where did all that anger come from? A lot of it . . . had to do with being failed parents—or perceiving themselves . . . as having failed. . . . If you talked with them long enough, some of them would tell you about taking the children to church . . . of living by the Bible— and then a kid would take off, heading for [some city] . . . to live with someone. . . . Screwing around. Drinking. Smoking dope. . . . They wanted to blame someone or something—television, the government, the press, psychiatrists, Jews. One lady . . . told me through clenched teeth that George McGovern and the Democrats were responsible for the homosexuality of a boy she knew. A boy from a fine Christian family, she said—the family . . . turned out to be her own. The boy, of course, was her son. (*Detroit Free Press*, May 24, 1981, p. 3B)

Harold Lasswell argued that much of political behavior could be understood in terms of externalization. He suggested that politics was largely the product of the displacement of personal concerns onto public objects and of the rationalization of private motives in terms of the public interest (1960, 1965). However, considerable research suggests that externalization is not that prominent a source of political orientations (see, e.g., Lane, 1962; Pettigrew, 1958). While it may account for some of the more extreme views that get injected into politics, object appraisal and social adjustment would seem to be the more common sources of self-activated symbolic attachments. An even more important source of a person's orientations toward symbols is likely to be found in basic patterns of socialization. Here, perforce the individual assumes a more passive role in establishing orientational linkages to symbols.

Passive Linkage Formation: Socialization

Much of the research on political socialization rests on two basic assumptions, sometimes referred to as the "primacy principle" and the "structuring principle" (Searing et al., 1973). The first of these suggests that early learning, while subject to some future modifications, tends to have an enduring effect on one's political orientations. The second follows from the first and suggests that "basic orientations acquired during childhood structure the later learning of specific issue beliefs" (Searing et al., 1973, p. 415).

Much of the literature on political socialization has served to demonstrate that children begin to acquire identifiable political orientations at a very early age. However, the political relevance of this early learning has been a matter of some controversy. Some have argued that "the closer a learning experience is to adulthood, the greater its influence and political relevance" (Weissberg, 1974, p. 25). The conflict between this recency argument and the primacy principle can be resolved by recognizing that "certain political orientations are learned very early in life and are highly resistant to change while different political orientations may be suscepti- ble to continual modification with recent learning being most important" (Weissberg, 1974, p. 25). The critical questions, then, are what aspects of early learning are likely to persist and how do they affect a person's sub- sequent orientations toward political symbols.

The Primacy of What?   Children's early images of politics are character- ized by orientations toward political objects about which they have little in the way of substantive knowledge. These objects are typically charac- teristic symbols of the political culture or subculture into which the child is being socialized. The child's orientations toward these symbols are pri- marily affective in nature and tend to reflect culturally (or subculturally) prescribed sentiments. They are largely devoid of cognitive content beyond vague associational meanings. With respect to symbolic objects that serve to define social differences within a culture or a subculture, the child's orientations will depend on the type of cues he receives from his immediate environment. It is not surprising, then, to find considerable correspondence between parents and children in terms of their basic iden- tifications and political preferences (see Dalton, 1980). This correspond- ence increases the more the cues available to the child are clear and consistent. Thus, the stronger the parents' views and the greater the agreement between them, the more likely the child will adopt their views as his own (see Jennings and Niemi, 1968, pp. 173–174; Tedin, 1974).

The affective sentiments that dominate a child's early images of poli- tics are likely to have an enduring effect. They will condition subsequent learning (Nimmo, 1974, p. 59) and provide the foundations of basic loyal- ties and identifications (Easton and Dennis, 1969, pp. 128–137; Hess and Torney, 1967, pp. 32–50). As the child matures and acquires more information about the political system, he may assign greater substantive meaning to the symbols with which he identifies. However, this meaning will be based on an emerging dispositional structure, the content and organization of which are likely to have been permanently colored by his earlier, affectively laden symbolic identifications. Having learned that the "Constitution" is good or that "communists" are bad, for example, it is unlikely that he will be very receptive to information or ideas that might contradict these conclusions. Information that confirms or justifies the affective assessments he has already internalized, on the other hand, may be readily accepted and integrated into his basic dispositional structure. Thus, it would seem that the primacy principle operates primarily through basic identifications and early affective orientations toward prominent political symbols. These sentiments tend to persist, structuring subse- quent learning through childhood and coloring an individual's interpret- ations of reality as an adult.

As one might expect, as a person matures, he tends to develop clearer and substantively more meaningful cognitive orientations as a result of the growing body of knowledge and information he possesses (Hess and Torney, 1967, pp. 23–59). However, as Lasswell argues, this process of substantive specification is likely to remain incomplete:

> The environment of the infant and child is teeming with words of ambiguous reference, which take on positive or negative significance long before there is enough contact with reality either to define their frames of reference, or to distinguish those whose frames of reference are wholly indeterminate. As an "adult" the individual continues to respond to those articulations in many childish and juvenile ways, very often imputing some special significance to them. Such words are "law and order" [and] "patriotism". . . (1965, p. 30)

Research on public opinion and popular knowledge about politics suggests that symbolic orientations are often predicated on limited information and commonly remain substantively improverished (see Erikson et al., 1980, pp. 19–25). This is true of symbols of substantial and enduring affective significance as well as more fleeting objects of orientation.

This is amply illustrated by the stability and strength of partisan loyalties found in the United States—loyalties that are commonly acquired early and persist as behavioral cues even in the absence of any knowledge of how the parties differ on specific issues (see, e.g., Erikson et al., 1980, p. 74). Despite this lack of substantive specification, popular images of the two parties have remained remarkably stable over the last 50 years. Gallup reports that "voters today perceive the GOP to be 'the party of the rich' and the Democrats 'the workingman's party' just as they did during the New Deal, nearly a half century ago" (*Providence Journal*, November 22, 1981, p. 17). These images have probably been sustained in part by associational meanings arising from relatively stable patterns of social identifications within and across generations. However, the prevalence and stability of these images also suggest some modicum of agreement in the substantive meanings that people attribute to the symbols "Democrat" and "Republican."

Although the substantive content we are talking about involves little more than the attribution of some general biases to the parties in terms of the social interests they represent, the fact that considerable agreement exists with respect to this limited content is noteworthy, especially given the dearth of specific knowledge regarding parties and party positions found in the population. Since these substantive orientations apparently do not rest on specific information, where do they come from and what accounts for their persistence? The answers to these questions are to be found in the myths and rituals that characterize the political culture. The broad substantive meanings commonly accorded not only parties but other prominent political symbols are shaped largely through indoctrination into the perceived truths and cultural understandings that myths embody. The lessons that myths convey are regularly reinforced through various rituals, i.e., behavioral routines and ceremonies, that serve to affirm or to give testimony to the essential accuracy of the myths. Thus, the myths of the "Great Depression,"of "FDR" and his efforts to create a "New Deal" for the "common man," and of "Herbert Hoover" and his alleged insensitivity to the plight of the "poor" have instructed the popular conceptions of the two major parties since the 1930s. These myths have received repeated reinforcement through the rituals that attend such political events as the quadrennial National Democratic Convention.

Myths present culturally defined truths in the form of stories, parables, and aphorisms that simplify, highlight, or dramatize basic cultural premises and prescriptions. They offer socially constructed accounts of exemplary behavior and significant events in the life of the polity. Their primary purpose is to instruct, and much of the substantive instruction one receives in the course of the political socialization process will be by means of such myths. They are instrumental in shaping the values and beliefs that come to define one's basic dispositional structure. Because myths are frequently couched in terms of or revolve around specific symbols, they not only give substantive content to one's political world view but also tend to define how that content is to be linked to specific political symbols. In this sense, myths represent prepackaged symbolic orientations that are simply internalized. Because myths represent fragments of the political culture that is itself not always consistent, the lessons conveyed by them do not necessarily form a coherent whole. Often the lessons learned from them are never fully integrated but rather remain fragmented, forming more or less discrete "opinion molecules" (Bem, 1970, pp. 38–39).

There are countless myths circulating in a society at any time; new ones are constantly being created, and old ones, revised and elaborated on. Nimmo and Coombs (1980) have examined in some detail both some of the myths and the dynamics of mythmaking in American politics. Bennett has similarly explored a sampling of American myths, arguing that such myths

> give life to the values and beliefs from which public opinion emerges. They give rise to the powers of symbols used by politicans. They set the boundaries of most public policy debates. They legitimize the status quo in times of tranquility, and they chart the course of change in times of stress. (1980, p. 380)

In chapter 4, we will examine some of the substantive lessons conveyed through myths in American politics by examining some of the tenets and tensions of the American political culture. For the moment, we would simply note that myths provide an important vehicle through which some substantive content is given to the often affectively ladened symbolic orientations that emerge through the processes of political socialization.

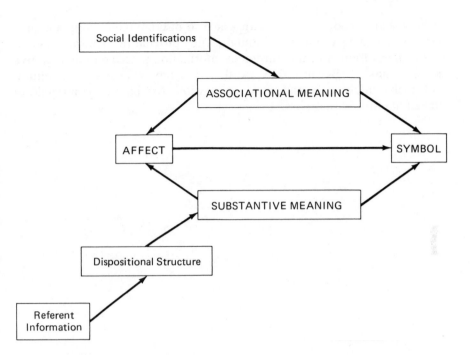

FIGURE 2.6   Linkages in an Individual's Symbolic Attachments.

CONCLUSIONS

In this chapter, we have explored the nature and dynamics of an individual's symbolic attachments. The political significance of these attachments arises from the fact that the symbols involved provide socially defined objects of individual meaning and serve to synthesize diversity. In attempting to sort out the complexities of individual symbolic involvements, we have identified a number of elements and linkages, which are summarized in Figure 2.6. The essential point is that the significance that a political symbol assumes for an individual can have many sources and can take many forms, all potentially idiosyncratic. Yet, ultimately, the individual's orientations toward the symbol are manifested in ways that are socially patterned.

These patterns, their social functions, and their political implications will be explored in subsequent chapters. Here we would simply note that symbols are created and sustained by individuals. Their social and political potency ultimately rests on the functions they serve for the individual. Confronted with a diverse, confusing array of stimuli emanating from the political arena, the individual would be overwhelmed without some system for filtering and organizing this variety. Symbols provide him with a socially shared coding system with which to discriminate among and give personal meaning to incoming stimuli. They provide behavioral cues and relieve him of much of the burden of information search and deliberative decision making. Because they are shared, symbols facilitate his cultural and social integration and make it possible for him to communicate "meaningfully" with others.

3

Patterns of Symbolic Usage
and Responses

The social significance of symbols arises from the fact that they are common objects of personal meaning and emotive sentiment. As we saw in the previous chapter, what a particular symbol means and the feelings it indexes vary from one individual to another. Nonetheless, because symbols are simultaneously objects of personal and of social significance, they are critical to communications and can be used to arouse or to reassure people having diverse motives and concerns. How symbols are used and the responses they elicit, however, are dependent upon a number of factors.

The way a person uses or responds to a symbol is directly dependent upon his or her peculiar affective and cognitive orientations toward it. Although no two people are likely to have precisely the same set of orientations, it is possible to identify some broad general patterns of symbolic attachment that help to explain differences in the way people use and respond to symbols. We will inquire into the extent to which these patterns can be generalized across symbols and how they are distributed in the population. We will then turn to some of the contextual or situational factors that influence a person's response to a symbol. While the power of a symbol to arouse or to reassure is ultimately a function of the emotions and meanings people associate with it, this power will be realized only if the symbol is used in a manner consistent with the meanings people attribute to it and in a context that they find personally meaningful. In other words, people's responses to a symbol will be contingent upon their. assessments of the circumstances of its usage. As Rokeach has pointed out, behavioral responses are dependent not only on "attitudes toward objects" but also on "attitudes toward situations" (1968, pp. 126–129). That people's responses to a symbol are conditional upon the way it is used serves to constrain the potential abuse that might otherwise be made of it. Inquiry into factors bearing on an individual's assessments of the situational relevance and appropriate usage of a symbol can help us understand not only how and why people respond to the symbol but also the nature and limits of its effective usage.

COMPOSITE MODES OF SYMBOLIC ATTACHMENT

In the last chapter, we suggested that an individual's orientations toward a symbol could be decomposed into two basic attitudinal dimensions—an affective dimension and a cognitive one. As we saw, these affective and cognitive orientations emerge as a consequence of a variety of social and psychological processes and may develop more or less independently of one another. To understand how they develop, it was useful to treat the two dimensions separately. However, as we explore the behavioral consequences of these orientations, it is necessary to consider them jointly in terms of the composite patterns they form. Although these patterns are potentially as variable as the people they characterize, this variation can be summarized in terms of four distinctive patterns or modes of symbolic attachment. These general patterns result from differences among people in the intensity of their affect toward a symbol and in the richness and specificity of the substantive meaning they attribute to it. Distinguishing people with high affect from those with little or no affective feelings toward the symbol and those with relatively well developed substantive orientations from those with diffuse or inchoate ones, the four orientational configurations shown in Figure 3.1 can be identified. Each of these combinations marks a distinctive mode of symbolic attachment and is likely to be associated with a distinctive pattern of behavior with respect to the symbol.

The behavioral inclinations associated with these modes of symbolic attachment can be characterized in terms of instrumental and expressive behavior. Instrumental behavior refers to activities undertaken for the purposes of promoting or achieving some larger goal. The behavior is a

		Affect Attached to a Particular Symbol	
		High	Low
Cognitive Meaning Attributed to a Political Symbol:	Well Specified	Ideological	Pragmatic
	Diffuse	Reactive	Apathetic

FIGURE 3.1   Modes of Symbolic Attachment.

means toward an end and is, at least in principle, subject to some assessment of success or failure and relative efficiency. Expressive behavior, on the other hand, serves as an end in itself. It consists of giving vent to one's feelings and expressing one's values and beliefs. The purposes of the act are satisfied by the action itself.

The distinction between instrumental behavior and expressive behavior, then, resides not in the act but in the motives that prompt it. Consider, for example, the act of voting. For a person motivated by the desire to influence the outcome of an election in a particular way, voting is an instrumental act. For a person who, for one reason or another, is indifferent about the outcome but votes out of a sense of civic obligation, the act is an expressive one. Although the instrumental/expressive distinction is often treated as if it defined mutually exclusive forms of behavior, it is more appropriately regarded as a way of describing the functions of behavior—functions that are not mutually exclusive. Viewed in this way, it is possible to speak of behavior that is both instrumental and expressive in nature. It is surely the case that the act of voting for some is simultaneously an instrumental and an expressive act.

In general, symbolic attachments involving high affect will be associated with expressive actions. Those involving well-developed cognitive orientations will be associated with instrumental behavior. The nature and predictability of a person's response to a symbol will tend to vary with the intensity of affect toward it (Himmelstrand, 1960, pp. 47–54), but the probability of a person's initiating action using the symbol will depend heavily on the clarity and richness of his or her cognitive orientations.

If a person's orientations toward a symbol involve both considerable affect and well-specified cognitive meaning, his or her attachment to the symbol may be described as "ideological." For such persons, actions associated with the symbol will be both instrumental and expressive. Moreover, the behavioral predispositions that are activated by the symbol will tend to be stable and predictable. Persons of this orientational type will be active guardians of the symbol, seeking to preserve and promote the meanings they attribute to it. They may initiate actions in the name of the symbol or use it to challenge the actions of others.

Consider the "Equal Rights Amendment" (ERA) as an object of ideological attachment. For committed feminists, "ERA" may be the object of strong emotive sentiment and index a well-developed understanding of the historical struggle for women's rights, an understanding that finds the traditional role of women in our society to be at odds with their beliefs and values. For antifeminists, "ERA" may be the object of equally strong feelings, albeit in the opposite direction; and it may also reference well-developed conceptions of the historical experience and appropriate role of women in our society. In both cases, the mode of orientation toward "ERA" is ideological. Both are likely to use the symbol to provoke or arouse others and are themselves likely to be aroused or provoked by its usage.

The orientations that define the second mode of symbolic attachment are primarily referential in character. This pattern of affectively neutral but substantively well-specified meaning is perhaps the hallmark of the "pragmatist," or "political realist." It might also be used to describe the "cynic" or "inside dopester." A person of this orientational persuasion is unlikely to use that symbol or to be activated by its use except when it serves some ulterior purpose. As a consequence, his behavior will not be predictable from a knowledge of his orientation toward the symbol per se. His approach may be that of the rational activist, if not the Machiavellian manipulator, or that of the detached observer, depending on the motives that prompted his cognitive investment in the symbol.

Returning to our "ERA" example, one can readily imagine a political leader who is thoroughly familiar with the history of the Equal Rights Amendment and the issues associated with it but who lacks any strong feelings toward it. For him, "ERA" is merely a referential symbol. However, being aware that it is the object of strong feelings on the part of others, he may use the symbol or react to it in a manner calculated to maximize his political advantage or minimize his potential political losses. Depending on the circumstances he finds himself in and the nature of his constituency, this may mean that he will warmly embrace "ERA," actively oppose it, or avoid responding to it in any way.

Symbolic attachments lacking substantive specification but high in affect are not likely to prompt people to initiate any actions using the symbol. However, they may occasion strong expressive reactions. Despite the absence of well-defined meaning, the reactions of persons with this mode of symbolic attachment may be fairly predictable. They will tend to respond in a manner consistent with the behavioral cues provided by those persons or groups with whom they identify and regard as reliable sources of guidance. This pattern of response will be stable insofar as the sources upon which they rely are consistent and remain credible. With respect to a given symbol, persons of this type are typically "followers." They are available for activation by those who initiate actions using the symbol, and they are ultimately vulnerable to manipulation through it. They are protected only by the integrity of those that they would follow, the safeguards afforded by stable institutions, and a vaguely defined set of general expectations regarding the use of that symbol.

With respect to our "ERA" example, persons of the reactive mode are likely to be only vaguely aware of the facts and issues surrounding the history of the Equal Rights Amendment. Nonetheless, they will have relatively strong positive or negative feelings about "ERA." As we saw in Chapter 2, these affective orientations may arise from a variety of sources that have little or nothing to do with the substantive matters that the symbol was created to reference. For example, affective sentiments toward "ERA" might be predicated on (1) the summary opinion guidance of others upon whom one depends or with whom one identifies, (2) vague perceptions that the symbol somehow represents a threat or a challenge to one's status or life-style, on the one hand, or relief from perceived deprivations, on the other, (3) visceral reactions to those who are identified in some way or another with the symbol, or (4) presumptions based on the structure or form of the symbol or some other equally irrelevant criteria; e.g., the belief that clenched fists and any kind of "power" are bad but that "equal rights" and anything "democratic" are good. Conover, Coombs, and Gray (1980) have documented in detail the prevalence of such dynamics in accounting for attitudes toward "ERA."

Regardless of their source, the strong affective orientations of those of the reactive mode predispose them to respond to the symbol in characteristic fashion and to render evaluative judgments of persons and things they associate with the symbol that are consistent with their affect toward it. At the extreme, these are people in the streets chanting empty slogans for reasons they do not really understand. As Graber, quoting Blanksten, observes:

> Many people who give lip service to a common ideology may not understand the basic doctrines involved. Nevertheless, they "derive slogans, phrases, or words" from the ideology, which then "become magnified as political symbols and taboos" channeling political action. Words like "imperialist," "capitalist," "colonialist," "Communist," have become effective street slogans even when those who use them to stir up emotional reactions have only the haziest notion of what they mean, conceptually. (1976, p. 53)

Many political conflicts are reduced to a battle over slogans and words which connote valued or desirable things. The actual preferences of a populace with respect to substantive issues may be at odds with their emotive responses to the language in which the debate over those issues is couched. In one recent poll, 51% of those who had heard of the "right to lifers" said they agreed with their position on abortion. Yet only 16% of the same sample disapproved of abortion under all circumstances. Given the potency of an opposing symbol which reifies the sanctity of human life, proponents of abortion rights have been hard put to come up with an equally powerful slogan. While "pro-choice" is not as powerful a symbol, its emphasis on "freedom" and "individual choice" undoubtedly helps to neutralize the appeal of "right to life." As one columnist has written:

> If the battle over abortion remains undecided, it is because the other side has a pretty good slogan: "pro-choice" . . . . If the "pro-choice" people had made the error of calling their position "pro-abortion" they would have lost the right long ago. (William Raspberry, "Needed: Some Catchy New Slogans," *Providence Journal*, July 10, 1981, p. A–12)

Persons whose orientations toward a symbol are largely devoid of both affect and cognitive content are apathetic, if not aliens, with respect to that symbol. They will be essentially indifferent to the symbol. They will exhibit no consistent behavioral inclinations with respect to it and will be largely invulnerable to appeals based on it. The apathetic with respect to "ERA." to continue our example, are likely not to even recognize the symbol, let alone have any feelings toward it.

GENERALIZING ACROSS SYMBOLS

Up to this point, attention has centered on different patterns that may characterize an individual's orientations toward a single symbol. A person is likely to exhibit different patterns with respect to different symbols. He might, for example, be ideological in his orientations toward some symbols, pragmatic with respect to others, and reactive or even an alien with respect to yet others. Still, a person is likely to exhibit a fairly consistent mode of orientation toward symbols relating to a particular area of social or political life, the patterns varying with the level of his interests and involvement in the area. For example, with respect to the symbols associated with civil rights policy, a person may be ideological in his orientations, but with respect to most other political symbols, his orientations may be those of a reactive or even an apathetic.

As was noted in the first chapter, politics in general is not an area of sustained interest and involvement for many. Not surprisingly, then, one finds relatively few who might be described as "consistent ideologues" in their orientations toward political symbols. Although it is impossible to estimate their number exactly, research on public opinion and popular involvement in politics (see Pierce, 1970, 1975; Margolis, 1977; Nie, Verba, and Petrocik, 1980; Erikson, Luttbeg, and Tedin, 1980) suggests that 15 to 20% would be a generous estimate. A more stringent reckoning might reduce their number by half. Although there is some evidence to suggest that the ranks of this group have grown in recent years (e.g., see Nie and Anderson, 1974; Nie, Verba, and Petrocik, 1980; Stimson, 1975), it is likely to remain a small segment of the populace. Persons with this characteristic mode of orientation toward political symbols more or less define the attentive public and include among their number most of those actively involved in the political process.

Persons of a consistently pragmatic orientation are probably quite rare. We would guess that well under 5% of the population could be so characterized. Since it implies little emotive commitment to symbols but a substantial cognitive investment, this mode of attachment is unlikely to be sustained without some material or status inducements. Because politics is an area that may provide these inducements, one would expect persons of this bent to be found disproportionately among those actively involved in the political process. Because of this, their political significance may be substantially greater than their number. Within the political process, they may be expected to use and respond to symbols in a distinctly instrumental, if not exploitive, way. This type of calculus was repeatedly reflected in the Watergate revelations. In many issues, the Nixon Administration was more concerned with how "it would play in Peoria" than with the substantive merits of the issues themselves.

The reactive style is probably the most common. We suspect that fully 40 to 60% of the population could be characterized in this way. For such people, a wide variety of political symbols are probably of some significance. This significance, however, arises largely from acquired affection that is predicated on neither substantive knowledge nor firsthand experience. While the symbols serve as objects of emotive sentiments, they remain ambiguous in their referents and diffuse in meaning. Although the behavior of persons with this characteristic pattern of orientation will often be important to the operations of the polity, that behavior is not likely to be self-generated or extensive.

While at odds with the classical conceptions of responsible citizenship, the reactive mode is undoubtedly found by many to be well suited to their needs and desires regarding politics. It provides an economical way of satisfying a sense of civic obligation and is probably adequate to their needs and to those of the polity, at least during periods of stability. During periods of political unrest and social upheaval, persons previously of this orientational bent may well develop a more sophisticated approach toward political symbols. There is some evidence to suggest that this is precisely what happens (Pierce, 1970; Nie and Anderson, 1974; Nie, Verba, and Petrocik, 1980; Stimson, 1975). The danger, of course, lies in the time required to make the transition. In the face of a sudden crisis or a major discontinuity, those of a reactive mode remain vulnerable to manipulation at the hands of unscrupulous or demagogic leaders.

Perhaps a third of the population might appropriately be regarded as primarily apathetic in their orientations toward most political symbols. They represent the least informed and least involved members of the political system. For some, this pattern of noninvolvement is a matter of choice; but for many, it is probably a matter of circumstance. For the latter, the demands of the moment may simply preclude concern with politics, even though this may be contrary to their larger self-interest. Among apathetics, participation will be rare, irregular, and of little consequence to the normal operations of the polity. Were they to become engaged, however, their potential impact would be profound. In this sense, they represent a latent threat to the status quo. This threat is remote, however, given the difficulties involved in mobilizing them and the numerous obstacles that can be erected by defenders of the status quo.

The distributional patterns we have characterized pertain to the universe of political symbols. If attention is restricted to a more limited set of symbols, the distribution of the various modes of symbolic orientation will change. Although most people's interest and concern do not encompass the whole of politics, many have a special interest in a specific area or domain of politics. Here persons otherwise of a reactive bent and perhaps even some who are generally apathetic may exhibit orientations similar to those of the ideologue. Thus, with respect to the symbols associated with a specific area of politics, the ranks of the ideologues may swell upwards to 40% or more of the population.

The focal points of interest and involvement of these "partial ideologues" may be different levels of government or politics (e.g., local, regional, or national) or specific areas of issue or policy (e.g., social security, agricultural policy, or foreign policy with respect to South Africa). These, or some combination of them, will define political specialists whose modes of orientation toward selected symbols may be atypical of their general pattern of symbolic attachments. Thus, for example, there are members of "issue publics" (Converse, 1964; RePass, 1971), whose status as ideologues (or simply reactives) may be restricted to symbols of immediate relevance to a particular issue area, and "communalists" (Nie and Verba, 1972), whose symbolic orientations are well developed only with respect to matters of local concern.

Variation in popular modes of symbolic attachment is also likely to be found across the different types of symbolic objects identified in the previous chapter. There we distinguished between community, regime, and situational symbols, suggesting that they tend to form a natural hierarchy in terms of generality and durability. In terms of the four modes of symbolic orientation, the reactive mode is likely to be most common with respect to community symbols. Even among the attentive public, we suspect that these symbols are often objects of intense affect but rather diffuse meaning. Lamb (1974, p. 224), for example, reports that a significant portion of a sample of "affluent technocrats" were unable to give any meaning to the symbol "democracy" beyond vaguely equating it with the American system. Regime symbols also tend to be objects of widespread reactive orientation. However, here greater variation in patterns of symbolic orientation is likely to be found. Substantial segments of the population have relatively well developed conceptions of "Congress," "Separation of Powers," "Federalism," and other symbols of the regime, although for many they remain objects of affective sentiment but diffuse meaning.

With respect to most situational symbols (certain current authorities being the most prominent exception), the most common mode of symbolic orientation is the apathetic one. For example, in 1966, as the American involvement in Vietnam rapidly expanded and the controversy over our involvement there became heated, 64% of the American public did not recognize the symbols "hawk" or "dove" in association with positions about that war, even though these terms were widely used by the media to distinguish proponents and opponents of expanded military action (Smith, 1972, p. 269). In 1979, only 23% of the people in a national survey could identify the U.S. and the U.S.S.R. as the two nations involved in the Strategic Arms Limitations Talks, commonly referenced by the symbol "SALT" (Erikson, Luttbeg, and Tedin, 1980, p. 19).

Such popular ignorance of the symbols associated with the topical concerns of government and politics is commonplace. This fact has important consequences. It helps to explain why in the course of a specific political conflict participants seeking outside support commonly attempt to define the controversy in terms of higher-order symbols. While this allows the controversy to become relevant to a larger number of people, it also leads to a politics of exaggeration as participants strain to define the situation in terms of the highest-order symbols that can be credibly applied.

DISCRIMINATIONS BASED ON SYMBOLIC ORIENTATIONS

The fourfold typology of different patterns of cognitive and affective orientations toward political symbols might be viewed as an extension and a refinement of a number of notions developed by Edelman. He suggests that organized elites relate to politics through referential symbols and tend to act instrumentally whereas the unorganized masses relate through condensational symbols and expressive behavior (1964, pp. 22–23). This argument parallels our distinction between the pragmatic and the reactive modes of symbolic orientation. We have identified two additional patterns of symbolic attachment: namely, the ideological and the apathetic modes. These distinctions emerge as a logical consequence of variation in how people relate to symbols and are important in that they have different behavioral implications.

Thus, our scheme serves to place the distinctions Edelman draws between organized elites and the unorganized masses in a larger context. Organized elites manipulate symbols for specific material ends, using them to arouse or to placate the mass public (1964, pp. 89–95). For reasons of background, strategic location, and, most importantly, personal interests and involvement, one would indeed expect elites to have more highly developed and instrumental orientations toward political symbols. Elite status implies and tends to demand symbolic attachments that are either pragmatic or ideological in nature. At the same time, and for largely the same reasons, large portions of the population have orientations toward these same symbols that are essentially reactive.

What the scheme obliges us to note, however, is that elites need not be characterized by a single mode of orientation. While it recognizes that some elites may employ symbols solely for their own gain, it also suggests that elite behavior may be more selfless and motivated primarily by an emotive commitment to the substantive meanings attributed to symbols. Similarly, the scheme acknowledges that a large segment of the population may simply react to the manipulation of symbols by others. However, it does not require that the mass public be viewed as totally undifferentiated in this regard. It suggests that a portion of the population will have little or no attachment to the symbols involved and as a consequence will be largely immune to manipulation through them.

Edelman also identifies four different styles or types of political language—hortatory, legal, bargaining, and administrative (1964, pp. 134–149). Each language seems to be distinguished by symbols that are the objects of a particular distribution of the various modes of symbolic attachment we have identified. For example, hortatory language is characterized by an abundance of what we have called higher-order symbols—symbols that are the objects of widespread reactive attachment and which may be used by ideologues and pragmatists alike to marshall support. Hortatory language is the language in which political leaders or would-be political leaders normally address the public. A striking example is provided by Senator Edward Kennedy's stirring speech to the 1980 National Democratic Convention. He exhorted his "fellow Democrats" and "fellow Americans" to rally to a cause that he identified with the Democratic Party:

> Our cause has been, since the days of Thomas Jefferson, the cause of the common man—and the common woman. . . . It is the glory and the greatness of our tradition to speak for those who have no voice, to remember those who are forgotten, to respond to the frustrations and fulfill the aspirations of all Americans seeking a better life in a better land. . . . We are the party of the New Freedom, the New Deal, and the New Frontier. We have always been the party of hope. So this year, let us offer new hope—new hope to an America uncertain about the present, but unsurpassed in its potential for the future. ("Continue Democratic Principles of Past," *Congressional Quarterly Weekly Report*, August 16, 1980, pp. 2423–2424)

Bargaining language, on the other hand, would seem to be distinguished by symbols of pragmatic significance to the participants but to which most people are apathetic. As an example of this, consider the following exchange at a congressional hearing between Robert Myers, an actuary expert from the Social Security Administration, and Wilbur Mills, for many years the chairman of the House Ways and Means Committee. The exchange relates to changes in the benefits and financing of the social security program.

> The CHAIRMAN. What is the cost of the change in the disability program?
> Mr. MYERS. That is 0.03 of payroll.
> The CHAIRMAN. You have 0.08 as I go over it hurriedly.
> Mr. ALGER (a representative from Texas). What is payroll again?
> The CHAIRMAN. When we say payroll, what is it in dollars?

Mr. MYERS. The current taxable payroll under the $4800 earnings base is a little under $220 billion a year. If the base were increased to $5400, it would be about $235 billion a year. . . . (Derthick, 1979, p. 59)

Legal language also involves symbols that engage differential patterns of attachment. For most, the mode of attachment is either apathetic or reactive; but for those who use the language, the orientational pattern tends to be distinctly pragmatic. Consider the following majority decision from the U.S. Supreme Court on the legality of abortion in 1973:

A state criminal abortion statute of the current Texas type, that excepts from criminality only a life-saving procedure on behalf of the mother, without regard to pregnancy stage and without recognition of the other interests involved, is violative of the Due Process Clause of the Fourteenth Amendment. (Quoted in Brigham, 1977, p. 21)

Administrative language is similarly characterized by symbols pragmatically interpreted by their users, but it is distinguished by the fact that the symbols tend to be affectively and cognitively meaningless outside this narrow circle. Consider the following statement of policy as proposed by the Chairman of the Federal Communications Commission in 1969:

In any comparative hearing within the same community for the frequency or channel of an applicant for renewal of a broadcast license, the applicant for renewal of license shall be awarded the grant if such applicant shows that its program service during the preceding licensing term has been substantially, rather than minimally, attuned to meeting the needs and interests of its area, and the operation of the station has not otherwise been characterized by serious deficiencies. (Quoted in Krasnow and Longley, 1978, p. 142)

ASSESSING SITUATIONAL RELEVANCE AND THE APPLICABILITY OF A SYMBOL

Edelman argues that the responses associated with symbolic stimuli vary with perceptions of threat or of reassurance (1964, pp. 4–16; 1971, pp. 38–39). Such perceptions will, of course, depend upon the individual's particular orientations toward the symbols involved. Symbols that are the objects of positive sentiments will normally be found reassuring and serve to promote quiescence. For example, to promote popular acceptance of the actions and policies of his administration, President Nixon repeatedly defined them as programs for "peace and prosperity without inflation." Symbolic objects of strong negative affect, e.g., "communists" for most Americans or "abortion" for persons of a "pro-life" persuasion, tend to arouse anxieties and to communicate threat. Symbolic usages that involve the negation of positive symbols, e.g., the burning of the Flag or the term "un-American," invite perceptions of threat.

While basic orientations are important, other factors are also involved in the perception of threat or of reassurance. Most notable among these are the perceived relevance of the situation to the individual and the perceived appropriateness of the symbol to that situation; i.e., the event, issue, or circumstances to which the symbol is being related. We suspect, for example, that for most Americans, the claim that overcrowding in prisons is "unconstitutional" is not likely to spark a responsive chord, even though "unconstitutional" is a potent negative symbol. Prison life is simply too remote from the personal lives of most to be of much relevance. Moreover, many would undoubtedly find the use of the term "unconstitutional" inappropriate with respect to the issue of overcrowded prisons.

Situational Relevance

Situational relevance is simply a matter of having a perceived personal stake in the situation; the greater the stake, the more relevant the situation. This stake may be material or economic in nature, but status considerations and social values and beliefs may also be involved. As Sears and his associates have shown, these latter considerations may be even more important than material self-interest in shaping perceptions of a stake in a situation. They find that sociocultural beliefs and political identifications acquired through the socialization process are more important than material interests in accounting for people's responses to social issues (1979 and 1980), the energy crisis (1978), and Vietnam (Lau, Brown, and Sears, 1978).

Situational relevance is largely a function of proximity. Lack of immediacy militates against the perception of relevance. Proximity may be reckoned socially, as well as physically in terms of time and space. Social distance is defined by a person's group identifications and self-conceptions. These group identifications may be based on any of the social attributes that people use to locate and distinguish themselves with respect to others. They may range from specific membership groups such as a particular union to broad and ill-defined social categories such as the "middle class" or the "common man." A situation will normally be seen as relevant only if it bears fairly directly upon the individual or those with whom he identifies. However, he may be convinced (and normally he will have to be persuaded in this regard) that it involves indirect effects or a potential precedent of significance to him.

Of course, what an individual views as proximate or immediate depends to some extent on that individual's world view and, more specifically, on the temporal and spatial horizons that constrain it. Variation along these lines has given rise to such distinctions as "cosmopolitans" versus "locals" or "future-oriented" versus "present-oriented." The former distinguishes between persons with broad interests that transcend their immediate locale and those whose interests and concerns do not; the latter distinguishes those whose concerns transcend the present and prompt them to postpone current gratifications for future benefits from those who tend to think and live for the moment. The outlooks suggested by these distinctions tend to be fairly stable personality attributes, but they tend to vary from one group or subculture to another. Lane (1962, pp. 283–306), for example, finds that the time and spatial perspectives of the working class tend to be relatively constrained. Banfield (1974) argues that differences in time perspectives mark important and characteristic differences in social class, the upper class being the most future-oriented and the lower class, the least. Whatever their origins, temporal and spatial horizons are likely to play an important role in the reckoning of situational relevance.

While a person's response to a symbol tends to be contingent upon his perception of situational relevance, some symbols may be so important to him that their very application to any situation renders that situation personally relevant. For many Americans, "social security" is such a symbol; for many Jewish Americans, "Israel" and "anti-Semitism"; for many blacks, the "KKK." Except in such cases, an individual's predispositions with respect to a symbol are likely to be activated only if the situation in which it is used touches him fairly directly or he is somehow persuaded that he has a stake in the situation. The latter may not be difficult if one can command people's attention, but getting people's attention is often one of the most difficult tasks in politics.

Linking Symbol and Situation

Assuming perceived situational relevance, the question becomes one of how symbols are credibly linked to the situation. For the individual to whom a symbol is important, the problem is one of assessing the appropriateness of its application. The more certain he is in this judgment, the more likely he is to respond to the symbol. If his cognitive orientations toward the symbol are well developed, instrumental actions are likely to be initiated. For example, when the Reagan Administration nominated Ernest Lefever, a prominent critic of former President Carter's human rights policy, for Undersecretary of State for Human Rights, "human rights" activists mobilized to defeat the nomination.

If a person's mode of orientation is primarily reactive, expressive behavior in the form of either uncritical support or anger and hostility is likely to result. Consider, for example, popular reaction to the attack of the Chicago police on demonstrators at the 1968 Democratic National Convention. An official investigation into the incident found the police action unjustified, terming it a "police riot," and the media reporting the incident were generally critical of the police. Nonetheless, the reaction of a majority of Americans, many of whom had witnessed the attack on television, was one of support for "the police" and "law and order" and of anger and hostility toward the "demonstrators" and other "trouble-makers."

The criteria used to assess what constitutes a credible application vary from individual to individual. They depend upon the person's mode of orientation toward the symbol, his general expectation regarding its usage, and the type of information he has available and upon which he is willing to rely. While persons with more highly developed cognitive orientations are clearly better prepared to render an independent evaluation, their judgments are often predicated on much the same criteria used by those who must depend upon others for "linkage guidance" (Sartori, 1969, p. 407). If a symbol is to retain its potency, however, it is essential that its use be restricted by the vigilance of at least some of those with an ideological bent toward it. Indiscriminate use of a term can water down its effectiveness and distinctiveness. This can be seen in the continuing battle between environmentalists and developers. Environmental zealots have used the term "environmental hazard" so indiscriminately and in so many different contexts that the potency of the symbol has been reduced and many people have become immune to such warnings. Similarly, health researchers have argued that so many practices may have "cancer-causing effects" that many people have despaired at doing anything about such perils.

Autonomously Based Evaluations

For the "vigilant ideologue" (i.e., for the person for whom the symbol is an affectively charged object of well-developed meaning and who is anxious to safeguard the integrity of its use), the criterion for evaluating the situational applicability of a symbol is simple. He must simply assess the extent to which the "facts" of the situation are consonant with the meanings he attributes to the symbol. There are two potential problems, however. The first of these is information. Frequently, the person will lack firsthand knowledge of the situation and will have to rely upon information provided by others. His judgment thus becomes dependent upon the reliability and credibility of his informational sources.

Objectively, the information a person receives is more likely to be reliable, the broader his sources. But emotive attachments to the symbol may lead him to rely fairly exclusively on sources that share his biases and whose credibility rests on little else. He may also fall into the trap that lies in the general psychological tendency

> to seek a single sufficient or satisfactory explanation for any given event, rather than one that is the best of all possible explanations. . . . Thus, when more than one satisfactory explanation is potentially available to an individual, which one he adopts may depend primarily on which of the various possible explanations is most *salient*. (Knouse, 1971, p. 11)

This suggests that the more important the symbol is to a person, i.e., the greater his affective and cognitive investments in it, the more inclined he will be to accept its application. When conflicting definitions of a situation are offered, the one involving the most important symbol or symbols will tend to be the most readily accepted.

For example, "national security" is probably more important to most people than "the public's right to know." As a consequence, when confronted with competing definitions of a situation involving these symbols, most people will be inclined to accept the "national security" explanation. Indeed, as the Watergate hearings revealed (see *The Senate Watergate Report*, 1974), this tendency was repeatedly played upon by the Nixon Administration to cover or to justify actions that might otherwise have been interpreted as illegal or inimical to the "rule of law" and the "public's right to know." "Executive privilege" was another symbol used by Nixon to justify the suppression of information. Lacking the importance typically attributed to "national security," however, it was much less likely to enjoy presumptive acceptance over competing explanations framed in terms of other salient symbols; e.g., "abuse of power."

The danger involved in this tendency is compounded by the fact that the first information a person receives is often from like-minded people or sources that share his biases. The problem that must be overcome is the tendency "to accept the first causal explanation that is sufficient by itself to account for the phenomenon...and to retain it even when... presented with an opportunity to accept a better alternative" (Knouse, 1971, p. 12).

As a consequence of all these problems, the "vigilant ideologue" may abuse the very symbols he seeks to safeguard. A striking and prominent illustration of this is provided by the reaction of President Lyndon Johnson to the Dominican crisis in 1965. It would seem that in his concern with the threat of "communism," he readily fell victim to misinformation regarding the nature of a political revolt in the Dominican Republic. The consequence was a costly and unseemly American military intervention, diminished Presidential credibility, and the attenuation of the potency of "communism" as a political symbol.

A person with a pragmatic orientation toward a symbol, like the ideologue, may engage in a fairly elaborate cognitive assessment of its appropriateness to a situation. His concerns, however, will be different, and his judgments will tend to be dominated by considerations largely unrelated to the meaning he attributes to the symbol. The central question will be how use of the symbol may affect his interests. Unless he has a personal stake in the situation or perceives the opportunity to exploit it to his advantage, he will be largely indifferent to the symbol's application. Even if he finds the situation congruent with his interpretation of the symbol, he is likely to oppose the symbol's application if he sees himself being adversely affected. On the other hand, when it is to his advantage, he

may attempt to use the symbol in situations wherein, by his own definition, it has doubtful relevance. The calloused use of the "national security" cover during the Nixon Administration is surely a case in point.

In assessing substantive congruence, the pragmatist's lack of emotive
commitment may give him some advantages over his ideological counter-
part. He may be open to more inclusive informational sources and less
prone to misinterpret the information available to him. This advantage is
partially obviated, however, by the fact that unless his interest in the
situation is both immediate and obvious, he is not likely to invest much in
the search for information.

The situational information of concern to the pragmatist will often
center less on the question of congruence with his own interpretation of
the symbol than on the question of how credible the symbol's application
will be to others. Mayhew argues, for example, that the incentives of public office frequently lead congressmen to be more concerned with appropriately positioning themselves vis-à-vis a situation than with addressing
the substantive issues involved. "The electoral requirement is not that he
make pleasing things happen, but that he make pleasing judgmental statements" (Mayhew, 1974, p. 62).

In fact, the pragmatist's dilemma, more often than not, would seem
to be one of finding credible symbols to attach to situations in which he is
already involved or has a stake. Since pragmatists are most frequently
found among those actively involved in politics, it is not surprising that
specific institutional practices often function to facilitate this search,
administrative and legislative hearings being prime examples. The re-
marks of an Illinois state legislator reported by Steiner and Gove serve to
illustrate this widely observed phenomenon:

> Our arrangements were concluded before the hearing ever started, but it was
> absolutely essential that members who had agreed to vote against the bill be
> furnished with a 'cover'—with an impressive witness whose competence was
> unquestioned so that they could offer an explanation of their votes. . . . When
> we return the favor on legislation in which others are interested, we shall ex-
> pect to be furnished with a 'cover.' The more consistently a legislator can
> furnish a good 'cover' to support his position, the easier it is for him to enter
> into logrolling arrangements. (Quoted in Edelman, 1964, p. 136)

Source-Based Evaluations

Those for whom a symbol is important but lacks well-defined meaning
(i.e., the reactives) are, of course, ill equipped to evaluate the substantive
appropriateness of its application in any systematic way. Sartori puts the
argument starkly:

> The inarticulate public not only lacks, without guidance, the grasp of what
> goes with what in the deductive chain of a highflown abstract argument; it
> equally and especially lacks the information and the inductive capability of

deciding on his [sic] own how a specific event relates to a general principle, and specifically to which principle. (1969, p. 407)

Yet such people are not likely to be totally indiscriminant in their assessments regarding the use of a symbol. Their discriminations, like those of people who could but do not engage in more substantive evaluations, will be influenced by several factors. Perhaps the most important of these is the "linkage guidance" provided by others, including friends who serve as opinion leaders, spokespersons for groups with which they identify, and prominent authority figures.

The form and informational content of this guidance may vary. It may be filtered through the mass media, or it may be communicated through group processes. In any case, the credibility of the communicator or source will be critical to whether or not the guidance is accepted.

> Research findings suggest that people often use source credibility as a basis for accepting or rejecting message conclusions without paying much attention to the supporting arguments. If the message does not contain evidence to support the conclusion, the source's credibility is apt to have a greater effect than when adequate evidence is presented. . . . On the other hand, if there is no credibility information available, then people are forced to pay more attention to the arguments that are presented. . . . (Oskamp, 1977, p. 183)

The clarity of the cues a person receives varies with the number of sources of information available to him or upon which he is willing to rely. If his sources are not exclusive, he may receive discrepant guidance. This can result in confusion and ambivalence. Frequently, however, the discrepancy will be resolved on the basis of his assessment of the comparative credibility of the sources. This assessment will hinge upon his perception of the relative expertise, trustworthiness, and likability of the sources (Sears and Whitney, 1973, p. 5).

The problem of disparate cues may also be resolved, or even avoided, as a result of the psychological tendencies that were noted with respect to the "vigilant ideologue." The person may simply accept the first credible guidance he receives and ignore any subsequent cues. Or if confronted, more or less simultaneously, with conflicting information, his inclination may be to accept that which supports the use of the symbol or symbols that are most important to him personally (Knouse, 1971, pp. 11–12). This tendency probably accounts for much of the popular reaction in support of "the police" and their efforts to maintain "law and order" in Chicago during the 1968 Democratic Convention.

Given the critical role that source credibility plays in most people's assessments of the situational applicability of a symbol, the standing of political leaders and other prominent sources of political cues is of considerable importance in understanding the way people respond to the use of symbols. As we noted in Chapter 1, there has been a general decline in popular trust in not only government but all major social institutions over the past two decades. This, coupled with a long-standing cultural suspicion of politics and politicians, leads one to suspect that the credibility accorded most sources of political information is relatively low. Indeed, since the mid-1960's, the phrase "credibility gap" has become a regular part of·the parlance of American politics. However, Sears and Whitney suggest that the prevalence of such a "credibility gap" is easily exaggerated. They find that "political sources have, on the average, generally high credibility" and that "in America even the best known members of the opposition political party are typically regarded as positive sources, and command positive influence" (1973, p. 11).

That political leaders and official sources continue to enjoy considerable credibility, despite widespread disillusionment with politics, is surely a testimony to the *credenda* and *miranda* of power (Merriam, 1964, p. 109), which we noted in Chapter 1. Political sources of linkage guidance frequently represent or embody prominent symbols of authority, symbols that reinforce, if not establish, the authoritativeness of the messages they seek to convey. This is the *credenda* of power. Its significance can be readily appreciated if one simply considers the attention-riveting effect of prefatory phrases such as "a source close to the President."

Similarly, the *miranda* of power acts to reinforce the credibility of political sources. The settings and accoutrements of power provide a context that tends to give visible testimony to the authoritative and serious nature of the communication. Such contexts serve to heighten sensitivity and to inspire a sense of confidence (see Edelman, 1964, pp. 95–113). Thus, independent of the situation itself, who is applying the symbol or communicating its use and the setting from which this information emanates will influence the perceived appropriateness of its application. In general, the more that both the source of linkage guidance and the specific application of the symbol itself are reinforced by other prominent symbols, the more credible the application will be.

Perhaps the most striking concentration of symbolic resources for reinforcing specific uses of symbols is found in the American Presidency. As Theodore Roosevelt once observed, it is a "bully pulpit." These resources have been used rather clumsily by recent Presidents. In fact, Nixon's efforts to exploit them to vindicate himself during the Watergate affair were sometimes so contrived and blatantly self-serving as to reduce rather than enhance his credibility. Nonetheless, as Ronald Reagan demonstrated during the early months of his administration, the *credenda* and *miranda* of Presidential power, when skillfully used, afford the incumbent of that office great leverage in controlling the definition of a situation and the symbols that apply.

Of course, while a President or any other political source of linkage guidance may benefit from the presumptive credibility accorded him by virtue of the offiice he holds, the perception of personal integrity and of commitment is also important. The appearance of impropriety or of a willingness to tolerate it can thus detract from the credibility of a political source. Although this lesson is seen most vividly in Nixon's Watergate experience, it is also revealed in the damage done to Carter's credibility when he refused to dissociate himself from Bert Lance, a friend and key adviser who had come under suspicion of having been a party to illegal banking practices.

In addition to dissociating themselves quickly from persons or situations of doubtful propriety, there are other things that political sources of linkage guidance can do to enhance or safeguard their credibility. Most notable among these are symbolic gestures that attest to their courage and convictions. Students of political persuasion (see Sears and Whitney, 1973, p. 5; Nimmo, 1978, pp. 98–130) have found that people tend to attribute greater credibility to sources who appear not to be catering to their immediate audience or making self-serving arguments. As Bennett (1980, p. 293) notes, President Ford probably enhanced his credibility as "an independent leader who would rather face adversity than court easy favor" by choosing "one of the least supportive audiences he could have found—the seventy-fifth annual convention of the Veterans of Foreign Wars" to announce his intention to create an "amnesty" program for Vietnam draft evaders. President Reagan undoubtedly benefited in a similar way when he chose the 1981 meeting of the National Association for the Advancement of Colored People as a forum to reassert his conviction that economically "rising tides lift all boats" and that the interests of blacks, along with everyone else, were better served by economic growth in the private sector than by government programs.

General Expectations as a Constraint

Persons lacking well-developed cognitive orientations toward a symbol are not likely to initiate its use. For the most part, they simply react to its use, relying upon the substantive evaluations of others for guidance regarding the symbol's applicability. However, their dependence is not total or their vulnerability unlimited. Their assessments of the credible application of a symbol depend not only on the more substantive assessments of others but also on a set of general expectations regarding the context wherein the symbol may be used. These expectations are sufficiently diffuse to allow considerable latitude and flexibility in a symbol's use, and they help sustain what Key has called the "permissive consensus" (1961, pp. 27–51). Still, they are not so diffuse as to pose no constraints on those who would use the symbol.

The expectations involved may be defined in terms of who can appropriately use or evoke the symbol, the general types of events or situations to which it may be applied, and the relative frequency of circumstances that might justify its use. For the most part, these expectations tend to be more proscriptive than prescriptive. The person may not have a clear idea of exactly who may apply the symbol to what situation, when; but he may have very strong feelings about certain groups and situations that preclude his acceptance of their association with the symbol. For example, a person might be delighted to see members of the U.S. Olympic Team wrap themselves in the American flag but totally reject the use of this or any other physical or discursive symbol of patriotism by a "draft resister" or anyone else engaged in or supportive of unconventional, disruptive, or illegal behavior. Similarly, a person may believe in "free speech" and "freedom of the press" but draw the line well short of the use of these symbols to defend unpatriotic conduct, atheism, or pornography.

Particularly in the absence of a well-defined cognitive interpretation of the symbol, a person's expectations regarding its use are likely to rest heavily on the precedents established by the previous situations in which he can recall the symbol's being used. As a consequence, his expectations are likely to have a strong status quo bias. The symbol's application to situations or circumstances similar to those wherein it was used in the past generally will be accepted. New or novel usage, however, will be accepted only with great hesitation, if at all. Consider, for example, President Carter's 1977 effort to mobilize support for a program emphasizing conservation as an approach to the nation's energy crisis. In a nationally televised address, he sought to rally the American people in a "moral equivalent of war" on the nation's energy problems. As dramatic as the war symbolism may have been, the address largely failed in stirring public support. The vast majority of Americans simply did not believe that there was a real energy crisis in the sense of a serious energy shortage. While Carter's war imagery had ample precedent in the memories of most Americans, e.g., Johnson's War on Poverty as well as several real wars in the sense of military conflict, the situation did not correspond with past precedent. Uncertain as to the problem and unclear as to the enemy, most people were unwilling to accept the war analogy and the sacrifice it implied.

Lessons Regarding Symbolic Usage

Just as past images of a symbol's use shape current expectations, current applications color the credibility of future use. Perceived misapplication tends to dilute the potency of a symbol. These facts have important implications for those who would use the symbol and are eager to see its power preserved. As Merelman observed, there must be some continuity in usage if the symbol is to retain its potency. He notes that when policymakers attempt to associate symbols of legitimacy with policies they wish to implement, failure to establish and maintain the desired association cheapens the symbol and makes it less effective in all areas (1966, pp. 553).

For example, the "FBI" has long stood as a symbol of the vigilance, competence, and integrity of federal law enforcement. For years, the imprimatur of the "FBI" conveyed almost instant legitimacy. However, in the early 1970s, information began to surface suggesting that the FBI had been used to harrass civil rights and antiwar activists, that its long-time director, J. Edgar Hoover, had regularly used its resources for his own personal and political purposes, and that L. Patrick Gray, the acting director who replaced Hoover, had allowed himself to become a party to the Watergate scandal. As a consequence of these negative associations, the potency of the "FBI" as a legitimacy symbol was substantially reduced. Similarly, in the late 1960s, Ralph Nader emerged as a leading spokesman for consumer interests and his name became virtually synonymous with "consumer protection." His efforts to promote legislation and to spur the Federal Trade Commission to become more aggressive in protecting consumer interests won him wide acclaim. His name alone conveyed considerable legitimacy. However, as he began to expand the scope of his concerns in the mid-1970s and became associated with other causes, his symbolic standing as an unimpeachable champion of consumer protection suffered from a growing impression that he was merely a general gadfly.

Because of the importance of maintaining continuity in the usage of a symbol, leading Democrats were appropriately aghast when Republican Ronald Reagan began appealing to the name of Franklin Roosevelt in support of his candidacy and policies. Revered by many Americans as the father of the "New Deal" and the defender of the common man, "FDR" has long served as an important symbol to Democrats, defining a tradition of the active use of government to promote social welfare. Understandably, then, Democrats identifying with this tradition were offended when Republicans, who were known to be hostile to this tradition, began to invoke his name. Senator Edward Kennedy expressed the Democrats' protest in a speech before the 1980 National Democratic Convention:

> The same Republicans who are invoking Franklin Roosevelt have nominated a man who said in 1976—and these are his exact words: "Fascism was really the basis of the New Deal." And that nominee, whose name is Ronald Reagan, has no right to quote Franklin Delano Roosevelt. (*Congressional Quarterly Weekly Report*, August 16, 1980, p. 2424)

Closely related to the problem of maintaining continuity in symbolic usage is what Merelman has called the problem of "connotative overflow" (1966, pp. 553–554). When a particular symbol is used in conjunction with several other symbols, they may all become linked in the eyes of the general public. Not only can this limit the future applicability of the original symbol, but a sort of "guilt by association" may develop. Negative connotations associated with any or all of the other symbols may spill over, making both the original symbol and its application suspect.

The controversy surrounding United States involvement in the Vietnam War provides a good illustration of the problem of "connotative overflow." Proponents of American involvement commonly appealed to patriotic symbols, especially the flag. Flag decals and lapel pins came to be regarded as a way of expressing support for the war effort. Opponents of the war had the peace symbol and were generally regarded as "liberals," but they had few other prominent symbols. They used protest symbols and demonstrations to dramatize their opposition to the war. Since most Americans have never been particularly sympathetic to protests or to any other form of "disruptive" conduct, this alone probably served to alienate the antiwar movement from a substantial segment of the general public. Even worse, however, in terms of "connotative overflow" was the fact that it became commonplace for war protesters to attack the symbols of patriotism they associated with the war. Draft cards were burnt, and the American flag desecrated. Regardless of their previous feelings toward the war, many Americans found such actions intolerable. Countermobilizations were organized, with many people, including a large number of "hard hats," marching as much to demonstrate their disgust with the actions of the war protestors as their support for the war. Perhaps even more importantly, the actions of the antiwar activists created in the minds of many an enduring association between liberal activism and a lack of patriotism. To love the flag was to reject liberalism, and vice versa As Jack Beatty has observed: "The stereotypes of the Vietnam era have stuck, making patriotism seem the exclusive property of the right. . . . 'Peacenik' begat 'flag-waver'" ("The Patriotism of Values," *The New Republic*, July 4–11, 1981, p. 18).

Just as association with other symbols may dilute the power of a symbol, so too can its overuse. The power of a symbol to sensitize and galvanize the attention of a mass audience rests in part on its ability to suggest or call to mind matters that transcend the ordinary. If its use becomes so commonplace or so frequent that this special quality is lost, much of its power to focus the attention and mobilize the energies of those for whom it was once salient is destroyed. During the late 1960s, for example, the symbols "discrimination" and "police brutality" provided potent rallying cries for civil rights groups. Many people, both black and white, were appalled at the thought of unfair and arbitrary treatment and the unnecessary use of force. However, as such charges became more frequent and were heard more and more from persons and in circumstances that made them seem self-serving, the charges began to ring hollow.

Finally, the above arguments lead to another and more general prescription; namely, that proper feedback must be maintained. Unless the consequences of the application of a symbol are minimally consonant with popular expectations, both the application and the symbol itself are called into question (Merelman, 1966, p. 554). Given the diffuse nature of most people's expectations and the fact that most are not likely to experience the consequences firsthand, this is often not a very stringent requirement. Moreover, the consequences of specific actions are frequently difficult to discern with any clarity owing to the complexities of social life. Nonetheless, maintaining appropriate feedback is important. Popular confidence in the user and the symbol alike requires at least some vindication. This lesson was not lost on the Viet Cong during the Vietnam War. In the early months of 1968, they launched the so-called "Tet offensive." Although regarded by U.S. military authorities as an act of desperation resulting in a devastating defeat of the Viet Cong, it appeared to most to be a dramatic refutation of the repeated assurances of the Johnson Administration that the battle for the "hearts and minds" of the South Vietnamese was being won. As a consequence, more and more people began to question the wisdom and the purpose of our involvement in Vietnam and grew increasingly skeptical of assurances of those who claimed to see "light at the end of the tunnel."

An equally striking case of the failure to maintain appropriate feedback is provided by the "War on Poverty" and "Great Society" programs of the Johnson Administration. Arguing that poverty and hunger had no place in an affluent society, President Johnson promised to lead an assault on the "causes of poverty" and the barriers to "equal opportunity." In committing himself and presumably the resources of the United States government to these great goals, he sparked the imagination and aroused the expectations of both the advantaged and the disadvantaged. However, neither the hodgepodge of programs nor the relatively meager resources committed to the task were equal to the promise. While progress was made in reducing poverty and in enhancing education and job opportunities, these results paled in comparison to the expectations that had been aroused. The poor grew bitter and restive, while the more advantaged segments of society grew increasingly resentful not only of the effort but of government itself.

SUMMARY AND CONCLUSIONS

We have argued that the response that a symbol evokes is a function of the nature of an individual's attachment to the symbol, the perceived relevance of the situation to which it is being applied, and the credibility of its application. Based on differences among people in their cognitive and affective orientations toward the symbol, four broad types of attachment have been identified. We have labeled these: "ideological," "pragmatic," "reactive," and "apathetic." Different behavioral predispositions are associated with each. For all but the apathetic, however, the behavioral response that may be anticipated with respect to the symbol also depends on the situation and the perceived appropriateness of the symbol to that situation.

The problems of situational relevance and of credible application are, of course, largely irrelevant to the apathetic. Such persons will be predictably nonresponsive to the symbol. Insofar as there is any correspondence between their behavior and the use of the symbol, this is likely to be a mere artifact of external sanctions or of the exigencies of the moment.

For others, the problem of reckoning situational relevance is relatively simple. It is largely a matter of the degree to which they perceive themselves as having a stake in the situation. Assessments of appropriate symbol applications are somewhat more involved. Cognitive evaluations, which many are not well equipped to make, are required. The guidance provided by others is thus likely to be critical. In any case, the number and credibility of the informational sources available to people have important bearing on their assessments regarding the use of the symbol. These assessments are also influenced by the operation of various psychological dynamics. In general, they simply reinforce a tendency to accept the guidance of those sources that are personally most credible. However, they also lead to a readiness to accept the application of those symbols that have the greatest personal significance. This inclination may be of substantial importance, particularly in circumstances wherein conflicting symbolic definitions are involved. When confronted with a conflict between symbols, the application of the most important one will tend to be accepted.

While the characteristics of those of a reactive mode and the nonvigilance of the more ideologically oriented make large portions of the population vulnerable to symbolic manipulation, this vulnerability is far from total. Popular expectations regarding the use of a symbol, albeit often diffuse and vaguely articulated, define important limits to its use. While these limits are often fairly broad, they do pose real constraints on those who would exploit the power of the symbol. The price of this protection lies in the restrictions it imposes on departures from the status quo. While new or novel usage may be accepted, considerable persuasion is likely to be required. Moreover, unless care is taken to assure appropriate feedback, the potency of the symbol is likely to be diminished.

4

Cultural Aspects of Symbolic Usage

In previous chapters, we have noted that the symbols which are important to a person, his orientations toward these symbols, and the limitations he imposes on their usage will all be influenced by the culture of which he is a part. Here we seek to extend these observations to give greater definition to the role of culture in symbolic usage. Both the shaping and the constraining effects of the culture are of interest. To illustrate these effects, consideration will be given to prominent features of the American political culture. We will also consider possible dynamics of cultural change and how these are reflected in the use of symbols.

SYMBOLS AND THE POLITICAL CULTURE

A culture embodies the historical experiences and derived "wisdom" of a people. It is characterized by a variety of myths, assumptions, and prescriptions regarding nature, man, and society. These are the heritage of a society. They represent historically derived "solutions" to the problems of interpreting and giving meaning to external reality and human experience. They condense the sum of all that has been "learned" from past experience and transported from generation to generation down to the present.

Sustained through the processes of socialization, a culture serves to give continuity and predictability to social life. Here we are concerned with those aspects of a culture that bear upon and shape the politics of a society. We will refer to these aspects of culture as the "political culture." There are numerous ways of characterizing the elements or components involved (e.g., see Pye, 1962; Almond, 1956; Rosenbaum, 1975). Our own conception is a broad one and encompasses all those cultural elements that are relevant to an individual's political world view. In other words, a political culture includes all the socially shared information and "knowledge" that inform the various individual dispositions that may be engaged by a political symbol.

The premises and prescriptions of a political culture tend to be experienced as "givens" and accepted as self-evident truths. They are referenced by symbols and manifested in the form of individual orientations toward these symbols. In this sense, symbols index properties of a political culture in much the same way that they index an individual's beliefs and values.

Symbols themselves, at least higher-order ones, may be regarded as important and characteristic elements of a political culture. As socially common objects of affect and attributed meaning, they serve to give definition to a political community, indexing common understandings and relatively stable patterns of preference. However, symbols stand apart from the meanings they index at the cultural level, just as they do at the individual level. The cultural meaning of a symbol arises from the interpretations popularly accorded it. The clarity of this meaning depends upon the degree of consensus that exists regarding its interpretation. The meaning that will tend to dominate the political process, while circumscribed by general expectations, will be that which is most prevalent among those with well-developed cognitive orientations toward the symbol and who are most likely to use it actively (i.e., those defined in Chapter 3 as having an ideological or pragmatic mode of attachment).

Over time, a symbol may take on new meanings, and new or different symbols may assume its previous role. Through all of this, the cultural premises and prescriptions that were originally indexed by the symbol may remain largely unchanged. For the most part, changes in the meaning of a culturally prominent symbol are gradual and serve to sustain its societal role. However, even the most prominent political symbols may become divorced from the cultural meanings with which they were once associated. This may or may not reflect changes in the basic characteristics of the political culture itself. It may simply represent the use of old symbols for new purposes. The essential point is that the characteristic symbols of a political culture can take on a life of their own. This can be readily appreciated if one considers the changing meanings of such symbols as "liberal" and "conservative," "Republican" and "Democrat" in the context of American politics.

In this regard, it is interesting to note that while contemporary Republicans have laid claim to the "conservative" label and have generally sought to associate Democrats with the "liberal" label, this has not always been the case. During the 1930s, both Republicans and Democrats tried to appropriate the "liberal" symbol (see Rotunda, 1968). Although it was Franklin Roosevelt and the Democrats who succeeded in capturing the label, "Herbert Hoover insisted that he was a 'true liberal' and . . . called the New Deal 'false liberalism'" (Graber, 1976, p. 300). The comparative value of "conservative" and "liberal" as legitimacy symbols has obviously changed substantially over the years, but as we shall see in Chapter 6, they remain for most people political symbols of diffuse meaning. One would err in assuming that changes in their comparative social appeal necessarily represent fundamental shifts in beliefs and values.

As we saw in the previous chapter, the potency of a symbol can be degraded by patterns of usage that violate previous expectations, create negative associations, or fail to produce appropriate feedback. Thus, while the culture does provide guidance regarding what meanings go with which symbols, this guidance is imperfect and changing, reflecting the changing circumstances and experiences of a society. The cultural premises and prescriptions that inform and give substance to an individual's basic dispositions tend to be more stable. These premises and prescriptions provide the common core of meanings available for attribution to political symbols.

The social significance of symbols arises not only from the common meanings they index but also from the affective sentiments they serve to focus. As we have seen, for many, attachments to characteristic symbols of a political culture are likely to be more a function of acquired affection than of well-specified cognitive meaning. Particularly with respect to community and regime symbols, these affective ties are largely culturally prescribed. In fact, it is here that the impact of the political culture is most manifest. The cultural mandate is simply clearer, more explicit, and less ambiguous with respect to appropriate affective sentiments than it is with respect to cognitive orientations. The lessons we learn through the socialization process generally leave little doubt as to whether something should be regarded as good or bad, positive or negative, even though they may leave us uncertain as to why. This is undoubtedly due in part to the fact that affective cues are easily communicated and readily discerned whereas substantive arguments are not.

In effect, affective orientations condense cultural premises and prescriptions into their simplest form. As a consequence, one may be guided by a cultural script of which he or she is at best vaguely aware and unable to articulate. A culture may be sustained in large measure through the learning of appropriate affective orientations toward socially significant symbols that largely ignores their underlying philosophical, ideological, or historical justifications. In terms of sustaining the culture and coordinating social action, perhaps the most important thing about a symbol is that it is a socially recognized object of more or less common affective sentiment. Excepting those most actively engaged in the political process, homogeneity and specificity in meaning may be less important to the continuity of the culture than the fact that the symbols are broadly recognized objects of common affect and support habitual patterns of behavior.

Most Americans, for example, esteem "democracy" and tend to accept it as a description of the American political system. That the symbol "democracy" itself is for many an object of diffuse and inconsistent meaning may be less important than the fact that it is commonly accepted as a legitimacy symbol that people rarely see as conflicting with their customary behavior. Because of its widespread acceptance, however, it can be used in specific situations to mobilize support or win acceptance for actions (e.g., the Civil Rights Acts) of those for whom the symbol has greater substantive meaning.

Of course, as we saw in the previous chapter, popular orientations toward culturally prominent symbols, while often predominantly affective in nature, are never totally devoid of cognitive meaning. These meanings are manifested in the form of general expectations that serve to constrain the use of symbols. While these limits are often broad, even this degree of constraint is dependent upon a modicum of commonality of perspective that only a shared culture can provide. While the interpretations of ideologues and of pragmatists may give a symbol its operative meaning, those of the reactive bent define the range of acceptable usage. Both this range and the core meaning are reflective of the culture itself.

The constraints imposed by a culture lie not only in the affective prescriptions and symbolic meanings it provides but also in the range of symbols it sanctions. These symbols give definition to a particular world view, providing a frame of reference and a language for interpreting reality and communicating experience. The various elements of this world view, having been historically accumulated and transmitted piecemeal, will typically be only loosely organized. There will be gaps, inconsistencies, even contradictions. Still, the paradigm formed by these elements will likely possess considerable internal logic, and there will be a notable degree of "systemness" arising from the interdependence of these elements. Were it otherwise, it would be difficult to account for the stability and historical continuity that tend to characterize at least the major components of a culture.

Because we are embedded in it, it is often difficult to appreciate how profoundly our culture influences the way we look at the world and to recognize the constraints it imposes on our vision. Most of us never have occasion to question why we think as we do or to realize that what separates "sense" from "nonsense" is largely culturally determined. To appreciate such cultural constraints, Tribe suggests that it may be instructive to consider the following assertion attributed to a certain Chinese encyclopedia:

> Animals are divided into: (a) belonging to the Emperor, (b) embalmed, (c) tame, (d) sucking pigs, (e) sirens, (f) fabulous, (g) stray dogs, (h) in-

cluded in the present classification, (i) frenzied, (j) innumerable, (k) drawn with a very fine camelhair brush, (l) et cetera, (m) having just broken the water pitcher, (n) that from a long way look like flies. (1972, p. 76)

As Tribe, quoting Foucault, observes:

> What we apprehend in one great leap in the "wonderment of this taxonomy" is not only the "exotic charm of another system of thought" but—even more pointedly—"the limitation of our own, the stark impossibility of thinking *that*." (1972, p. 76)

PRESCRIPTIONS FOUND IN THE AMERICAN POLITICAL CULTURE

In defining the range of symbols that are available to give social definition to a situation, a political culture acts to limit the range of problems and problem-solving alternatives that are likely to be considered, or for that matter, even entertained or recognized. While this tends to limit the demands that are placed on the political system and facilitates the development of routine modes of coping with problems, it can also blind a polity to potential dangers and severely limit its ability to speak effectively to those problems that are recognized. Thus, the shaping and constraining effect of a culture has two faces. While restricting the extent to which the members of a polity are vulnerable to exploitation and manipulation, it also restrains the possibilities available for serving their needs.

That culture colors perceptions and constrains problem definition is revealed daily in the topical concerns of American politics. To illustrate this more fully, it may be useful to consider some of the premises and prescriptions of the American political culture that inform the repertoire of meanings that an individual has available for interpreting political reality. In doing this, our intent is not to offer a detailed or comprehensive description of the American political culture. Rather, it is simply to provide examples of how a particular culture shapes and constrains the politics of a community. The cultural premises and prescriptions of interest are those corresponding to the various dispositional dimensions identified in Chapter 2.

The American political culture has been the object of extensive inquiry, and there exists impressive agreement on many of its distinguishing features. Numerous observers have remarked on the singular and unchanging character of the ideology or world view it endorses (e.g., Hartz, 1955; Lipset, 1980; Devine, 1972). This world view has its foundations in seventeenth-century liberal thought, particularly as expressed in the work of John Locke. This perspective was transported, largely to the exclusion of all others, to the arcadian lands of North America. Both the circumstances and the environment seemed to vindicate its premises. The abundance of land and the rich physical environment mirrored the idyllic setting envisioned in Locke's fictional state of nature. The voluntarily formed community that sprang up in this pristine environment gave reality to the myth of the social contract.

As the community grew and flourished, there was little reason to doubt the essential "rightness" of this world view. Nineteenth-century laissez faire economics was found to mesh well with this outlook and was readily accommodated by it. With this, the essential elements of the paradigm were complete, and they have remained largely the same throughout our brief history. America became, and largely continues to be, a society dominated by a single, unitary political tradition, a tradition so pervasive that it is seldom recognized as such. It is the elements of this tradition that instruct the dispositions and occasion the dilemmas discussed below.

Empirical Premises

Perhaps the most basic guidance a culture can provide is that regarding the nature of the physical world, man's relationship to it and with one another. The questions involved are about the most basic facts of existence, facts of an ontological character that lie beyond empirical confirmation and which must simply be accepted as a matter of faith. To a significant extent, all else is subordinate to the way these questions are resolved, and the culture plays a prominent role in providing the answers.

Premises Regarding Physical Nature. From its inception, the American political culture has invited the view that the physical world is one of ample, if not endless, abundance to be exploited by man. Indeed, experience has tended to reinforce this assumption because in fact "economic abundance and an environment susceptible to human manipulation" (Devine, 1972, p. 47) have provided the backdrop for American politics. While never sanctioning a wanton disregard for the natural environment, the cultural mandate has been that it should be put to use and aggressively exploited to the material ends of man. The impulse to exploit nature's bounty encouraged by Lockean liberalism has been strongly reinforced by a religious imperative traceable to the Puritans. To conquer the land and to extract its riches was to do God's work. Thus:

> American capitalist culture is firmly rooted in a secularized Christian myth and mystique of struggle with nature. The basic article of faith in this mystique is that you prove your worth by overcoming and dominating the natural world. You justify your existence and you attain bliss (temporal, eternal, or both) by transforming nature into wealth. This is not only good but self-evident. Until transformed nature is useless and absurd. (Thomas Merton, quoted in Coleman McCarthy, "How Watt Occupies the Land," *Detroit Free Press*, May 21, 1981, p. 9A)

The culture itself has offered little or no vision of the natural limits of this exploitation of resources. Even though the question of limits began attracting considerable attention in the 1970s and symbols such as "gas lines," "rationing," "water depletion," "energy conservation," and "environmental protection" became a regular part of the rhetoric of American politics, most Americans still have difficulty in conceiving of nature's resources as being much short of inexhaustible. As shown in a 1981 *Newsweek* poll, a majority (58%) support efforts to protect the environment but even a larger majority (75%) see no conflict between "strong economic growth" and "high environmental standards" (*Newsweek*, June 28, 1981, p. 29).

Despite repeated warnings from experts and declarations by three Presidents (Nixon, Ford, and Carter) that the nation faces a major "energy crises," a majority of Americans have remained unconvinced of the existence of a real energy shortage. In a nationally televised speech in July 1979, Jimmy Carter protested: "The energy crisis is real. It is worldwide. It is a clear and present danger to our nation. These are facts and we simply must face them" (*Congressional Quarterly Weekly Report*, July 21, 1979, p. 1471). A nationwide poll conducted shortly thereafter showed that about 35% of the people surveyed were willing to concede that there was an energy shortage (Bennett, 1980, p. 96). While this represented a significant increase over the 26% of this opinion prior to the speech, most still did not believe that the "energy crisis" was real.

Another striking example of this culturally sanctioned tendency to conceive of physical resources as nearly boundless is found in attitudes toward water resources in the American Southwest. Despite the fact that it is an arid land, dependent upon water from distant sources, the population has been prodigal in its use. Speaking specifically of Southern California, Hobson notes that they have

> built a land which denies the true nature of the land. . . . Since it was a world of ample water, the idea of drought was and is without real meaning. If there is no conception of water shortage, is there any wonder that [the] conception of water conservation is so shallow? . . . [As] Carey McWilliams wrote, "the problem of water in Southern California is a cultural problem." The successive waves of immigrants to the area brought cultures . . . [that] were inherently antithetical to conservation and the collective action necessitated by the semi-arid environment of the land. This cultural indifference to the land is as pervasive today as it was in 1946 or 1910. (Timothy Hodson, ". . . Or for Asking Why We Waste Water as We Do," *Los Angeles Times*, March 19, 1977, Part V, p. 5)

The optimistic (some might say foolhardy) view of nature's abundance encouraged by the American political culture may militate against effective resource management and long-range planning. Perhaps more importantly, however, it also poses a potentially more profound dilemma.

As a basic premise, it supports a variety of other culturally sanctioned principles. For example, it predicates a conception of distributive justice that has enabled the American political system to avoid confrontation with many of the more wrenching questions regarding how the wealth of the nation should be distributed. To change this premise, as has been tried by those who argue for the "limits of growth," is to call into question many of the more salient features of the American political culture. Potentially, this could precipitate a major cultural crisis.

Premises Regarding Human Nature. Just as Americans tend to be optimistic regarding the state of nature, so too have they tended to take a fairly sanguine view of human nature. While viewing man as basically motivated by self-interest, they have also been impressed by the human capacity for growth and reason. The attribution of inherent rationality, coupled with the assumption of a benign environment, has inclined them toward a generally positive view of man's trustworthiness. In a five-nation study reported in the early 1960s, Almond and Verba found that Americans tended to exhibit greater social trust and "faith in people" than respondents in the other nations studied. Eighty percent of the Americans they polled agreed that "human nature is fundamentally cooperative." When asked to choose between the statements "most people can be trusted" and "you can't be too careful in your dealings with people," 55% indicated that the former best expressed their view (Almond and Verba, 1963, p. 213).

Almost identical results were obtained when the same question was asked in a 1968 survey (Devine, 1972, p. 100). Social trust measured in this way declined in the early 1970s, but in 1976, a majority (51%) were again choosing the most trusting alternative (Converse et al., 1980, p. 28). It is also noteworthy that in six different surveys conducted by the National Opinion Research Center over the period 1972 to 1980, approximately 60% in each survey rejected the assertion that "most people would try to take advantage of you if they got a chance" in favor of the belief that "most people try to be fair" (*Public Opinion*, August/September, 1980, p. 35). These data leave little doubt that the American culture is basically a trusting one and that it encourages a generally positive view of human nature.

The culturally sanctioned image of human nature, of course, is not without its negative overtones. Heavily influenced by a strong religious tradition, the culture acknowledges human weakness and corruptability. At the same time, it celebrates the ability of human beings to overcome and transcend the flaws inherent in their nature. Mankind is seen as endowed with a remarkable capacity to perceive truth ("the laws of nature and nature's God" that Jefferson invoked in the Declaration of Independence) and to know right from wrong.

These views of human nature have led Americans to attribute extraordinary capacities to the common man and to be suspicious of authority. They serve to undergird basic political values, such as freedom, equality, and human dignity. In terms of public policy, they have justified massive expenditures on public education; and at the same time, they have sanctioned the legislation of individual morality—"those who had not fallen to temptation . . . having an obligation to protect those who might fall" (Zurcher and Kirkpatrick, 1976, p. 114). Perhaps most importantly, these cultural views of human nature have mandated individual responsibility and culpability for almost everything. As Hacker observes, "The person is to be held accountable for his own fate" (1971, p. 79).

These premises are revealed in popular orientations toward symbols such as "welfare," "poverty," and "crime." The problems these symbols reference are typically viewed as matters of personal failing for which the individual must bear responsibility. "You have no one but yourself to blame" is the common refrain. Needless to say, this tends to limit the acceptable range of socially supported ameliorative action. In keeping with the notion that the problem lies within the individual, "education" and "rehabilitation" tend to be the prescribed palliatives. The problem, of course, is that while these may change the person, they may do little to change the conditions that occasioned "his or her" problem.

Culturally sensitized perceptions of human nature are similarly found in such contemporary concerns as "pornography," "promiscuity," and the "breakdown of morality." While these concerns may be motivated in part by status anxieties, they also tend to reflect a common view of human weakness and vulnerability. This view, which owes much to the American Puritan heritage, helps account for recurring efforts to use government to combat "deviance" and to reassert "traditional values." However, whether government is used to promote "self-discipline and chastity" or to provide "sex education" and "family counseling," such policies share a common premise: social problems are people problems that must be addressed at the level of the individual. The thought that problems might be structural or contextual is alien to the American political culture.

Premises Regarding the Nature of Society. The cultural conceptions of man sketched above support a peculiarly atomistic conception of society. "The degree of atomization in the United States is perhaps greater than in any other culture" (Almond, 1960, p. 48). Based in part on the beliefs in natural law and in the myth of the social contract, the culture encourages the view that the individual is logically prior to society. From this individualistic perspective, social borders tend to be seen as fluid and nonbinding, if they are recognized at all. Group identities, including social class, are conceived to be largely matters of personal choice.

Americans are uncomfortable with the thought that their status might be determined by factors beyond their control. They find the idea of a stable class structure offensive. They resist using the concept of social class to distinguish themselves from others and tend to deny that such distinctions make any difference.

> People are to be judged for what they are here and now; parentage, background, and the normal labels indicating prestige in society don't count. Not only *should* America have a classless society; [one ought to] behave as if it *does*. (Lamb, 1974, p. 133)

This is not to say that social comparisons are illegitimate. To the contrary, precisely because social distinctions are viewed largely to be the result of individual choices, these choices are subject not only to criticism but to harsh judgment. The criteria for these judgments are themselves culturally prescribed in the form of the social norms that will be considered momentarily. Defined largely by the white, Anglo-Saxon, Protestant population that dominated the country's early history and founded on the premises that we have been describing, those norms have been used to condemn broad segments of the population (e.g., the poor) and to justify ethnocentrism and race prejudices that are otherwise at odds with the cultural paradigm. Owing to the conditional and contingent nature assumed to characterize most social relations, it is not surprising to find the social order viewed as somewhat fragile. In this sense, the culture perhaps gives reason for the low tolerance widely shown toward dissent and nonconformity, sentiments that find expression in symbols such as "law and order" and "America—Love It or Leave It."

The culturally endorsed conceptions of society that we have described very much tend to shape the content and the character of American politics. They tend to sanction a mode of problem solving that Roche has described as "every man for himself." He suggests that these orientations are vividly revealed in episodes such as the frenzy to build private fallout shelters in the early 1960s and the national response to the gas shortages of 1973–74. The former prompted him to write in 1961: "I doubt if any free society has ever matched the nauseating display of callous individualism we are now observing." Recalling those words in 1974, he observed:

> We are seeing a rerun of the same syndrome in the manic quest for gasoline. One filling station operator was quoted as saying "they are behaving like animals." . . . As I have observed before, if you scratch an American you find an anarchist. (John Roche, "The Quest for Gas," *Philadelphia Bulletin*, February 25, 1974, p. 9)

The problem-solving biases created by these culturally rooted orientations are of profound consequence. They foster little sympathy or concern for social problems that are not experienced directly and immediately. "Problems" and their "solutions" tend to be conceived exclusively in terms of their personal costs and benefits. Planning is spurned insofar as it implies restrictions on individual discretion. Collective benefits are discounted, and a premium is placed on divisible or particularized benefits. It is not surprising, then, to find limited sympathy with such concerns as "regional planning" and "the urban crisis." Hacker puts the argument starkly:

> Americans prefer to see their society as a conglomeration of private individuals and activities entitled to pursue profit and pleasure as they choose. Health, housing, transportation, even relations between races, classes, and sexes are deemed to be private matters: to behave as one pleases in these and countless other areas is a cherished liberty no free citizen will easily relinquish. . . . Americans are temperamentally unsuited for even a partial merger of personality in pursuit of a common cause. A society so inordinately attached to personal pursuits cannot be expected to renounce them simply because social survival demands such an adjustment. (1971, pp. 142–143)

Normative Premises

The norms that instruct individual dispositions regarding the ends and means of social behaviour depend in part on the empirical premises of the culture. Although not strictly determined by them, the normative premises that serve to justify certain behaviors and to proscribe others must be minimally consonant with cultural assumptions regarding the empirical world and the way it works. Conceivably, the same empirical premises could support a different set of normative principles, but it is doubtful that a given set of normative premises could be sustained by a significantly different set of empirical assumptions.

In our discussion of the empirical premises of the American political culture, we have anticipated some of the culture's normative premises. Here we extend that discussion, considering additional normative principles sanctioned by the culture.

Premises Regarding Social Obligation. Most Americans believe that they have an obligation to "love their country" and "defend it against all enemies." These sentiments are expressed in strong attachments to symbols of patriotism and in a profound hostility toward those who fail to honor them. They led Americans in the early 1970s to favor giving authorities the right "to censor TV, radio, newspaper, and the theater for unpatriotic or revolutionary content" by a 57% to 37% margin, freedom of speech and freedom of the press notwithstanding (Harris, 1973, p. 280). This same intolerance of those who would "shirk their duty" was revealed in the strong opposition to any form of "amnesty" for draft evaders following the Vietnam War.

Beyond this sense of duty to country, the American political culture suggests that an individual's social obligations are limited. For the most part, they reduce to little more than being self-reliant and responsible. Being responsible, of course, includes the obligation to honor contractual commitments. Since society itself is viewed as a sort of voluntaristic, contractual arrangement, this means that the individual is duty-bound to abide by the law, at least insofar as it is seen as a legitimate expression of the terms of that "contract." Voluntarism and legalism thus play a critical role in the cultural conception of social obligation.

Even with respect to duty to country, Americans have had reservations regarding the scope of their social obligations. Voluntarism has often failed to satisfy the manpower needs of the military, and American history is replete with draft riots and the unabashed use of legal means to avoid military service. A 1981 Gallup poll found that only 48% of Americans favored reviving the "draft" to meet the nation's military manpower needs. A two-thirds majority of those who would be most affected— young adults between the ages of 18 and 24—opposed it (*Providence Journal*, August 23, 1981, p. A–15). All this suggests that even with respect to commonly acknowledged social obligations, the personal sacrifices Americans are willing to make or expect others to make to further social ends is limited.

About all that is required of a person to vindicate his culturally prescribed social obligations is that he be "law-abiding." No other nation has made such a fetish of the law. In a society that sees itself as little more than a quasi-legalistic arrangement, heavy reliance on legal solutions to all manners of problems, public and private, is to be expected. Given the impulse to define virtually all relationships in terms of individual rights and legal obligations, it is easy to understand why Americans are the most litigious people in the world.

Perhaps because the social order is seen as being held together by such fragile stuff, Americans have been particularly sensitive to obvious threats to the security of the social order. "Crime in the streets" prompts the demand for quick and harsh punishment. "White-collar crime," on the other hand, typically does not. Concern with the "criminal element" has sometimes inclined Americans to "take the law into their own hands." This is reflected not only in vigilantism but also in the predilection of people to arm themselves. Nearly half (48%) of the population claim to have a gun or revolver in their homes (*Public Opinion*, February/ March, 1971, p. 23). Surely in no other land will you find people so quick to perceive "public safety" to be a matter of individual responsibility rather than as a "public good."

The limited sense of social obligation encouraged by the culture and its view of man and society helps to explain the low priority that is generally accorded "public" as opposed to "private" goods. Impoverished public facilities and services are tolerated in a fashion that other, less affluent societies find unacceptable. It is not that Americans would not like more and better public services. Indeed, most Americans feel they are entitled to them (see *Public Opinion*, April/May, 1981, p. 16). The problem is that they are unwilling to pay for them. "Officeholders are defeated, school budgets are rejected, and governmental programs gutted under the never furled banner of 'No New Taxes'" (Hacker, 1971, p. 134). Comparatively, Americans are not heavily taxed, but they tend to be unwilling to sacrifice personal gains to public purposes or, for that matter, to ask anyone else to.

Premises Regarding Authority. As we have previously suggested, the American political culture credits the common man with extraordinary capacities and assumes that he is the best arbiter of his own fate. As a consequence, it tends to enshrine "common sense" as the embodiment of wisdom and to sanction a suspicion of any claim to authority. Historically, this has been manifested not only in a tradition of anti-elitism but also anti-intellectualism. It is not surprising then that Rokeach finds that when asked to rank attributes they value, Americans tend to place "imaginative," "obedient," "intellectual," and "logical" at the bottom of their lists (1973, p. 58).

While embracing "science and technology" as an important avenue of "progress," Americans are suspicious of "experts" and are not reluctant to challenge even the authority of science. In a 1979 poll, for example, 42% agreed that "you can't trust what experts like scientists and technical people say because often what they say isn't right" (L. John Martin, "Science and the Successful Society," *Public Opinion*, June/July, 1981, p. 17).

Suspicion of authority, of course, is even more pronounced when it comes to political authority. Americans have tended to be more impressed by the possibilities for the abuse of political power than they have with the need for political authority. Convinced that "power corrupts," they not only have insisted that political power be fragmented but have remained suspicious of the fragments. Even as expectations of government have grown, Americans have been reluctant to grant it the authority and the resources needed to satisfy those expectations. The results have often been something like a self-fulfilling prophecy, perceived governmental failures serving to confirm suspicions regarding the untrustworthiness of public authority.

That political authority should be viewed as a "public trust" that must be vigilantly monitored for signs of abuse is perhaps not surprising, given the empirical premises that characterize the American political culture. It is interesting to note, however, that the same stringent standards tend not to be applied to the exercise of private power. The presumption seems to be that private activity is inherently legitimate whereas public activity is not. Supported by the myths that only private activities can be creative and efficient, this view has facilitated the concentration of corporate power and has led Americans to ignore or passively accept the social consequences of private actions. The legacy of simpler times, "American ideology possesses neither the language nor the inclination for a critical review of the society's private institutions" (Hacker, 1971, pp. 140–141).

Premises Regarding Distributive Justice. To úse Lasswell's phrase, the question of "who gets what, when, and how" is perhaps the central question that a polity must resolve. At issue is the question of the operative meaning of distributive justice. The American cultural prescriptions in this regard are well known and find expression in the familiar imagery of "hard work," "competition," and "individual achievement."

> It has been part of the fundamental pathos of American culture to believe that virtue should and will be rewarded—and more particularly that such economic virtues as hard work, frugality, and prudence should receive a proportionate reward. (Williams, 1970, p. 479)

Ironically, "there is 'virtually no evidence' that personal attitudes such as self-confidence, ambition, and motivation have much to do with economic improvement" (Gerald Volgenau, "Work Hard, Avoid Poverty? Wrong!" *Detroit Free Press*, July 26, 1977, p. 1).

True to its empirical premises, the American political culture has rejected any form of categorical privilege and has mandated open competition as the vehicle to ensure the just distribution of rewards. "Just deserts" are to be determined individually on the basis of industry, achievement, and luck. As to how these virtues are themselves to be reckoned, the culture suggests that they are evidenced by individual achievement itself, achievement attesting to virtue. Accommodating the American Puritan tradition and incorporating elements of the "natural selection" doctrine of Social Darwinism, this prescription has served a dual function in American politics. It both provides criteria for allocating rewards and serves to justify their existing distribution. As a consequence, the "American culture has never found it overly difficult to tolerate great differences in certain types of individual privileges or rewards" (Williams, 1970, p. 477).

Presuming "equal opportunity," the American political culture thus offers "a vindication of a system of inequality" (Form and Huber, 1969, p. 27). If one assumes that a person deserves what he gets and gets what he deserves, any inequalities that result are justified. Since what a person gets tends to be taken as the measure of what he deserves, it is difficult to challenge any inequalities as violating the cultural principles of distributive justice. However, the cultural justification of inequality is predicated on the assumption that inequalities are the product of individual differences, and stable social patterns of privilege and deprivation would seem to belie this assumption. The persistence of social- or group-based inequalities suggests that either opportunities are fundamentally unequal or the competition is inherently unfair.

Recognition of these problems has brought the American cultural premises regarding distributive justice under increasing strain. In a 1966 Harris poll, 45% of those sampled agreed that "the rich get richer and the poor get poorer." In a comparable poll in 1973, 75% agreed, a 31% increase in less than a decade. A 1977 poll again found 76% agreeing (Hill and Luttbeg, 1980, p. 117). Doubts about the fairness of prevailing inequalities have prompted a sizable number of Americans to feel "that the government in Washington ought to reduce the income differences between the rich and the poor, perhaps by raising the taxes of wealthy families or by giving income assistance to the poor." The National Opinion Research Center reports that 44% felt this way in a 1980 survey (*Public Opinion*, October/November, 1980, p. 25). None of this, however, should be taken as a wholesale rejection of the traditional concept of distributive justice based on individual achievement. Only 21% of a national sample in 1980 agreed that the amount that a person could earn should be limited to $100,000 a year. This result is remarkably similar to the 26% who endorsed the idea of an income ceiling in a 1940 survey. It is also noteworthy that among those earning less than $5000 in the 1980 survey, nearly two-thirds rejected the income ceiling idea (*Public Opinion*, June/July, 1981, p. 32).

Those who have found themselves disadvantaged by existing patterns of inequality have, nonetheless, become more and more insistent on greater substantive equality. An estimated 68% of the nonwhite population, as opposed to only 42% of the white population, favors government action to reduce income differences (*Public Opinion*, October/November, 1980, p. 25). "The demand for various kinds of substantive equalities— amounting to categorical and preferential status in the view of many white, middle-income persons—has become a political reality" (Williams, 1970, p. 479). While such demands are as offensive to many Americans as the injustices that gave rise to them, this does not mean that most are insensitive to the unfairness arising from past deprivations. As Lipset and Schneider observe in a review of recent public opinion studies:

> Relatively few Americans object to compensation for past deprivations in the form of special training programs, Headstart efforts, financial aid programs, community development funds and the like. . . . Americans will go along with special compensation up to the point where they feel that resources have been roughly equalized and the initial terms of competition are once again fair. But the data show that every attempt to introduce any form of absolute preference where the results are "set aside" according to fixed racial or sexual proportions meets with stiff and determined resistance. ("America's Schizophrenia on Achieving Equality," *Los Angeles Times*, July 31, 1977, Part IV, p. 6)

Premises Regarding Personal Virtue. Competition has been embraced within the American political culture not only as an instrumentality of distributive justice but for the personal qualities that it is presumed to foster. Competition is viewed as "character building," and those qualities that are assumed to facilitate "success" in the competitive struggle are widely admired. Thus, as one might expect, Americans tend to rank "honest," "ambitious," and "responsible" at the top of the attributes they value (Rokeach, 1973, p. 58). In fact, the linkage between "success," defined largely in terms of individual material achievement, and personal virtue has tended to be so tightly drawn that the former is typically taken as *prima facie* evidence of the latter.

The relevant cultural premises are largely embodied in what has been called "the work ethic." Derived in part from a Puritan heritage that posited industry and piety as signs of divine grace, this ethic has placed a premium on individual achievement, viewing it as an external manifestation of moral virtue. Within such a system, material success is seen to be not simply the fruits of labor but a testimony to personal worth. As a consequence:

> In our culture, failure is still more likely to be charged to defect of character than to blind fate, capricious accident, or impersonalized social and economic forces, and the wealthy and powerful still either desire or find it expedient to justify their positions in the name of "service" and "stewardship." (Williams, 1970, p. 456)

While the assumption that success attends virtue has supported rather callous and harsh judgments of the less advantaged (even by themselves), the culture does not relieve its members from all concern with their fellow man. The principles of morality embodied in Lockean liberalism mandate that a person do "as much as he can to preserve the rest of mankind" (Devine, 1972, p. 225). However, the overriding assumption that personal failure is largely attributable to deficiencies in individual character or skill has colored the acceptable ways in which humanistic concerns may be manifested. For the most part, emphasis tends to be placed upon "correcting" the flaws in an individual's character or experience so as to make him more self-reliant and more virtuous. Failing this, help may take the form of protecting the individual from himself. These orientations perhaps find their clearest expression in popular attitudes and public policy toward "welfare." However, they play a shaping and constraining role in numerous other areas of social policy. For example, they support the myth of contributory social insurance that undergirds the American social security system, even though that system is in reality a program of income transfer from one generation to another In general, cultural conceptions of personal virtue militate against any policies that are or appear to be more than mildly redistributive. They also serve to justify public concern with "deviant" patterns of private behavior (e.g., homosexuality) and encourage rather strict conformity to conventional standards of behavior and belief.

Premises Regarding Life Values. While the American political culture sanctions, within broad limits, the "pursuit of happiness" as defined by its individual members, it presumes that the acquisition and use of private property will be central to this pursuit. Property is valued not only for the comfort it affords but also for the achievement it indexes and the personal qualities to which it gives testimony. Just as freedom to acquire and use property and equality in this right are seen as essential to human dignity and happiness, so too is the security of that property. Within the American political culture, civil society finds its justification largely through its ability to secure these conditions and has no more ultimate purpose.

The sanctity attached to private property and the premium placed on its pursuit through "private enterprise" have served both the material desires and the individualistic impulses of the American people. They have contributed to an ethos that has brought historically unparalleled standards of personal comfort and private consumption, but often at the price of wanton waste of human and material resources and an impoverished public sector. They have justified the development of a capitalistic economy whose corporate structure has become the locus of enormous but largely unrestrained power. Still:

> To many people in America, the large corporation represents "private property"—they attach to corporate organization the values historically associated with control of property by individual entrepreneurs . . . even though it is a fiction if one compares the modern corporation to private property as defined in earlier periods of history. (Williams, 1970, p. 435)

The materialistic individualism that sustains and is sustained by the values placed on private property militates against effective collective action and planning for public purposes, while sanctioning both for private gain. The well-worn doctrine of "noninterference" in private enterprise remains a potent barrier to any definition of the public interest that transcends a simple accomodation of private interests. As a consequence, only in promoting the immediate security of property itself (e.g., "law and order") and in protecting the community from foreign encroachment (e.g., "national security") are governmental officials likely to be granted broad latitude in exercising political authority.

Political Prescriptions

Dispositions of the members of a polity will be influenced not only by a set of culturally prescribed empirical and normative premises but also by a number of prescriptions specific to the conduct of political affairs. These will generally reflect the more basic characteristics of the cultural system of which they are a part. They will likely, however, provide the most vivid manifestations of the tensions and inconsistencies contained within that system and thus serve to provide the cutting edge of significant cultural changes. Because this is particularly true of political values, we will give them a somewhat more extended treatment than the other cultural elements to be considered under the rubric of political prescriptions.

Prescriptions Regarding Political Values. We have previously noted that within the American political culture, perhaps the ultimate value to be promoted and protected through the political process has been that of "private property." Closely associated with this value and instrumental to its realization, as conceived in the American context, are two distinctly political values: namely, liberty and equality. It is through these values and their pursuit that many of the empirical and the normative premises we have discussed find their most direct political expression. As typically conceived, these values strongly reflect the materialistic and individualistic impulses of the culture.

The inherent conflict between liberty and equality is long recognized and well documented (e.g., see Lamb, 1974; Lipset, 1980). The tension between them provides an important dynamic element in the American political culture, the question of the relative priority to be given to one or the other being a matter of continuing controversy. It seems fair to say that in general, the American response to the dilemma posed by the conflicting imperatives of these two values has been to give priority to liberty values and to define equality so as to accord with that emphasis. Rokeach, for example, finds that Americans generally tend to assign greater importance to "freedom" than to "equality" (1973, pp. 57–58). Still, the culture offers no definitive resolution of the competing claims of liberty and of equality; and one finds considerable ambiguity, as well as ambivalence, in how they are to be interpreted.

The American conception of liberty rests on the view that people should be free from arbitrary external restraint and should be morally responsible for their own conduct. Liberty is not license, but rather individual responsibility. This is manifested "in the tendency to think of rights rather than duties, a suspicion of established (especially personal) authority, a distrust of central government, a deep aversion to the acceptance of obviously coercive restraints through visible social organization" (Williams, 1970, p. 480).

Historically, Americans have been sensitive to any form of explicit control exercised over their lives by identifiable social organizations, most particularly, government, which has been seen as the chief threat. At the same time, they have been largely oblivious to, or have accepted as legitimate, equally restraining but more diffuse forms of control exercised through impersonal and less visible economic, social, and cultural forces. Thus, "social planning" tends to be found unacceptable, while even severe social dislocations and deprivations may be accepted simply as "acts of God" to be coped with individually as best as one can.

In terms of more specific "liberty" themes, Americans endorse the ideas of freedom of the press, speech, and assembly; but they are often willing to compromise the exercise of them, particularly when used by unpopular groups to give expression to unconventional thoughts (e.g., see McClosky, 1964; Monroe, 1975, pp. 168–171; Sullivan, P(ie)reson, and Marcus, 1979). They value the right of choice in matters of religion, employment, consumption, and location, even though for most, no active choice is ever actually exercised (Lane, 1962).

Equality as a value theme in the American political culture represents an historical rejection of hereditary privilege and of a closed class system. These sentiments still find expression in the absence of any fixed habits of deference and in recurring themes of anti-intellectualism and anti-elitism. While asserting the moral equality of man, the American egalitarian impulse has never assumed biological equality nor has it sought vindication through the equalization of the material benefits of society. "The dominant culture value is not an undifferentiated and undiscriminating equalitarianism, but rather a two-sided emphasis upon basic social rights and upon equality of opportunity" (Williams, 1970, p. 478).

"Equality before the law" in the sense of formal rights and obligations and political equality in the sense of access to the political system (e.g., "one man, one vote") have been major tenets of America's conception of the value. More substantively, equality in terms of wealth is an idea that tends to be abhorrent to most. It is assumed that wealth is the due reward of merit and that a benign and abundant nature provides more than an ample basis to ensure all their just deserts—the economic struggle being seen as a continuous positive-sum game.

From this perspective, equality of conditions tends to be viewed as inappropriate and unfair—an arbitrary distortion of the natural order of things and a fearful prospect even for those who might stand to benefit (Lane, 1962). What Americans do consider important is "equality of opportunity." They have insisted, however, on no strict reckoning of the equality involved, emphasizing instead the notion that all should have at least some chance ("opportunity") to get ahead and better themselves.

Prescriptions Regarding the Scope of Politics. As has been alluded to several times above, the American political culture has encouraged suspicion of political authority and suggested that its exercise should be limited. Throughout much of our history, this prescription has effectively constrained the scope of governmental activity. However, with the improvisations of the New Deal, a new element was injected into the political culture, namely, the idea that the community through the agency of government bears some responsibility for individual welfare. The government thereby became a benefactor and a supporting partner for private endeavor. What is striking about this change is that it was accomplished without displacing the standing prescription of limited government. The resulting dilemma has been how to give definition to the appropriate limits of positive government—a dilemma that the culture has yet to resolve and perhaps never will.

The resulting duality parallels and, to a large extent, reflects the tension between the political values of liberty and of equality that we noted earlier. Symbols such as "limited government" and "freedom from governmental interference" retain their potency because they are in keeping with the premium placed on individual achievement and freedom from arbitrary restriction. On the other hand, equality values and basic conceptions of fairness prompt the belief that government should promote the "public interest," protect the "weak," and help the "deserving poor." Thus, in a national poll reported in 1978, 58% agreed that "the government has gone too far in regulating business and interfering with the free enterprise system"; however, when asked about specific types of regulation such as setting "safety standards" and requiring "changes in job conditions if it thinks they're harmful," 67% of the same sample endorsed governmental action (Adam Clymer, "More Conservatives Share 'Liberal' View," *New York Times*, January 22, 1978, pp. 1, 30). Similarly, in a 1981 survey, Harris found that 59% agreed with the adage "the best government is the government that governs the least"; at the same time, 72% agreed that the federal government was responsible for "seeing to it that the poor are taken care of, that no one goes hungry, and that every person achieves at least a minimal standard of living" (*Public Opinion*, June/July, 1981 p. 60).

The cultural prescriptions regarding the scope of politics are thus of two faces. They sanction the view that government has almost limitless responsibility, while at the same time supporting the belief that government threatens to become too powerful and that any additional claims it makes on the citizenry are of questionable legitimacy. In essence, the culture invites the view that responsibility and power can be effectively divorced, suggesting that one can be increased while the other is restricted. Such a proposition would seem a ready-made prescription for unrealistic expectations which make popular disillusionment with political authority almost inevitable. Moreover, it serves to limit policy innovation of a redistributive nature, as the more advantaged segments of society willingly partake of collective benefits but grudgingly give of their private resources.

Prescriptions Regarding Decision Protocols. The rules and institutions that the culture prescribes for the management of social conflict and collective decision making have remained remarkably stable throughout our history. They strongly reflect the values, priorities, and concerns of Lockean liberal thought (Devine, 1972, pp. 139–179). Preeminent among these prescriptions are the rule of law, the fragmentation of governmental power, and the ultimate sovereignty of the people.

The rule of law, as conceived by Americans, is embodied in the Constitution. The institutional structure and decisional protocols it mandates are the objects of widespread pride and confidence.

> The Constitution enjoys a veneration that makes it a substantial barrier against sudden or far-reaching changes in the structure of the state. There is a "psychology of constitutionalism," a widespread conviction that the Constitution is sufficient to cover all emergencies, that deviations from its provisions are unnecessary and dangerous, that a breach of the Constitution would bring down the whole structure of order and lawful government. (Williams, 1970, p. 253)

Even with the tremendous expansion in the scope of governmental responsibility dating from the New Deal, the essential logic and organizing principles of government have remained unchanged. Political authority has been fragmented and diffused across a "maze of competing and overlapping governmental agencies . . . [so as] to prevent exactly what classical liberalism sought to prevent: the ability of government to exercise unified and central authority in response to the interests of the people as a people" (Lamb, 1974, pp. 286–287). The effects of all this frequently have been to accentuate and reinforce the concentration of private power and existing patterns of privilege. In this scheme of things, government often becomes little more than a reflection of the existing balance of power among organized interests in society.

The American conception of democracy is realized through the principles of popular sovereignty and majority rule. True to these principles, American history records the successive removal of numerous barriers to popular participation in the political process. Still, the fragmented and decentralized structure of government serves to obscure the meaning of any popular mandate and makes even minimal accountability difficult. Within such a system, positions taken rather than performance tend to become the basis of candidate evaluations, and public policy becomes more a response to the mobilization of private power between elections than the result of broad electoral mandates.

Prescriptions Regarding Standards of Political Conduct. The American political culture prescribes exacting standards for those who hold or would hold public office. As Edelman observes:

> A higher moral standard is expected in public affairs than in private ones. Therefore, an act that evokes a disapproving reaction when a public official

performs it is regarded as shrewd business tactics in a private setting. (1964, p. 107)

Because public office is seen as a public trust, no aspect of a public official's life is beyond scrutiny. Interestingly, probity in one's personal life seems to be as important as official conduct in office, and intentions are judged as much as performance in the execution of official responsibility.

While positing demanding standards for those who would serve the public, the culture also seems to encourage the expectation that these standards will be violated. Politics tends to be seen as an inherently compromising, if not a corrupting, endeavor—as a "dirty business." Similarly, public bureaucracies tend to be viewed as wasteful, inefficient, and self-serving. As a consequence, public servants, be they politicians or bureaucrats, are accorded an ambivalent status at best. The culture seems to demand integrity, dedication, and self-sacrifice in those who would serve the public, while promising them continuing suspicion of their actions and motivations.

The manifest characteristics of American politics, particularly electoral politics, frequently serve to reinforce latent suspicions and anxieties regarding politics and politicians. These characteristics are themselves reflective of basic cultural premises. Most particularly, the emphasis placed by the culture on "winning" in a "competitive struggle," coupled with the material and symbolic benefits at stake, can readily lead some to regard elections as "the civilian equivalent of warfare and everything goes" (Richard Baisden, quoted by Tracy Wood, "Politicians Paying the Price for Win-at-Any-Cost Philosophy," *Los Angeles Times*, August 29, 1977, Part II, p. 8). Furthermore, in a politics governed by a singular political tradition, it is frequently found expedient to exaggerate minor differences and to personalize conflicts by drawing sharp distinctions between oneself and the opponent.

The resulting mobilization of energies and resources simply feeds further suspicion. Contemporary concerns with "campaign practices" and "campaign financing" represent an effort to curb some of the excesses involved, but a politics of exaggeration seems an endemic condition of American life. Crises and/or imminent threat, be they real or contrived, are often required to arouse the attention and concern of a people bent on the "private pursuit of happiness."

Prescriptions Regarding a Citizen's Role. The citizen's role as envisioned in the American political culture involves both a subject and a participant dimension. As a subject, the citizen is expected to provide largely for his own well-being and to protect his own interests. While he is expected to abide by the law and to support the political order, his formal obligations are few. The culture suggests that the primary flow of obligation is from the state to the individual, and not vice versa. In the course of history, this doctrine has been stripped of much of its radical elan, but it still serves to sustain a limited sense of individual responsibility to the larger community.

The culture places somewhat greater emphasis on the participatory aspects of the citizen's role, but always within the context of voluntarism. The citizen is seen as having both the ability and the right to participate in his own governance. In fact, the culture suggests that he must bear some responsibility for the direction of the polity. What is implied by this charge, however, is left for the individual to determine. There is evidence to suggest that it is experienced as a sense of civic duty that frequently goes unattended. For example, almost invariably postelection surveys find substantially more people claiming to have voted than actually showed up at the polls.

Perhaps the most distinctive feature of the American conception of citizenship is the tendency to view it as a status attained rather than a simple matter of circumstance. As Lipset observes, Americanism tends to be an

> ideology rather than simply a nationalist term . . . a creed to which men are converted rather than born. . . . Just as foreigners may become Americans, Americans may become "un-Americans." This concept of "un-American activities," as far as I know, does not have its counterpart in other countries. American patriotism is allegiance to values, to a creed, not soley to a nation. . . . More than any democratic country, the United States makes ideological conformity one of the conditions for good citizenship. (1955, pp. 181–182)

The American political culture thus proscribes certain identities (e.g., "communism") and tends to restrict the range of beliefs that citizens may legitimately hold to those that accord with its dominant liberal tradition. The mere advocacy of innovation outside of this tradition can become the invitation to opprobrium.

SUBCULTURAL VARIATION

We have attempted to describe some of the major premises and prescriptions that tend to characterize the political culture and inform the dispositions of individual members of the American polity. Transferred across generations, generally with only minor modifications, and validated through interpersonal interaction, these premises and prescriptions serve to give a degree of substantive commonality to the political world views of the population. In fostering common dispositions, the culture constrains the meanings that are likely to be attributed to political symbols and establishes a general set of expectations that limits the ways in which they may be used.

While the American political culture rests upon a singular political tradition, it has accommodated some variation on its basic theme. For the most part, this variation has been a simple matter of differential emphasis of the same basic elements. Much of it may be regarded as idiosyncratic, but some of it is sufficiently patterned to allow the identification of more or less distinctive subcultures.

Such subcultures reflect the peculiar historical experiences and traditions of different groups or segments of society. These differences tend to be associated with shared social attributes, racial or ethnic characteristics, or geographical location; and it is commonplace to distinguish subcultures in these terms. However, it is a shared world view and not common demographic characteristics that defines a subculture. In Chapter 5, we will explore more fully the relationship between demographic attributes and ideational variation. Here we will simply note some of the major patterns of subcultural variation that have been identified in the American political culture.

In a compelling synthesis of the observations of numerous observers, Elazar (1972) suggests three major patterns of subcultural variation: namely, the individualistic, the moralistic, and the traditional subcultures. These distinctions rest primarily on differences in what we have called "political prescriptions"; but more basic cultural premises are also involved, most notably, those regarding the nature of society and of social obligation.

The individualistic subculture embraces a distinctly atomistic view of society and posits minimal social obligation. It tends to be uncompromising in its support of private enterprise and is generally antistatist in its orientation toward government. Politics is conceived largely as an alternative channel for the pursuit of private gain, and participation is assumed to be motivated primarily by narrow self-interest.

As an illustration of the individualistic subculture, consider the state of Ohio. Elazar suggests that it is one of many dominated by this subcultural type. It is a state characterized by what Fenton has called "issueless politics" based on the "middle-class" myth. Fenton writes:

> Ohio has been called the "great middle class state." There middle class myth was a blend of Horatio Alger and the rugged individualist attitudes associated with the frontier. It found concrete expression in a dedication to the homely virtues of honesty, thrift, steadfastness, caution, and a distrust of government. Freedom was prized, and restraints tended to be associated exclusively with government. (1966, p. 153)

The moralistic subculture places greater emphasis on the individual's obligation to the community and encourages the individual to assume some responsibility for the commonweal. It tends to take a more sanguine view of government as a vehicle for promoting the common good but insists on the most exacting standards of political conduct. Participation is conceived as a civic duty, but it is frowned upon unless motivated by principle.

The distinctive properties of the moralistic subculture are perhaps illustrated in the following excerpt from a statement of principles issued by the Democratic Party in the state of Michigan, a state that Elazar finds to be of this subcultural type.

> So long as one human being is hungry and we can feed him and do not, so long as one person is naked and we can clothe him and do not, so long as one person is sick and we can administer to him and do not, so long as one worker or farmer is deprived of a just living and we can remedy it and do not, so long as one person is unwillingly illiterate and we can educate him and do not, so long as one nation is subjugated by another against its will and we can work for freedom and do not, the American task is not done. (Quoted in Fenton, 1966, p. 21)

While it is possible to imagine such a broad statement of social obligation and such a positive view of the possibilities of political action being widely embraced as operative political principles in some other states, such as Minnesota or Wisconsin, it is difficult to imagine them serving as guiding principles in the politics of many others, e.g., Indiana or Ohio.

The traditional subculture suggests a more organic conception of society. One's social obligation is largely to accord oneself with the existing order. While not encouraging governmental activism, it brooks a degree of governmental paternalism. Politics tends to be viewed as something of an estate of a traditional elite, and the subject aspects of the citizen's role tend to be given priority over participation.

Elazar identifies Virginia with the traditional subculture. In his classic study, *Southern Politics*, V. O. Key observed:

> Of all the American states, Virginia can lay claim to the most thorough control by an oligarchy. Political power has been closely held by a small group of leaders. . . . The Commonwealth possesses characteristics . . . akin to those of England at about the time of the Reform Bill of 1832. It is a political museum piece. Yet the little oligarchy that rules Virginia demonstrates a sense of honor, an aversion to open venality, a degree of sensitivity to public opinion, a concern for efficiency in administration, and so long as it does not cost much, a feeling of social responsibility. (1949, p. 19)

While much has changed since Key made these observations, many vestiges of the political order of which he wrote remain, including a voter turnout rate that is one of the lowest in the nation.

In recognizing this subcultural variation, it is important that the differences involved not be exaggerated. For the most part, they are differences of degree, not differences in kind. All three tend to endorse both the premises and the conclusions of Lockean liberal thought and to accept the major tenets of the dominant culture we have previously characterized.

Still, the variations indexed by these subcultures may be useful in understanding the alternative interpretations given to different political symbols and the range of meanings that any particular symbol is likely to engage.

While acknowledging that these subcultures have become intermingled and have taken on hybrid qualities, Elazar argues that they tend to be differentially concentrated geographically. Their ecology is a function of different regional experiences and of the historical patterns of migration of different ethnic groups in the United States. More specifically, he finds the moralistic subculture dominant along the northern tier of the country and the traditional subculture concentrated in the South. The individualistic subculture is seen as prevailing throughout the rest of the country.

Wilson and Banfield (1964, 1971) find similar subcultural variation in American urban politics. They identify two types of political ethos: public-regardingness (subsequently relabeled the "unitary ethos") and private-regardingness (renamed the "individualist ethos"). The patterns involved are similar to those that Elazar associates with the moralistic and the individualistic subcultures. Like Elazar, Wilson and Banfield find some association between these patterns and ethnicity.

Sale (1975) offers an additional hypothesis to account for subcultural variation. His observations regarding the presumptions that tend to govern the politics of the "Sun Belt," and the Southwest in particular, suggest that subcultural differences may in part be understood in terms of patterns of economic development. It would seem that the "rugged individualism" encouraged by the individualistic subculture tends to thrive in eras and areas of rapid economic expansion.

DYNAMICS OF CULTURAL CHANGE

A political culture (and the subcultures it subsumes) promotes not only uniformity but also continuity in the life of a polity. Transporting "lessons" from the past, it facilitates a socially meaningful construction of present realities and provides a guide to the future. Neither the symbols of a culture nor the premises and prescriptions they index are, however, static. Changes can occur in any and all elements of the culture and may be occasioned by a variety of factors. Some of these changes are more common and less consequential than others.

Forms of Change

Perhaps the least disruptive and most superficial form of cultural change simply involves changes in the ensemble of socially significant symbols. In the previous chapter, we noted ways in which symbols could be transformed in meaning or used to the point that they lose all potency. A certain amount of turnover of prominent symbols is inherent in the normal operations of the policy. It is a particularly commonplace occurrence with respect to lower-order symbols.

Symbolic objects, such as candidates and issues, regularly change without precipitating any attendant changes in the underlying dispositions that may have been engaged. These changes, however, are not without significance. As Stokes observes, "A turnover of stimulus objects can alter dramatically the facts of social structure which are relevant to political choice" (1966, p. 27). Insofar as they serve to focus attention and to structure the options immediately available for giving political expression to personal preferences and priorities, lower-order symbols determine what dispositions are likely to be mobilized in the political process and whose biases are likely to prevail.

Changes in the basic premises and prescriptions of the political culture tend to be of even more profound consequence, because they alter the operative characteristics of the political system. Such changes find expression both in new symbols and in the redefinition of old ones.

> Thucydides said long ago that social revolutions occur when old terms take on new meanings. The wisdom of this statement is apparent in the dramatic, recent change of the meaning for the term "black"—a word that has become a badge of intense pride which borders on racial superiority: "Black is beautiful." (Caplan, 1970, p. 67)

The significance of this kind of change tends to be greater the more basic or primitive the premises involved. We have observed that the various elements of a political culture tend to be interrelated to form a more or less coherent structure. The configuration, taken as a whole, tends to have a logic of its own. The alteration of one element is therefore likely to have ramifications for others. The more central the element, the more profound the implications of its change are likely to be.

Consider, for example, the empirical premises regarding the natural environment found in the American political culture. Whether or not the faith Americans tend to place in nature's abundance and man's extractive genius is justified, there can be little doubt that a fundamental shift in these assumptions would have profound and multifaceted consequences. Comparative research, particularly in less developed areas of the world (e.g., see Banfield, 1958; Scott, 1968) and studies of subcultural patterns found among persons living in impoverished environs in the United States (e.g., see Jaros et al., 1968) suggest that such a change would necessitate widespread revisions in the cultural system, if a viable civil society were to be sustained. In any case, major alternations could be expected in American political, economic, and social life.

Sources of Change

Cultural change can be both a response to and a cause of changes in the social and the physical environment. While external events and circumstances provide the immediate impetus for cultural change, these precipitating conditions may themselves reflect cultural imperatives. In this sense, the seeds of change may be contained within the culture itself. These may take the form of the conflicts, inconsistencies, and gaps that are almost inevitably found in any cultural system. The continuing tensions between liberty (achievement) and equality in American politics, for example, almost assures an element of cultural dynamism.

John Agresto suggests that such cultural tensions are found in the contemporary debate over alternative energy sources. "The poles of the debate, nuclear vs. solar, imply a whole range of old divisions and dilemmas—commerce vs. agriculture, production vs. conservation, competitive individualism vs. egalitarianism" (*Providence Journal*, August 30, 1981, p. B–19). Each side appeals to a different but deeply rooted set of values. While the "nuclear" side offers a vision of America based on "progress," "technology," "industry," and "know-how," the "solar" group emphasizes "community," "cooperation," the values of the "simple life," and the "virtues of "self-sufficiency." In this sense, the energy debate is not simply a matter of alternative forms of energy but of competing cultural images of who we are and what we are about.

Yet another source of "autonomously" induced change lies in the culture's own internal logic, the implications of which tend to be constantly in the process of being worked out. That the premium placed on equality and property in America would ultimately lead to revised assumptions about the nature and role of government was forseen by de Tocqueville almost a century and a half ago in his classic study, *Democracy in America*. He argued that in rejecting the idea that anyone was entitled to special privileges and insisting that individuals be treated equally, the American political culture fostered a climate of opinion favorable to the gradual concentration of power in the central government. This tendency, he observed, was further compounded by the love of well-being and a concern with protecting one's property. De Tocqueville, in fact, anticipated much of the historical evolution of our political culture. His prescient observations are a testimony not only to his genius but to the powerful imperatives implicit in the cultural paradigm.

In a more proximate sense, cultural change is occasioned by events that alter or threatened to alter the current "facts" of social life. Insofar as these events are routine and anticipated (e.g., change in political authority figures), they normally affect little more than the available array of lower-order symbols. The attention and concerns of the polity may be refocused as a consequence, but the basic premises and prescriptions remain intact. When events conspire to produce anomalies or lead to unexpected consequences, more fundamental cultural changes may ensue. As Whyte has observed, "People grow restive with a mythology that is too distant from the way things actually are" (1956, p. 6).

The events associated with major cultural modifications may be sudden and dramatic (e.g., a depression) or gradual and cumulative (e.g., growing international interdependence). The coincidence of the two tends to facilitate the most pronounced change. The latter serve to undermine prior convictions making change more palatable, while the former gives change more poignant justification and provides its symbolic definition. Regardless of the circumstances, the response is likely to involve improvisations that seek to accommodate the new realities while doing minimal violence to the central characteristics of the culture. Even in dire situations, resistance to major change or innovation is likely to be strong. Such changes will be entertained grudgingly and accepted only gradually and unevenly. "Often it takes the replacement of one generation by another to let the impact of external changes take full effect" (Deutsch and Merritt, 1965, p. 183).

Inglehart (1977) has demonstrated how over generations changing life experiences and societal conditions can alter values and value priorities to the point of constituting a "silent revolution." He finds evidence that such "revolutionary" changes have been occurring throughout the Western world over the last quarter-century. They are marked by a "shift from overwhelming emphasis on material consumption and security toward greater concern with the quality of life; and an increase in the political skills of Western publics that enables them to play a more active role in making important political decisions" (1977, p. 363).

Miller and Levitin's (1976) analysis of the "New Politics" that emerged in the United States in the 1960s lends support to Inglehart's arguments. They find American politics increasingly defined by value differences similar to those identified by Inglehart. Ladd (1982) finds that the same value differences—differences that he dubs "Old Liberalism" versus "New Liberalism" are responsible for a profound cleavage in the Democratic Party. This cleavage has proved a major burden to recent Democratic candidates for the Presidency and has threatened the majority status, if not the viability, of the Democratic Party itself.

Cultural Constraints and Policy Manipulation

While a political culture imposes important constraints on the politics of a community and limits the ability of elites to manipulate public policy, these constraints are broad ones and afford considerable latitude for political action. The actions undertaken as part of the "normal" politics sanctioned by the culture can themselves provide, or at least influence, the events that occasion cultural changes. Thus, while major policy innovations may have to await basic cultural changes, these changes may be prompted through the political process.

Within the "normal" politics sanctioned by the American political culture, the policy process tends to be incremental and disjointed. Neither the culture itself nor the institutions it serves to support are conducive to bold or programmatic policy initiatives. Even marginal policy changes may require a substantial mobilization of political resources. Still, major policy departures can and do occur as the result of purposive actions. To be successful, however, such policy innovations need cultural moorings. A crisis or a spectacular event can provide the immediate justification for change, but the imperatives of a singular event are not likely to be sufficient to assure a particular policy direction. Justification in the larger cultural context is needed.

Cultural accommodation of a major innovation is facilitated by cumulative events that serve to weaken prior presumptions and gradually move a society to recognize new problems or to accept redefinitions of old ones. Such a succession of events provides perhaps the surest basis upon which to rest major policy departures. In any case, to serve the ends of specific policy changes, events (be they cumulative, spectacular, or both) must be exploited through effective symbol management. Minimally, this involves the focusing of popular attention through the use of culturally significant symbols. Whether or not the events themselves are actively manipulated will be less important than the guidance provided regarding what symbols are applicable and thus what cultural premises or prescriptions are relevant to the interpretation of events. Gradually, through the selective use of higher-order symbols, new symbols can be created and old ones redefined (or discredited) so as to create a climate conducive to a significant policy innovation. Some patience, however, is likely to be required. Dramatic gestures and efforts to force this process can readily backfire, precipitating reactions that have effects opposite to those intended.

Examples of both effective and ineffective symbol management in contemporary American politics abound. Earlier we noted how the differences between Richard Nixon and George McGovern in their advocacy of fundamentally similar welfare reform proposals occasioned almost contradictory responses. The lessons involved did not totally escape the Carter Administration. In accord with popular perceptions conditioned by at least a decade of cumulative events, Carter declared in 1977 that the "welfare system was 'anti-work,' 'anti-family,' 'unfair' and 'wasteful of taxpayer's dollars.'" In its stead, he proposed a "program for better jobs and income" that bore remarkable resemblance to the earlier reform proposals of Nixon and McGovern. Harris reported:

> By any measure, the initial reaction to Carter's welfare reform package must be viewed as remarkable.... [As] far as the public is concerned, the president [sic] is off to a flying start in mobilizing public opinion behind his program. (Louis Harris, "Most Back Carter in Welfare Plan," *Detroit Free Press*, September 16, 1977, p. 2–B)

Remarkable as it might be, the response can be regarded as a predictable result of the exploitation of cumulative events and of effective symbol management. Carter's reply to a reporter who noted his avoidance of the word "welfare," except to say the system was a "failure," is perhaps instructive:

> I think there's a great deal of stigma to the word "welfare" and I can't shape the vocabulary of the nation, obviously, but we've decided to call this program . . . "a program for better jobs and income." . . . The people of the country don't like the word "welfare" but they do favor the programs that provide for poor people—both those who work and those who cannot work. . . . I think that the [proposed changes] . . . will do a great deal to restore the beneficial image of the word "welfare" if it is used. ("Transcript of Presidential News Conference," *New York Times*, August 7, 1977, p. 41)

Despite the initial positive response to Carter's welfare reform proposal, it was subsequently lost amid a flurry of other legislative initiatives and died as both Carter's popular standing and the state of the economy declined. Many of the issues involved surfaced again in the 1980 presidential campaign as part of Ronald Reagan's attack on "big government." Upon assuming the Presidency, Reagan effectively exploited the distressed state of the economy and popular disillusionment with government to alter substantially the direction not only of welfare policies but of much of the domestic activities of the federal government. Arguing that the nation was in the "worst economic mess since the Great Depression," he suggested that the source of the problem was government itself and proposed dramatic cutbacks in the federal budget along with a major tax cut.

Reagan appealed to the public for support, assuring them that the cuts would not be at the expense of the "truly needy" and that the government would continue to provide a "social safety net" for "those who through no fault of their own must depend on the rest of us." At the same time, he pledged to put a stop to the "wasteful ways" of government, including eliminating "benefits to those who are not really qualified by reason of need." This, he suggested, would help create the "incentives which take advantage of the genius of our economic system" and begin "to reward hard work and risk-taking" (*Congressional Quarterly Weekly Report*, February 7, 1981, pp. 286–288, and February 21, 1981, pp. 360–363). Through the use of culturally significant symbols to interpret the unsettled state of the nation and to support his definition of the problem, he successfully mobilized the support necessary to bring about a profound shift in American public policy.

CONCLUSIONS

Symbols, particularly higher-order ones, are a basic part of the political culture. The cultural premises and prescriptions they serve to index inform the dispositions of the populace and create expectations that limit the possibility of symbolic manipulation. To illustrate these constraints, we have considered some of the major characteristics of the American political culture and the subcultures it subsumes.

While the characteristic features of a political culture tend to be stable, they are neither fixed nor immutable. Changes occur and alter political priorities. These changes may be occasioned by the culture's own internal logic or by external events. The political process itself may be used to prompt cultural change and open up new possibilities for political action, even though the normal politics is one of incrementalism.

5

Social Functions of Political Symbols

Political symbolism is simultaneously a social and an individual phenomenon. Just as symbols serve critical needs of the individual, so too do they serve important needs of the larger society. Symbols are essential to the processes of social organization and vital to the operations of the polity. They structure social communications and define the stakes of social action. They provide the vehicles through which political demands are articulated and serve as the objects around which mobilization and countermobilization occur. Governments respond through symbols and, through them, assuage anxieties and promote the support essential to the stability and effectiveness of the political system. In this chapter, we will explore some of the social functions and political uses of symbols. We will find that these functions and uses arise from the basic properties of symbols as objects of individual-level orientations, properties that allow them to serve as vehicles for aggregating social diversity. Accordingly, we will attempt to delineate more fully the role of symbols in defining politically important patterns of consensus and cleavage.

SYMBOLS AND THE STAKES OF POLITICS

The allocation of material and symbolic benefits is a central function of any political system. How these allocations are made and rationalized bears heavily on the ability of the system to sustain itself. Of particular interest is the question of how the vast majority of people come to accept political verdicts regarding a distribution of benefits which may not be to their immediate advantage. This question would seem to be critical to an understanding of the nature of diffuse support, legitimacy, and other related concepts (e.g., see Easton, 1965; Kelman, 1969).

Edelman speaks to this question, hinging much of his analysis on the distinction between symbolic and tangible rewards. He argues that the political process normally operates to convey tangible benefits to organized interests while providing only symbolic reassurances to the mass public. He notes that many political acts which command widespread attention are highly significant symbolically but have little or no effect on the distribution of material resources. Such symbol-laden acts buoy public confidence and promote popular acquiescence to the conditions that sustain the current political order. These conditions enable the organized elites to pursue their material interests and to partake disproportionately of the tangible benefits allocated by the political system (1964, pp. 22–43).

Noting essentially the same phenomena, Lowi suggests that they are fortified in the United States by a deeply ingrained and culturally sanctioned public philosophy which he calls "interest group liberalism." He sees this ethos as a vulgarized version of the pluralist arguments that have been widely used to describe (or rationalize) the operations of the American polity. "Interest group liberalism" defines the "public interest" as a product of the accommodation of private interests. All significant private interests are assumed to be effectively represented through organized groups. The role of government then is to work with these groups as a cooperative "partner" rather than as an adversary. This ethos is manifested in the familiar calls for "government" to work together with "business" and "labor" to solve community problems. In effect, it simply serves to legitimate the demands of organized interests and to ensure governmental access to the most effectively organized (1979, pp. 42–63). Governmental responsiveness to the most powerful and best-organized interests becomes an operating principle of government, a principle that is presumed to serve the "public interest" even though it might otherwise be seen as making "conflict of interest" a virtue instead of a vice.

Both Edelman and Lowi stress the participation of organized groups in the distribution of the tangible outputs of government. However, the literature on status politics (e.g., see Gusfield, 1963; Hofstadter, 1967; Lipset, 1955; Lipset and Raab, 1979; Zurcher and Kirkpatrick, 1976) suggests that it is important not to assume that organized groups are concerned exclusively with material benefits. Gusfield contends that there are symbolic interests at stake in politics which may be as important as material interests, if not more so:

> We live in a human environment in which symbolic gestures have great relevance to our sense of pride, mortification, and honor. Social conflicts and tensions are manifested in a disarray of the symbolic order as well as in other areas of action. Dismissing these reactions as "irrational" clouds analysis and ignores the events which have signification for people. (1963, p. 183)

An example of such symbolic stakes is found in the continuing controversy over "women's rights" in the United States. That conflict has pitted supporters of "traditional family values" against advocates of "women's liberation." Although the Equal Rights Amendment and abortion have provided the focal points of debate, the stakes involved transcend those specific issues. As Conover, Gray, and Coombs write:

> Whichever side ultimately loses on the issues of abortion and the E.R.A. loses much more than those two issues; it loses the broader symbolic battle over which life style and which set of values will be accepted as the norm in American society. With the stakes so high, it is no wonder that the battle has been so intense. (1981, pp. 31–32)

Symbolic benefits may be important in and of themselves. They may also be necessary precursors to the attainment of more material goals. Symbolic victories that give "official" sanction to a group's cause lend legitimacy to both the group and the interest it represents. Without this legitimacy, the group may have little hope of commanding a share of the material benefits of politics. The history of the civil rights movement in the United States would seem to attest to this. As long as segregation and discrimination were officially sanctioned, there was little prospect of black political gains. Although the civil rights movement's early court and legislative victories did not put an end to these practices, they considerably altered the prevailing biases of the political system and paved the way for more substantive gains.

Government is unavoidably involved in the social allocation of prestige, the affirmation of values, and the legitimation of life-styles and standards of morality. To ignore conflicts over these matters, even though they may not involve the direct or immediate allocation of material resources, is to ignore a major and important part of political life. The passage of a law, regardless of whether it is implemented or enforced (or is even implementable or enforceable) can be an act of substantial social significance. For that matter, the mere recognition of an issue by a governmental body can represent a major victory. Attention itself can define "winners" and "losers," both in an immediate sense and in the general social order of things.

That the symbolic rewards produced by governmental action (or inaction) are highly valued and are matters of great public sensitivity is widely appreciated among political leaders. Many recognize that symbolic patronage can be as important as material benefits in maintaining a supportive constituency. If nothing else, successful leaders tend to be alert to the potential perils posed for them should they ignore the symbolic overtones of their actions. Thus, it is not surprising to find such things as the Pennsylvania State House voting to reinstate adultery and fornication as criminal violations in its new criminal code. The arguments used by Representative Martin Mullen in promoting this amendment are suggestive of the symbolic stakes involved:

I can't imagine anything more destructive of family life than adultery or fornication. As a practical matter, we can't stop it, but I don't think we should condone it. Any of you who believe in the Ten Commandments and sound family life will support my position. (*Philadelphia Bulletin*, April 4, 1973, p. 1)

SYMBOLS AND POLITICAL MOBILIZATION

Just as symbols are used to justify or rationalize the decisions of government regarding the distribution of valued things, they can be used to challenge those decisions and mobilize support for new demands. As most students of social movements would surely attest, symbols are essential to political mobilization. By considering the different ways people relate to symbols and by recognizing the importance of affective identifications in particular, we begin to appreciate the potency that symbols have both for mobilizing people and for stemming mobilization. When the emotional aspects of a symbol are removed, so too is much of its potency.

Through symbols, movements can appeal to diverse groups, interests, and individuals for different and even incompatible reasons. It is not homogeneity of motivations, but commonality of affective sentiment that unites them. An example of this phenomenon is provided by Brown and Ellithorp in their analysis of the symbolic appeal of Senator Eugene McCarthy during his 1968 bid for the Democratic Presidential nomination. They found that "persons with diverse perspectives resonate to the same stimulus object (McCarthy), but for different reasons as developed through different experiences" (1970, p. 363). Aberbach and Walker have similarly shown how a symbol such as "black power . . . may excite many different attitudes and may motivate individuals to express their loyalties or take action for almost contradictory reasons" (1970, p. 367). Blumer (1954) describes this process as one of "convergent selectivity." Lipset and Raab call it "selective support" (1979, pp. 496–515). Through it,

> members of a mass converge on a common object because of an idiosyncratic attraction by each of them to selected characteristics of the object. Their common convergence produces the impression of homogeneous mass behavior . . . and gives rise to the further but erroneous assumption of homogeneous motivation. (Brown and Ellithorp, 1970, p. 363)

Understandably, "the larger and more diverse a political movement's constituency, the more vague and imprecise its unifying symbols and rallying cries are likely to be" (Aberbach and Walker, 1970, p. 367). However, the peculiar unifying properties of symbols that facilitate movement expansion also carry attendant liabilities. Caught up in the exhilarating experience of being able to arouse the passions of others, the leaders of a political movement may fail to articulate their goals with sufficient clarity to define responsive governmental action. As a consequence, the very ambiguity that allowed the symbols to serve as a basis for mobilization can become as obstacle to the movement's success. As a sympathetic observer correctly anticipated, these problems were largely to doom the mobilization efforts of "black power" advocates in the late 1960s and early 1970s. He writes:

> "Black Power" is ideological without really being an ideology. It is not . . . a fully adumbrated scheme of ultimate goals which sanction immediate action. Its advocacy is an attempt to provide the symbols necessary for sustaining mass mobilization, but these symbols have not yet been evoked with clarity. The term "Black Power" does . . . seem to tap the welled-up aspirations of many Negroes for self-realization. . . . Beyond this striking term, however, there are only those vague calls for black solidarity and pride in a common heritage—presumably African. (Lewis, 1970, p. 186)

Even if a movement's demands are fairly well formulated initially, its unifying symbols are likely to become more abstract and imprecise as it attempts to expand its support. As a consequence, the clarity of the original demands may be lost, and the leaders of the movement may lose all control over the definition of what the movement is about. In the middle 1960s, for instance, the effort of the Students for a Democratic Society to mobilize public opposition to the Vietnam War was transformed from a mobilization against the war into a radical critique of American society— a transformation that was ultimately to destroy the organization itself. Thus, just as movements may fail from their inability to appeal to a large enough constituency, they may fail precisely because of their success in attracting diverse support. The alternative to such failures would seem to be selective appeals, ever more formal organization, and concomitantly greater reliance upon an elite (see Zald and Ash, 1966). In effect, this would simply transform the movement into another organized participant in the process of "interest group liberalism."

Most movements die out before reaching this stage. This may be the result not only of strategic failures but also of the march of events. Perhaps even more important, movements are likely to founder because of the expressive nature of the commitment of many of their adherents. Expressive needs tend to be more easily satisfied than instrumental ones (see Edelman, 1964, pp. 22–43; Zurcher and Kirkpatrick, 1976, pp. 332–333). Through simply identifying themselves with the movement in some way, adherents whose commitments are primarily expressive often exhaust the reasons for their involvement and cannot be counted upon to do much more. Thus, although political movements play a vital role in the life of a polity, they tend to be made of very fragile stuff.

SYMBOLS AND POLITICAL LEGITIMACY

The same qualities of political symbols that are so crucial to social movements and political mobilization are also critical to the processes of legitimacy. While the support given to a political system is partially a product
of demand-based satisfactions, it is generally agreed that the support tendered by most people is not predicated exclusively, or even primarily,
upon such a strict reckoning of personal payoffs (e.g., see Muller, 1970;
Gamson, 1968; Murphy et al., 1973).

No system is likely to be able to withstand the test of a constant and
self-interested evaluation of its performance on the part of all or even
most of its members. If most people were constantly engaged in the process of weighing the personal costs and benefits involved, it is doubtful
that much in the way of collective political action would be possible (see
Olson, 1965). However, most persons are not inclined to expend the
time, energy, and effort required by such a calculus. Loyalty is tendered
as much on the basis of long-standing affective sentiments toward the
symbols of the system as it is from any short-term satisfactions derived
from the immediate allocation of material or symbolic benefits. This more
basic support in the form of emotive ties to the basic symbols of the system arises largely from identifications acquired through the socialization
process. Appeals to these symbols serve to confirm general expectations
and to provide diffuse gratifications in the form of reassurance of the integrity of the system (see Merelman, 1969; Anton, 1967; Nimmo, 1974,
pp. 131–155).

As an illustration of the use of symbols to provide such reassurance
and to rally support, consider the following excerpts from President
Reagan's 1980 Inaugural Address:

> The orderly transfer of authority as called for in the Constitution routinely
> takes place as it has for almost two centuries. . . . We as Americans have the
> capacity . . . to do whatever needs to be done to preserve this last and greatest
> bastion of freedom. . . . This adminstration's objective must be a healthy,
> vigorous, growing economy that provides equal opportunities for all Amer-
> icans. . . . Our government has no special power except that granted it by the
> people. . . . Your dreams, your hopes, your goals are going to be the dreams,
> the hopes and goals of this administration, so help me God. . . . I believe we
> the Americans of today are ready . . . to do what must be done to ensure
> happiness and liberty for ourselves, our children, and our children's children.
> . . . When action is required to preserve our national security, we will act. . . .
> We are a nation under God, and I believe that God intended us to be free. . . .
> The crisis we are facing today does not require of us the kind of sacrifice
> that . . . so many thousands of others were called upon to make. It does,
> however, require our best efforts, and our willingness to believe in
> ourselves. . . . And after all why shouldn't we . . . ? We are Americans. (*Con-
> gressional Quarterly Weekly Report*, January 24, 1981, pp. 186–188)

The excerpts we have quoted amount to little more than an affirmation of faith in the American system. Through them, Mr. Reagan identifies himself and his administration with the basic legitimacy symbols of the American political system and assures all those who share a commitment to those symbols that their stake in the political system is in good hands.

Merelman suggests that such exercises play an important role in the dynamics of legitimacy. He argues that while the initial legitimacy of a political system may depend upon the allocation of specific benefits, the satisfactions that accrue are reinforced through symbols. Over time, these symbols become an alternative basis of legitimacy and a substitute source of gratification and satisfaction (1966, pp. 551–552). Allegiance to the system can then be reinforced through the ritualistic use of these symbols.

The Question of Consensus

It was once commonly assumed that political stability is a matter of either coercion or consensus. As doubt arose regarding the possibility of the maintenance of stability through force alone, the notion of legitimacy predicated upon some degree of value consensus came to be viewed as critical to any system's long-term stability. To sustain a democracy, a substantial consensus seemed absolutely essential. This assumption has suffered in light of contemporary empirical research. Even in the most stable democratic systems, research has shown that little in the way of a substantive consensus may actually exist (Mann, 1970; McClosky, 1964; Prothro and Grigg, 1960).

This research has repeatedly shown that while abstract statements of democratic principles are widely endorsed, this apparent consensus breaks down when those principles are framed in specific terms. For example, nearly all Americans agree that "every citizen should have an equal chance to influence public policy" and that "the minority should be free to criticize majority decisions" (Prothro and Grigg, 1960, p. 281), but nearly half the population would deny people the right to circulate a petition calling for the legalization of marijuana and roughly 40% would deny black militants the right to hold a peaceful demonstration (Lawrence, 1976, p. 88). The general conclusion emerging from this literature is that while there is widespread positive identification with such symbols as "freedom" and "equality," there is at best limited agreement on the substantive meanings attributed to them. As one might expect, there is more agreement on the meanings associated with these symbols among people who are politically active than in the general public (McClosky, 1974; Mann, 1970). This is attributable in part to educational differences. With increasing education, people are more likely to embrace not just the general value statements but also the specific applications that they seemingly imply (Lawrence, 1976).

From a symbolic point of view, these findings are hardly surprising. A symbolic consensus rests on the mutual attribution of significance to a symbol and on common affective sentiments toward it—not on agreement about its substantive meaning. Such a consensus breaks down, and much of the unifying power of the symbol is destroyed, when its substantive meaning comes into question. As Gusfield notes, "When politicians argue about the definition of sin instead of being uniformly opposed to it, then the underlying political consensus is itself threatened" (1963, p. 184).

That a symbolic consensus is based on "matters of principle" which are understandable in symbolic terms but not in terms of agreement on substantive meanings does not mean that such a consensus is unimportant or without social consequences. As Berelson observes:

> A seeming consensus which is accepted at its face value is far better than no consensus—and a seeming consensus is sometimes reflected in loyalty to the same symbols even though they carry different meanings. A sense of homogeneity is often an efficient substitute for the fact of homogeneity. (1952, pp. 320–321)

It may well be that for a stable polity, at least a democratic one, the electorate "must at least share the symbols describing the substantive ends to which political action is directed and in terms of which it is justified" (Berelson, 1952, p. 321). But such a symbolic consensus is always vulnerable, as some of the more difficult problems of contemporary American politics would surely attest.

The problem is frequently diagnosed as simply one of communication. Since most people are inclined to take the meaning they personally attribute to a symbol to be the only possible one, they naturally tend to assume that there is basic agreement on the meanings attached to shared symbols. As a consequence, differences occasioned by the use of shared symbols tend to be seen as matters of miscommunication, misinformation, or ignorance. All that is required is believed to be more discussion— "let us reason together," if you will. However, the pseudocommunication that can occur as a shared symbol of disparate meanings is invoked may only cloud the issue and blur the real problem. The prescribed palliative tends to be seen as more of the same, but the results may simply be ever-louder appeals to emotively charged but nebulously defined symbols.

Hall and Hewitt (1970) recount an episode of such pseudocommunication involving then-President Nixon and antiwar demonstrators gathered in Washington to protest the Vietnam War. Apparently frustrated by what he perceived to be a lack of understanding of his policies by the demonstrators, Nixon slipped out of the White House late one evening to talk directly with some of them. He sought in vain to convince them that he was as committed to "peace" as they and that he was doing everything possible to bring it about. Their differences with him, he suggested, were the result of misunderstandings and miscommunication. However, as each side appealed to the other to see the error of its ways in the name of "peace," little was accomplished beyond further convincing both parties of the unreasonableness of the other. Neither Nixon nor the demonstrators seemed to recognize that in speaking of "peace," they were talking about different things.

Another example of such pseudocommunication is found in the recent controversy over the content of science education in public schools. Some Christian conservatives have demanded that "creation science" be taught along with "evolution." Most of the scientific community, as well as groups committed to the "separation of church and state," has strongly opposed this idea. Both sides of the controversy have argued that the issue is one of "academic freedom" and "freedom of inquiry." However, despite repeated appeals to these symbols, it seems clear that little communication has occurred. The basic terms of debate simply do not have the same meanings to the parties involved.

The problem, then, is often neither a breakdown in communication nor a breakdown in value consensus (a consensus we suspect is always more imagined than real). Rather, the problem is a shallowness of agreement on what the shared symbols imply. A symbolic consensus is viable and can sustain the political community only as long as the content attributed to politically significant symbols is not brought into question. People may be talking past one another when these symbols are used, but this is of little consequence as long as their referent is, for most, remote, abstract, ambiguously defined, or poorly understood. As actions initiated in the name of a symbol become more proximate, immediate, and clearly understood by more people, the shallowness of the consensus is revealed and the unifying power of the symbol is destroyed. In such cases, political conflicts are likely to degenerate from the lofty plain of platitude and principle to the stark reality of differential power and influence.

SYMBOLS AND SOCIAL DIFFERENTIATION

Just as symbols can serve as a basis for social solidarity, they also can provide a basis for social differentiation. As Warner writes:

> Two types of symbol system[s] are present and necessary wherever societies are differentiated. Segmentary systems provide the symbolic means to express the sentiments of members within the limited solidarity of autonomous structures; the integrative systems allow common sentiments present in everyone to be expressed, giving participants the necessary symbols to express the unity felt by all members of the community. At different times certain symbol systems can be used for either purpose. (1959, p. 231)

Gusfield similarly recognizes this dual function of symbolism and emphasizes its importance to the political process. He distinguishes between gestures (symbols) of cohesion and gestures (symbols) of differentiation. Symbols of the first type

> serve to fix the common and consensual aspects of the society as sources of governmental support. They appeal to the unifying elements in the society and the grounds for the legitimacy of the political institutions irrespective of its specific officeholders and particular laws. They seek to mobilize the loyalties to government which may exist above and across the political conflict of parties, interest groups, and factions. (1963, p. 171)

Symbols of differentiation, on the other hand, serve as the basis for social discrimination. They index different social identifications and summarize different patterns of tastes, moralities, and general life-styles (Gusfield, 1963, p. 172).

Party labels provide a good example of political symbols of differentiation. They provide a basis for distinguishing among groups and individuals and mark important political distinctions. Within the shared-identification groups they define, these symbols serve to synchronize diversity. At least in the United States, there tends to be nearly as much heterogeneity in political orientations within the parties as there is across them. Nonetheless, the symbols of party identification remain an important basis for discriminating among political actors and for making political judgments. They are the objects of relatively enduring loyalties and serve as guides to political action for their adherents. They allow for coordinated action on the part of persons who may differ quite considerably in their interpretations of what the symbols mean.

As with other groupings defined by shared symbolic identifications, parties themselves can be decomposed into more limited and more exclusive subgroupings. Each subgroup distinction typically indexes greater homogeneity in political orientation than the party labels themselves do. The symbolic objects used to reference these subgroupings are typically a candidate (not necessarily a current one), an issue, or a general policy stance. Thus, distinctions such as "New Deal Democrats," "McGovernites," and "Moderate Republicans" act as important foci of identification and discrimination.

Parties are only one of many ways of drawing distinctions relevant to the operation of a political system. Others will be considered momentarily. For the moment, the important thing to note is that just as similarities in sentiments toward prominent symbols are critical to social integration, variations in these sentiments serve as important bases for social differentiation. Not only will symbols be objects of shared identification and serve to promote social solidarity, they will also be used for discriminating among and classifying other people. As Litt observed, "The shared symbols, interest, affection, and real or imagined traits which draw some men together into the group or community are the walls that separate those men from others" (1970, p. 4).

Symbols not only distinguish groups, they make the creation of groups possible. In their study of the public response to issues surrounding the Vietnam War, Rosenberg and his associates write:

> As a symbol, the "silent majority" is more important for the reality it creates than the reality it describes. Whether or not there was a silent majority before . . . [President Nixon's] speech, his use of the term goes a long way to making the silent majority real. It is a symbol that pits the opponents of the war against the bulk of the American population. As such, it may be self-confirming; for many Americans unhappy about the course of events in this country may find the silent majority a most congenial group of which to be a member. They may indeed begin to behave as the President expects the silent majority to behave. . . . Thus, a group is born. (1970, p. 19)

The group-defining functions of symbols arise from the same properties of symbols that we have previously discussed, namely, their ability to engage the selective support of persons of different dispositional persuasions.

The Demography of Symbolic Orientations

Insofar as the social attributes people share reflect similar patterns of socialization, common life experiences, or shared reference-group identifications, differences in these attributes are likely to be associated with differences in symbolic orientations. However, the ability of demographic attributes to summarize differences in symbolic orientations is limited by two factors. First, at all stages of socialization, the symbolic orientations that a person acquires are colored by his or her own peculiar social, environmental, and cultural experiences. As a consequence, the person's symbolic orientations are unique in at least some respects. Second, those symbolic orientations that are not idiosyncratic often reflect cultural conceptions of reality that are widely, if not universally, shared. Thus, the possibilities for sociodemographic properties to be associated with distinctive patterns of symbolic orientations are constrained by the political relevance that historically has been assigned to those properties and by the role they have played in structuring distinctive subcultural traditions. In other words, a polity lacking in a history of sharp social divisions is not likely to be characterized by sharply differentiated social patterns of symbolic orientation (Lipset, 1981, pp. 64–79).

Mitchell is probably correct when he asserts that "there are few sharply delineated symbol systems in American politics" (1962, p. 127). While one would err in assuming that this implies that there are no patterned differences in symbolic orientations with respect to sociodemographic attributes in the United States, it does suggest that caution should be exercised in attributing specific differences to these sources.

Social Class. A notable example of the lack of a socially distinct symbol system is found in the American class system. As Mills notes:

> No common symbols of loyalty, demand, or hope are available to the middle class as a whole. . . . The major instruments are not differentiated in such a way as to allow, much less to encourage them, to take upon themselves any specific political struggle. (Mills, 1956, pp. 351–352)

Shostak similarly notes that manual workers are discouraged from "class-conscious" politics and that "class" is not a symbol of any great significance to blue-collar workers (1969, pp. 225–227).

Owing to the absence of sharply differentiated, class-based symbols, all socioeconomic strata of American society tend to identify with the same basic symbols. This does not mean, however, that the mode of identification is necessarily the same or that there are not important class differences in terms of the cognitive content and the intensity of affect typically attributed to these symbols. For example, Handel and Rainwater find that there are many surface similarities between the working and middle classes in terms of the "values" they espouse. Yet as one penetrates beneath statements of positive sentiment, it becomes clear that symbols such as "a college education" or "owning a home" have quite different meanings for working-class and middle-class persons. Among the working class, "education" tends to be conceived largely as vocational training or job preparation, while "owning a home" means escape from subordination. The middle class tends to place a greater premium on the intrinsic value of education as means of self-development and to perceive home ownership more as a validation of status (Handel and Rainwater, 1964, pp. 38–39).

Similar differences are undoubtedly present with respect to other significant symbols. We are told, for example, that the stable American worker is

> traditional, "old-fashioned," somewhat religious, and patriarchical. The worker likes discipline, structure, order, organization, and directive, definite (strong) leadership, although he does not see such leadership in opposition to human, warm, informal, personal qualities. . . . He reads ineffectively, is poorly informed in many areas, and is often quite suggestive, although interestingly enough he is frequently suspicious of "talk" and "new fangled ideas." . . . (Miller and Riessman, 1964, pp. 28–29)

This suggests that stability tends to be of paramount importance to many members of the working class. Appeals to symbols such as "law and order" are, as a consequence, particularly likely to strike a responsive chord (Scammon and Wattenberg, 1970, pp. 37–43). Similarly, "protests and demonstrations" are likely to be diffusely defined objects of impatience and limited tolerance (e.g., see Dawson, 1973, pp. 44–46). The sanctity of community symbols may be defended as much for the stability and order they represent as for any substantive values they imply. It is not surprising, then, to find workers extraordinarily moved by the desecration of the flag. As Lane observes, "The working (and lower-middle) class defenses of the present order . . . are well-organized and solidly built" (1962, p. 72). Dawson offers evidence to suggest that these tendencies are most pronounced among skilled workers, who seem "to be the most reluctant to support and accept social and economic change" (1973, p. 120).

Working-class defenses of the existing order are revealed not only in a concern with stability but also in a commitment to traditional standards of morality. This is reflected in a pronounced tendency for persons of lower socioeconomic status to react in a hostile way to such symbols as "marijuana," "homosexuality," and "pornography." However, while they tend to be more conservative in terms of personal values and more intolerant of deviance and dissent than persons of higher social status, working-class people are typically more liberal in their conception of the role government in managing the economy and in promoting social welfare. They are inclined to respond positively to symbols such as "national health insurance," "help for the poor," and "guaranteed jobs." They also disproportionately tend to support the Democratic Party (see Erikson et al., 1980, pp. 153–168).

The social attributes typically used to distinguish the working class or persons of lower socioeconomic status are education, occupation, and income. The predilections we have identified are associated with variation on each of these attributes. Of the three, education (or the lack thereof) seems to be the most important in accounting for the relative intolerance exhibited by members of the working class. Their commitment to the use of government to help the less advantaged seems to be rooted more in their life experiences as reflected by their jobs and income. Of course, with respect to all the attributes used to define social class, one finds considerable heterogeneity. Moreover, over time, this heterogeneity has been increasing (see, e.g., Dawson, 1973, pp. 78–106). Thus, the power of these attributes to explain differences in people's political and social orientations appears to be declining.

This "destructuring" of class-based cleavages is undoubtedly attributable in part to the general growth in affluence in the United States since World War II and to increasing levels of educational attainment. Bogart is also probably right when he notes that the mass media have militated against class-based differences by providing "a common source of widely shared information, values, symbols, heroes, and fantasy figures for workers as for other elements in American life" (1965, p. 928). In effect, the media help to sweep workers and everyone else into "the mainstream of conformity to middle class values and aspirations" (Bogart, 1965, p. 417). Nonetheless, as we have seen, discernible class-based differences do exist. While many of these differences may be muted or remain submerged, they are likely to come to the fore and affect the direction of the polity during periods of social turmoil or severe economic dislocation.

Ethnicity.   Greeley argues that the resistance of members of the working class to social change and their defenses of the traditional sociopolitical order tend to be anchored in ethnic and religious ties. He suggests that these ties are central to understanding the recent patterns of political disaffection and mistrust:

> American ethnics are deeply troubled at what they consider the "changing of the rules" . . . the white ethnic feels that he is being told that the rules no longer apply, that others are to achieve what he has achieved (frequently, it seems to him, with his picking up the tab) by doing exactly the opposite of what the rules prescribed. (1970, p. 15)

Elazar similarly attributes great importance to ethnicity in structuring political orientations. As we saw in Chapter 4, he suggests that it accounts for many of the regional or sectional differences found in the American political culture.

> Because the various ethnic and religious groups that came to these shores tended to congregate in their own settlements and because, as they or their descendents moved westward, they continued to settle together, the political patterns they bore with them are today distributed geographically. (1972, p. 103)

As compelling as these arguments may be, a note of caution is in order. Historically, the political relevance of ethnicity has been broadly recognized albeit at times somewhat reluctantly. The persisting effects of ethnicity have been, however, a matter of some controversy (for a discussion of the main issues, see Knoke and Felson, 1974). Some would argue that ethnic identifications continue to structure political perspectives and social outlooks in critical ways (e.g., see Greeley, 1970). Others question this. For example, while granting that religious-ethnic identities "have in the past tended to give structure and shape to our politics and to serve as important reference points for determining political preferences, values, and allegiances," Dawson suggests that they may be waning as relevant factors, at least in contemporary national political life (1973, p. 134).

Thus, while the persistence of ethnic identifications is not really questioned (the myth of the "melting pot" notwithstanding), their continued political relevance is uncertain. Insofar as different ethnic backgrounds continue to represent distinct cultural traditions and life experiences, we would expect considerable homogeneity in orientations toward political symbols within these groups. However, the persistence of ethnic identifications may be less a reflection of the absence of acculturation (i.e., the adoption of beliefs, values, and symbolic orientations of the dominant culture) than it is of the absence of social assimilation (on this point, see Parenti, 1967). That is to say, ethnic identifications may remain important in structuring patterns of social interaction long after they have ceased to represent distinctive sociopolitical traditions and, thus, distinctive sets of symbolic orientations.

None of this is to deny the continuing importance of ethnic symbols. The persistence of ethnic politics bears testimony to the vitality and importance of such symbols, even if they index only sentimental attachments and are largely peripheral to the organization of individuals' political world views. There is strong evidence that certain ethnic identities index much more than this, that they play an important role in structuring distinctive patterns of symbolic orientation, at least with regard to what we have called situational symbols. Perhaps the most notable of these is the distinctive pattern of political orientations found among black Americans. Black perceptions of the realities of contemporary American life are frequently at odds with those of whites. For example, more than half of the whites in a 1980 national poll thought that blacks in America were a lot better off than they were 10 years ago; only 18% of the blacks shared this view. In a 1981 survey, only about 20% of the whites felt that blacks were discriminated against in getting skilled jobs and in the wages they were paid; 60 percent of the blacks thought they were (*Public Opinion*, April/May, 1981, pp. 33–35).

Polls have consistently shown blacks to be more tolerant of "protests and demonstrations." These differences result in part from the fact that blacks and whites often hold very different conceptions of what is and is not "violent." In a study of attitudes toward violence, Blumenthal and her associates found that blacks "were most apt to call police acts 'violence' and . . . blacks rather than other groups were more apt to say protest activities were not violence" (1972, p. 82). As one might imagine, blacks and whites also tend to differ markedly in their orientations toward symbols such as "busing," "open housing," and "affirmative action"; but black-white differences are pronounced on more than just racial issues. Unlike whites, blacks have been remarkably consistent in their support for federal social programs. They are also much more likely to identify themselves as "liberals" and to support the Democratic Party (see Adam Clymer, "Polls Find Black-White Gaps on a Variety of Issues," *New York Times*, August 28, 1981, p. 27). While blacks and whites share common commitments on many higher-order symbols, it is clear that they are polarized on many lower-order ones.

Although few ethnic groups are as consistently distinctive in their political orientations as are black Americans, there are other groups that also exhibit fairly distinctive patterns, at least with respect to specific symbols. Such patterns are indexed to some extent by the religious differences that are associated with, and help to define, different ethnic traditions. For example, people of the Jewish faith typically are much more sensitive than others to the symbols "anti-Semitism," "Israel," and "separation of church and state." They are also distinctive in their tendency to support social welfare programs and civil liberties. Perhaps as a consequence of their historical status as a minority, they tend to be more tolerant of both dissent and alternative life-styles than other predominantly white groups. Perhaps for much the same reason, Catholics also tend to be more liberal in their social and political orientations. Among the Protestant majority, which in general tends to be both less tolerant and less supportive of the use of government to promote social welfare, one find some variation in symbolic orientation corresponding to denomination. However, these denominational differences may be more the product of variation in social status than of distinct ethnic traditions. For example, members of Protestant fundamentalist sects tend to be intolerant of both dissent and deviations from traditional standards of morality, but in this regard, they differ little from others of comparably low socioeconomic status (see Erikson et al., 1980, pp. 176–179; *Public Opinion*, April/May, 1981, pp. 26–27).

Age or Generational Differences. Age-based differences in political orientations are commonly observed and have been the object of considerable attention (e.g., Blumenthal et al., 1972, pp. 42–43, 152–154). Whether these differences simply represent stages in the life cycle, are transitory period effects, or mark more basic cross-generational change is often difficult to determine. Certainly, compelling arguments have been made to suggest that age-based differences in many areas of contemporary social and political life reflect more than simple maturation or transient period effects. Rather, they would seem to be the result of fundamental differences in socialization experiences. As a consequence, these differences are likely to have enduring relevance (e.g., see Inglehart, 1977). Of course, maturational and generational effects undoubtedly tend to confound one another, and there is reason to believe that many age-based differences are the product of both life-cycle and generational forces (e.g., see Jennings and Niemi, 1975).

In any case, age does tend to discriminate the patterning of orientations toward political symbols, although not always in consistent ways across other demographic attributes. In general, members of the younger generation of contemporary Americans exhibit less affective attachment to symbols of both the political community and the regime than do their elders. They are less likely to identify with party labels and are more distrusting of government. With respect to situational symbols, sharp polarization along class lines within this generation is often in evidence. Thus, both the strongest support of and the strongest opposition to the Vietnam War was found in this generation. Similarly, this generation produced the most intense support and the most intense opposition to the presidential candidacy of George Wallace. They count among their numbers those most hostile to, and intolerant of, "protests and demonstrations" and those most open to, and supportive of, such activities (see Flanigan and Zingale, 1979, pp. 53, 114–116, 187–195). In general, however, they tend to be more liberal than their elders in their orientations toward symbols of social and cultural change and more sensitive to minority rights (see Erikson et al., 1980, pp. 170–175; *Public Opinion*, August/September, 1980, pp. 37–39).

SYMBOLS AND CONFLICT DEFINITION

Since symbols serve to distinguish groups as well as unify them, it is not surprising to find that political symbols typically play a major role in the dynamics of social conflict. The struggle over whose symbolic definition of a situation will prevail is often the central battle in a political conflict and a critical determinant of its outcome (see Cobb and Elder, 1972). What is at stake in any particular conflict is a matter not simply of the facts of the situation but of what facts are considered relevant and of the meanings people assign to them. Who has what at stake, then, is often itself an issue. Those whose definition attracts the greatest and most intense support are likely to prevail. Fainstein and Fainstein refer to this definitional process as "naming." It involves

> the application to a phenomenon of a symbolic term which evokes a response set from onlookers. Naming provides a definition of a situation; it informs the onlooker of what frame of reference to perceive and evaluate the "thing" in. . . . In many political disputes contending parties struggle over how an event should be named ("Our goals are educational, not political") or who has the right to appropriate complimentary names to their own action ("I am saying that the war is immoral because of my loyalty to the nation"). (1974, pp. 7–8)

The symbols used to define the stakes in a conflict define who has reason to be involved. Groups that find themselves disadvantaged by the existing mobilization of forces in a conflict will seek to expand the conflict or otherwise alter its biases by redefining what is at stake. They will attempt to do this by using symbols of importance to potential allies. These prospective allies may be specific groups or simply members of the general public. These dynamics are illustrated in the conflict over "women's rights" and help to explain

> the trend from initially rather easy acceptance of legal abortion and equal rights to the more recent hardening of opposition. At first these issues were defined in terms of the relatively narrow symbol of women's rights: the rights of a woman to control her own body and equality of rights under law. . . . Now these issues are increasingly symbolized in terms of the family—a broad concept of a high order—which attracts and holds increasing numbers of individuals. Note, for example, the symbols incorporated in the names of a number of groups (few of which existed before 1975) opposing E.R.A. and abortion: Pro-Family Coalition, . . . Citizens for Family Life, . . . Family America Inc., Women Concerned for America, and the group with the highest order

name of them all: FLAG (Family, Life, America, God). (Conover, Coombs, and Gray, 1980, p. 17)

While groups disadvantaged by a particular definition of a conflict will seek to redefine the issues involved by introducing new symbols so as to attract additional support, those advantaged in the conflict will try to prevent its redefinition. They will do this by exploiting their own symbolic resources to lend legitimacy to the existing definition and to undermine the credibility of those seeking redefinition. Professional groups, for example, may exploit their special status to maintain control over an issue by insisting it is a "technical" or a "professional" matter that should be left to the "experts." Alford (1975) suggests that this accounts in part for the tremendous control that the medical profession and the medical service delivery bureaucracy have exercised over health care policy in the United States. Edelman (1975) extends the argument, finding that much of the social policy in the United States is dominated, often in self-serving ways, by the "helping professions." By defining social issues in the often arcane language of their professions, they effectively limit the terms of debate and thereby the prospects of popular involvement.

Of course, the symbolic power of professional status varies with the nature of the profession and its social function. Because of their function, for example, the police tend to enjoy special status. The symbolic potency of that status was repeatedly seen in the controversies that raged in many American cities in the 1960s over the issue of civilian police review. More often than not, police organizations succeed in defining the issue as simply a question of "Do you support your police?" The professional status of educators has seemingly been a less potent but not insubstantial symbolic resource, as their mixed success in conflicts over "community control" of schools attests. The medical profession probably enjoys the most symbolically potent status. However, even it has not been above challenge. Consider the controversy in the late 1970s over the legalization of the drug Laetrile. Although promoted as a cure for cancer, the medical profession dismissed it as worthless in the treatment of cancer and potentially poisonous. Nonetheless, using a definitional strategy analogous to that used by opponents of the fluoridation of drinking water in the 1950s, proponents of Laetrile raised the specter of "big government" and were successful in at least some states in defining the issue as a matter of "individual rights" and "freedom of choice."

In addition to appealing to special authority symbols to gain and maintain control of the definition of a conflict, groups may attempt to secure control by discrediting their adversaries. For example, they may use terms such as "racist," "violent," or "un-American" to label their opponents. As Skolnick (1969, pp. 3–6) has observed, such terms are ambiguous symbols whose applicability to any given group or situation is less a matter of fact than of political definition. As a consequence, questionable applications of coercive force may be applauded in the name of "law and order," while unpopular but peaceful protests are defined as "violent."

Symbols play an important role not only in domestic conflict but in international conflict as well. Actions taken by governmental officials in the name of a nation-state are often based on symbolic images and idiosyncratic interpretations of the symbols involved. Symbols often support exaggerated self-images and superficial, inaccurate, and ill-conceived assumptions regarding other nations (e.g., see Janis, 1972). Holsti's (1967) classic study of former Secretary of State John Foster Dulles illustrates how profound the role symbols can play in foreign policy decision-making. He found that Dulles's deeply rooted aversion to "atheistic communism" so colored his world view that it precluded a rational assessment of Soviet behavior. In effect, he was a captive of his own symbolic images.

Because the objects of international conflict are typically remote from the experiences of most people, foreign policy decision makers have broad latitude in defining external situations and mobilizing popular support for their actions. They have at their disposal a virtual arsenal of ambiguous but widely recognized symbols over whose use they have fairly exclusive control. As a consequence, most Americans are likely to accept uncritically, if not actively support, interventions in the domestic affairs of a Latin American nation to "contain communist aggression," the giving of military aid to oppressive regimes to strengthen the "free world," the refusal to recognize a major actor in the Middle East conflict because of its "terrorist" activities, and massive expenditures on arms to restore a "balance of power."

Through the use of such symbols, governmental officials define international friends and enemies and redefine them almost at will. The rapid transformation of American-Chinese relations in 1971–72 by the Nixon Administration is surely a case in point. Dating from the Communist victory that established the People's Republic of China in 1949, "Communist China" had been regularly portrayed by American policymakers as an ominous enemy. In July 1971, President Nixon dramatically announced that he would soon be traveling to a nation whose government we had steadfastly refused to recognize. Almost overnight, China became respectable. Edelman (1971, pp. 46–47) notes that world history abounds with similar examples. He attributes such rapid changes in popular perceptions to the government's near monopoly of foreign policy cues. Comparably rapid and widespread shifts, he suggests, tend not to occur in domestic policy because on most issues there are multiple and conflicting sources of cues.

As in domestic politics, ambiguous symbols that invite the attribution of different meanings can be used to facilitate at least momentary accommodations among conflicting nations. For example, the rather fragile rapprochement forged between Egypt and Israel in 1979 through the good offices of President Carter has been sustained in part by the "spirit of

Camp David" and a commonly professed commitment to "the peace process." The problem, of course, is that such accommodations can easily break down, with the conflicting parties using the symbols that once united them as weapons to villify one another. Meg Greenfield notes that the symbol "human rights" has been used in this way. Through the United Nations, virtually all nations are committed to "human rights." However, when President Carter sought to establish it as a central theme of his foreign policy, it became the object of heated exchanges among a variety of nations, each claiming to be holier than the others. Greenfield reports that this politicizing of "human rights" prompted Thomas Hammarberg of Amnesty International to lament that is was being reduced to just another empty superpower slogan—"a concept without real content, roughly equivalent to the term 'peace' as lovingly embraced by the Soviet Union in the aftermath of World War II." Greenfield herself concludes, "Human rights as a rally cry is a little like 'environment'—a catchall so loose and ill defined that campaigns organized around it are peculiarly susceptible to posturing, pointlessness, and blather" ("The Risky Rhetoric of Human Rights," *Newsweek*, July 18, 1977, p. 96). Indeed, she is probably right; but such is the stuff people live and die by.

SYMBOLIC BASES OF SOCIAL AGGREGATION AND DIFFERENTIATION

We have identified and discussed several closely related and overlapping social functions that are served by symbols in the political process. All these functions are more or less predicated on the power of symbols are vehicles for social aggregation and differentiation. The key to this power lies in the nature of individual symbolic attachments. These attachments afford multiple points of possible correspondence or agreement in the orientations of different people. Any and all of these points of possible correspondence may serve as a basis for social aggregation or, in the case of disagreement, as a basis for differentiation. By exploring the various kinds of similarities and differences that may exist among people in their orientations toward a symbol or a set of symbols, it is possible to arrive at a set of principles or composition rules that describe symbolically based patterns of consensus and cleavage.

The most primitive and superficial of these principles arises from the mutual recognition and attribution of significance to a symbol. Here individuals are united in having some emotional or cognitive investment in the symbol and are distinguishable from those who have not. They may not share the same affective sentiments toward the symbol nor attribute similar cognitive meanings to it, but they are bound by the fact that the symbol is an object of some significance to each of them. Such mutual significance is a necessary condition for the symbol to serve any social function in the relationships among them. The presence of such symbols is necessary, although not sufficient, for the existence of a political culture. Since the significance attributed to a symbol derives from individuals' more basic affective and cognitive orientations toward it, the mutual significance of a symbol simply establishes a starting point for the operations of other principles of symbolic aggregation (or differentiation). It, in effect, identifies those who are likely to use or to be sensitive to the use of a particular symbol (or set of symbols).

Assuming that a symbol is of mutual significance, more specific principles of symbolically based social aggregation can be identified on the basis of similarities and differences in people's affective and cognitive orientations toward it. Juxtaposing the possibilities for general agreement or disagreement on each of these dimensions of symbolic orientation yields several possible patterns of social congruence and differentiation, as shown in Figure 5.1. Each of these patterns represents a potentially important composition rule for defining social aggregates.

The first pattern is based on shared affect and congruence in the cognitive meanings attributed to a symbol. It will be recalled that the cognitive meanings assigned to a symbol may be either substantive or associational in nature. If the shared cognitive orientations are primarily of a substantive variety, the people whose orientations conform to this pattern are united by what might be called a "substantive consensus." The strength of this consensus will vary depending upon the richness of

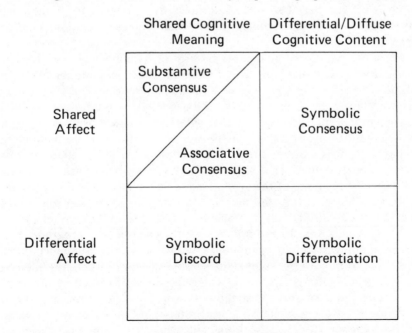

FIGURE 5.1   Patterns of Social Congruence in Symbolic Orientations.

the agreed-upon content. Because most people's orientations toward political symbols tend not to be substantively well developed, patterns of strong substantive consensus are not likely to be common and will generally be confined to relatively small groups. Members of the American Civil Liberties Union, for example, may be in substantive agreement on the meaning of "separation of church and state," but the meaning they assign to that symbol is likely to be quite different and generally much more specific than that attributed to it by others for whom it is also a significant symbol and commands comparable affect.

If the shared cognitive meanings assigned to a symbol are primarily associational in character, i.e., they rest more on common social identifications than on common substantive dispositions, the overall pattern is one of "associational consensus." Because this pattern is based on mutual identifications that often lead to reliance on the same sources of cues regarding the use of the symbol, it represents a potentially important political resource for those who provide the cues. The larger the solidarity grouping defined by these shared identifications and the fewer the sources of authoritative cues regarding how the symbol should be used, the more powerful the cue-givers will be. An example of this is seen in the extraordinary power exercised by the leadership of the Mormon church with respect to social issues in Utah and some of its neighboring states. As was evidenced in the response of the Salt Lake City woman to questions about the Equal Rights Amendment recounted in Chapter 2, the Mormon church is often a major source of authoritative guidance to its members on such issues as women's rights, family planning, race relations, and social welfare.

Perhaps the most important pattern of symbolically based social aggregation is that involving congruence in affective sentiment coupled with differences in the cognitive content attributed to a symbol. Included in this pattern are not only persons with manifestly different substantive or associational interpretations of the symbol but also those whose cognitive orientations are so diffuse or ill-specified as to preclude meaningful comparisons. This pattern is the product of what has been called selective convergence. It defines what we will call a "symbolic consensus." As long as the specific meaning of the symbol is not called into question, the common affect that provides the basis for this type of consensus will be sufficient to sustain a relatively homogeneous response to the symbol.

Many Americans, for example, dislike "social welfare" programs, considering them wasteful governmental giveaways. As a consequence, many were quick to rally to the support of President Reagan when he called for major cuts in "welfare" spending. This support was fortified by the President's repeated assurances that the cuts would not be at the expense of the "truly needy" and that the "social safety net" they depend on would not be affected (see, e.g., "President Reagan's Economic Proposals Text," *Congressional Quarterly Weekly Report*, February 21, 1981,

p. 361). Except for those people immediately affected by the cuts, the symbolic consensus surrounding these symbols has not been widely questioned as most have not had occasion to realize that they may sharply disagree with the President on what constitutes "social welfare," the "truly needy," and a "social safety net."

In situations wherein both the affect and the cognitive content associated with a symbol differ across individuals, the pattern is one of "symbolic differentiation." Symbols that are the objects of this pattern will typically distinguish major social cleavages and mark important group distinctions. What we have called situational symbols (encompassing current political authorities, prominent issues, and well-known persons and groups active in the political process) will typically be the objects of such symbolic differentiation. The prodevelopment statements and policies of Secretary of the Interior James Watt in the early days of the Reagan Administration, for example, quickly made him a symbolic object of such differentiation in the conflict between environmentalists and advocates of more aggressive resource utilization.

Figure 5.1 suggests the possibility of yet another pattern of social differentiation, one involving comparable cognitive orientations but different affective sentiments. We will refer to this as "symbolic discord." While it is difficult to imagine the same basic identifications or associational meanings supporting fundamentally different affective assessments of a symbol (except perhaps in cases of misperception or psychopathology), it is possible to imagine some circumstances wherein there may be considerable substantive agreement on what a symbol means but discordant affective feelings toward it. These circumstances will typically involve institutionalized or routinized forms of conflict among fairly specific interests whose differences are largely a matter of narrow self-interest. For example, many business and labor leaders probably share a fairly common understanding the symbols "collective bargaining" and "right to work" but feel quite differently toward them. Although such symbolic discord may be important in conflicts that remain confined to a limited and narrow range of participants, it is not likely to play a widespread or prominent role in defining major patterns of political consensus and cleavage.

Given symbols of at least minimal mutual significance, we have identified five symbolically mediated principles of social aggregation: (1) substantive consensus, (2) associative consensus, (3) symbolic consensus, (4) symbolic differentiation, and (5) symbolic discord. With respect to any given situation and any given set of symbols, any and all of these principles may be operative, although the first four are likely to play the most prominent roles in structuring the politics of a community. Some people may be linked to others on the basis of a substantive consensus and to yet others through an associative consensus. Both of these groups may be part of a larger amalgam sustained by a symbolic consensus. All these people in turn may be distinguished from others in a still larger population as a consequence of symbolic differentiation.

The co-occurrence of these patterns and their importance in explaining macropolitical phenomena are suggested in studies of both American and comparative politics. For example, Percheron (1973, pp. 217–228) has shown that similarities and differences in affective sentiments toward political symbols such as "de Gaulle," "communism," and "capitalism" serve as important bases of social aggregation and differentiation in French politics. The study found that these patterns are based on symbolic orientations acquired at an early age and that they tend to persist across generations. The political importance of these shared symbolic orientations is evidenced by the fact that they tend to play a more important role in structuring French political behavior than do specific party identifications.

Studies of political movements in the United States have revealed comparable patterns of symbolically based social aggregation. Evidence of each of the three forms of consensus we have identified, for example, can be found in studies of supporters of both Eugene McCarthy (e.g., see Brown and Ellithorp, 1970) and George Wallace (e.g., see Pettigrew, 1971) in the 1968 presidential campaign. Lipset and Raab's analysis of the Wallace movement is particularly revealing in this regard. They found that

> the more than one-fifth of American adults who indicated a preference for Wallace . . . included highly varied segments of the population, who supported him for apparently different reasons. The Wallace ideology . . . contained elements which could appeal to extreme racists, populists, antielitists, and rigid economic conservatives. The backing given to groups like the Birch Society seemingly went to Wallace. Hence, like the two major parties, Wallace had the support of many who believed in trade-unions and the welfare state and of others who thought the country was going down the road of socialism or Communism because of welfare legislation. (1979, p. 373)

Different symbols may evoke different patterns of social aggregation and differentiation. In particular, one would expect patterns to vary with respect to the major types of objects of political symbolism identified in Chapter 2. There we argued that individual symbolic orientations, most particularly affective ones, vary systematically in terms of a threefold hierarchy defined by community, regime, and situational symbols. This variation, of necessity, leads to different patterns of symbolic convergence. Lower-order symbols tend to be the objects of greater symbolic differentiation, whereas higher-order one typically serve as the foci of symbolic consensus. Substantive consensus is likely to be pronounced only among more highly differentiated groups; and there the degree of consensus is likely to be as great, if not greater, on lower-order symbols as it is on higher-order ones. Associative consensus is likely to be a common pattern with respect to many higher-order symbols, especially those relating to the political community. It is also likely to be prevalent with respect to specific situational symbols that are of special concern to the leaders of membership organizations or identification groups (e.g., "right to work" among labor leaders and "abortion" among leaders of the Catholic Church).

The different patterns of social aggregation found across symbols are strikingly illustrated in a number of studies comparing the political orientations of party elites (convention delegates and party activists) of the two major political parties in the United States with one another and with those of the rank-and-file party identifiers (see, e.g., McClosky, 1964; McClosky et al., 1960; Ladd, 1982; Verba and Nie, 1972, pp. 292–298; Nie et al., 1980, pp. 194–209; Martin Plissner and Warren Mitofsky, "Political Elites," *Public Opinion*, October/November, 1981, pp. 47–50). In general, the results of these studies suggest a pattern of considerable substantive consensus among the leaders *within* each party encompassing both higher- and lower-order political symbols. This substantive consensus holds up *across* party elites with respect to higher-order symbols, but pronounced symbolic differentiation occurs in terms of most situational symbols. Thus, while Republican and Democratic leaders are likely to be in agreement on symbols such as "due process" and "freedom of the press," they tend to be at odds with respect ot symbols such as "food stamps" and "ERA." Within the general public, a symbolic consensus, rather than a substantive one, tends to exist with respect to higher-order symbols; and there is a muted pattern of symbolic differentiation, rather than the sharp one found among the two sets of leaders, on most lower-order symbols.

Evidence of all these patterns can be seen in Table 5.1, which reports the orientations of party leaders and of rank-and-file identifiers with respect to selected contemporary issues. Each of these issues involves what we have called situational symbols, although the "prayer in public school" issue is commonly linked (at least in elite opinion) to regime norm symbols such as "the separation of church and state." This undoubtedly accounts for the fact that on this issue, unlike the others, the party elites are somewhat closer to one another than they are to their respective party identifiers. The distribution of positive and negative sentiments with respect to all the other issues conforms to the expected pattern of greater polarization between party elites than between rank-and-file identifiers. It is also noteworthy that in most cases, there tends to be greater agreement among the leaders within each party than is found among the party's rank-and-file.

Of the two dimensions of people's orientations toward political symbols that we have used in defining patterns of consensus and cleavage, the

TABLE 5.1   Issue Positions of Party Leaders and Identifiers.

	Republicans		Democrats	
	Leaders*	Rank and File	Leaders*	Rank and File
Orientations Toward:				
Constitutional Amendment Allowing "Prayer in Public Schools"				
Favor	46%	81%	19%	79%
Oppose	41	15	65	16
"ERA"				
Favor	29	46	92	62
Oppose	58	44	4	29
Too Much "Government Regulation of Business"				
Agree	98	72	35	59
Disagree	1	22	49	30
"Food Stamps" Increase spending or keep the same	21	33	80	53
Decrease spending	71	63	14	40
"Job Programs/CETA" Increase spending or keep the same	25	58	83	77
Decrease spending	66	39	13	17
"Reagan's Tax Cut"				
Aprove	97	44	17	26
Disapprove	0	5	73	14
Not Sure	3	51	10	60

* Members of the Republican and Democratic National Committees.
SOURCE: Martin Plissner and Warren Mitofsky, "Political Elites," *Public Opinion*, October/ November, 1981, p. 49.

affective dimension tends to be the more critical and contributes more to the systemic functions that symbols serve. In a sense, it provides the glue that holds large-scale political coalitions and voluntaristic organizations together. Because affective orientations toward commonly recognized symbols tend to be more uniform and less idiosyncratic than cognitive orientations, they provide a basis around which to organize collective action that would be impossible were substantive agreement on the meanings of symbols required. The normal operations of any political system are likely to depend on the mobilization of support of persons of diverse motives, interests, and concerns. Through the use of symbols that serve to synchronize this diversity, to pool common affective sentiments occasioned by selective and even idiosyncratic reasons, the necessary support can be mobilized and coordinate actions undertaken. The symbolic consensus that makes this possible, of course, affords opportunities not only for creative leadership but also for cynical manipulation. Both the danger of one and the prospects of the other are limited, however, by the problems of credible symbol usage, the maintenance of appropriate feedback, and the very fragility that characterizes a symbolic consensus.

Symbolic Convergence as a Social Composition Rule

If, as we have argued, important patterns of social aggregation are defined by symbolically based composition rules, this has important implications for political analysis. Not only does it suggest how an individual becomes linked to the larger polity, but also it suggests how the major dimensions of cleavage are defined for a political system. From a symbolic perspective, patterns of convergence in symbolic orientations structure the politics of a community. This structure may vary depending on the situation and the symbols involved. In any case, it is identified by the clustering of individuals on the basis of similarities and differences in ways they relate to mutually significant symbols. Such groupings serve to summarize social diversity in a political way. Their demographic correlates and macropolitical effects are appropriately matters of empirical inquiry.

Although this approach has not been widely exploited in political inquiry, it is generally consistent with a number of recent efforts to identify politically important patterns of social aggregation on the basis of shared behavior, perceptions, or predispositions (e.g., see Rusk and Weissberg, 1972; Jackson and Marcus, 1975). These efforts have been greatly facilitated by the developments in multivariate cluster analytic techniques (see Friedman and Rubin, 1967). For example, Verba and Nie have explored the structure of popular political participation using multidimensional scaling to identify specific types of citizen participators. Using this technique, they find that a high proportion of the population "fall into a relatively small number of clusters or types of participators that are internally homogeneous and distinct from other clusters" in terms of political behavior (1972, p. 76). Kessel has used this same technique to analyze the internal structure of political parties. By focusing on the issue orientations of party activists, he identifies groups on the basis of shared attitudes on public policy. By examining the characteristics of these groups, he suggests, we can learn "what the party is agreed about, what questions divide it, and something of the dynamics by which the party determines its positions on issues that cause internal division" (1980, p. 66). While technically sophisticated, the significance of these efforts is more conceptual than technical in that they represent an attempt to shown how micro-level properties are translated into macro-level political patterns.

Miller and Levitin (1976, pp. 63–97) employ a similar but less technically rigorous analytic strategy in their study of cleavage patterns in contemporary American politics. Based on national samples and using individual orientations toward symbols of social control and symbols of the counterculture, they distinguish three major groupings to characterize the "New Politics" that emerged in the United States during the 1960s. They identify these groups as the "Silent Majority," the "New Liberals" and the "Center." They argue that these three groupings define major patterns of political cleavage that are likely to dominate American politics for some time to come.

The groupings identified by Miller and Levitin bear striking resemblance to symbolically based groupings emerging from a study of the political behavior of white, male, heads-of-household in Philadelphia (Cobb and Elder, 1976). In that study, three basic ideational groupings were identified on the basis of shared affective orientations toward representative symbols of contemporary American politics. The nature of the groupings is implied by the names they were assigned: the "Anomic Communitarian" (intolerant patriots), the "Dissident Liberals," and the "Moderates." The latter group was found to break into two subtypes, distinguishable only on the basis of differences in orientations toward current situational symbols.

Lipset and Raab (1979, pp. 407–482), in their study of the nature and sources of political extremism, develop a similar set of typologies on the basis of an analysis of two national surveys. Initially using orientations toward federal welfare programs and black progress, they define four types of publics (leaving a large residual category undefined): "Tolerant Liberals," "Intolerant Liberals," "Tolerant Conservatives," and "Intolerant Conservatives." This typology was subsequently refined using a variety of indicators of cultural intolerance and economic conservatism. The resulting scheme distinguishes what they call "Rednecks," "Radical Rightists," "Consistent Liberals," "Old Guard," and "Others."

The distinctive feature of all these studies lies in the fact that individuals are grouped analytically on the basis of multivariate similarities in the ways they actually relate to the world of politics. This may be contrasted with the use of demographic variables which may or may not index homogeneity in political perspectives. It also stands in juxtaposition to the insistence on some unidimensional criterion such as liberalism-conservatism to describe people's political world views, an approach which often leads to the mistaken conclusion that the political orientations of most people are so inchoate as to define no meaningful patterns of social consensus and cleavage.

CONCLUSIONS

In this chapter, we have considered several social functions that symbols serve in a political system. We have found that they define important stakes in the political process and provide important vehicles through which social prestige is allocated. They serve as focal points for political mobilization and provide objects of allegiance that help sustain a polity. They provide bases for both social solidarity and social differentiation. Through their manipulation, the operative patterns of conflict and consensus within a political community are activated and defined.

The ability of symbols to serve these functions arises from their power to unite and to divided people. The key to this power is found in the nature of individual symbolic attachments. These attachments afford multiple points of possible correspondence and divergence among people. Similarities and differences in these attachments thus serve to define several possible principles of social aggregation and differentiation. We have identified five such principles: substantive consensus, associative consensus, symbolic consensus, symbolic differentiation, and symbolic discord. These, we suggest, play a critical role in structuring the politics of a community. Accordingly, we have argued that to understand the structure and dynamics of politics, analysis might appropriately begin with the identification of patterns of shared symbolic identification.

6

Politics from a Symbolic Perspective

We have argued that symbols play a vital role in the political process. Perhaps more importantly, we have suggested that by focusing on the symbolic nature of politics, one is afforded a particularly useful vantage point from which to study politics. We have touched on a number of the potential implications that a symbolic perspective might have for political analysis. In this concluding chapter, we will briefly summarize our basic arguments and assess more fully some of their possible implications for political inquiry.

Many of the arguments that have been presented are not new. Rather, they are anchored in modern social science theory and research. We have attempted throughout to document the many sources of insight and information upon which we have drawn. In our interpretations, we have taken some liberties in an effort to synthesize diverse insights and observations and to couch them in a more general framework. We have sought to illustrate the potential utility of this framework, but its ultimate utility can be demonstrated only through much more extended and repeated inquiry into the processes we have described.

ELEMENTS OF A SYMBOLIC PERSPECTIVE

The symbolic perspective we have outlined has considerable generality, affords a relatively parsimonious description of complex processes, and speaks to a significant theoretical problem in social and political inquiry; namely, what binds and structures a political community and shapes the concerns that dominate its attention.

The critical defining elements of the perspective center on the notion of symbols and people's orientations toward them. A symbol is seen as any stimulus object, the meaning or significance of which is socially generated and cannot be inferred from its physical form. Of interest are sym-

142

bols that are widely perceived as significant within a population and that characterize the politics of that population. These symbols constitute characteristic elements of a political culture. The objects of significant political symbolization include the major structures and processes of a political system, as well as major historical events in the life of the polity.

By definition, significant political symbols serve as common focal points for people's orientations toward politics. Those orientations constitute an important link between the individual and the larger polity, binding him to some, while distinguishing him from others. Thus, shared symbols become the currency through which personal, or micro-level, motives are given social, or macro-level, meaning. By the same token, through the social conventions and myths associated with these symbols, macro-level constraints are visited upon individual behavior.

Individual symbolic orientations themselves vary along two important dimensions which correspond to the major orientational components identified in attitudinal research. The first of these is an evaluative component referred to as affect, or valence. It relates to the intensity and direction of emotive sentiments toward a symbol. The second, a cognitive dimension, refers to the dispositional and associational meanings engaged by the symbol. The dispositional meanings a person attributes to a symbol are informed by the political culture and colored by his own particular life experiences. They are the building blocks of his political world view and reflect his substantive understandings of past and present realities and of future possibilities. Associational meanings arise from a person's social identifications and reflect the guidance provided by persons and groups with whom he identifies and whose judgments he accepts as authoritative. The greater a person's affective and cognitive investments in a symbol, the greater its personal relevance to him.

From our symbolic perspective, we take as axiomatic that the reality to which individuals respond is socially constructed. In the process of this construction, symbols are generated that become part of the common currency people use in relating themselves to others and to the external world. These symbols may persist as part of the cultural configuration long after the circumstances that occasioned their creation cease to exist. Although the logic underlying the evaluative sentiments associated with such symbols may be lost, the symbols themselves may continue to command characteristic responses and to support behavior in accord with a cultural script that transcends the individual belief systems of the members of that culture. The overall cultural configuration of which symbols are a part constitutes something of a social paradigm characterizable in much the same terms that Kuhn (1970) has used to describe a scientific paradigm (e.g., see Wolin, 1968). Individual understanding of this social paradigm is largely "tacit knowledge" which is acquired simply through experience and which often cannot be articulated explicitly (see Polayni, 1958, chapters 5 and 6).

We also take as axiomatic that mass political behavior is neither random nor devoid of subjective significance. Rather, it is predicated upon, and is generally consistent with, a fairly stable set of motivations. Those motivations are manifested in the form of cognitive dispositions and reference identities. They find expression in orientations toward significant political symbols. While these orientations may be highly idiosyncratic, lack logical structure, and even lack coherent substantive meaning, they are nonetheless meaningful reflections of personal motivations (which themselves may be inconsistent and ill-understood in any conscious sense).

Of the two basic components of people's orientations toward symbols, the affective dimension tends to be the more critical both in establishing social identities and in the logic of collective behavior. Not only are affective orientations often acquired early in the socialization process, they also tend to be more clearly and explicitly prescribed by a political culture or subculture. It is through these orientations that the culture has its greatest impact. The cultural mandate regarding the cognitive meaning or substantive interpretation to be attributed to a symbol tends to be much more ambiguous; and the socialization processes involved, more haphazard. As a consequence, the meanings are likely to be heterogeneous, even among those for whom the symbol is the object of comparable affect. In fact, a symbol may be important to an individual and serve to guide his or her behavior, even though its cognitive meaning remains diffuse and ill-specified.

Similarity and differences in orientations toward political symbols provide an important basis for social discrimination and identification. Homogeneity in these orientations creates a bond of consensus. However, the diversity that tends to characterize cognitive orientations severely limits the possibilities of substantive consensus. Even without substantive consensus, symbolic orientations are still an important basis for distinguishing social groupings. The fact that different people respond affectively in the same way to the same symbols tends to be important to mutual identifications and collective behavior, regardless of any differences the people may have in their substantive interpretations of the symbols. Thus, commonality of affect becomes an important principle of social aggregation and, ultimately, the basis for political community. By the same token, differences in affective orientations become an important basis for the social discriminations that underlie political cleavages.

MICRO- AND MACRO-LEVEL POLITICS AND THE LINKAGES BETWEEN THEM

The symbolic perspective we have outlined speaks to some of the most basic and perennial questions in political analysis. It addresses and suggests answers to three general types of problems. The first type is micropolitical, relating to individuals and their motivations and behaviors as political actors. The second set of problems involves the linkages between micro- and macro-level political phenomena. Of particular interest are questions of how individual-level orientations are aggregated and given collective expression. The third general type of problem addressed by the perspective relates to macropolitical patterns and the problems of sustaining a viable political community.

Micropolitical Behavior

Of central concern in understanding individual behavior is the identification of the motivational bases of political actions—actions that are often more expressive than instrumental. It is assumed that such actions have a motivational basis that is more fundamental, enduring, and broadly relevant than the proximate decisional factors commonly identified in political behavior research. Party, candidate, and issue evaluations, for example, represent conclusions that are expressed in voter choice. These evaluations are themselves political decisions. These decisions and the relative priorities assigned to them may be understood in much the same terms as the behaviors they imply; namely, as specific manifestations of more basic motivations. These motivations are found in the political world views and identity structures of individual members of the polity. They are given expression through orientations toward political symbols. Insofar as individual political world views and even identity structures are the product of political forces, the motivations underlying political behavior need not be regarded as arising exclusively, or even primarily, from nonpolitical sources.

The problems of characterizing political world views and their structures are a part of this individual-level puzzle. These problems have been approached from a variety of perpectives. It is often assumed, for example, that a person's political orientations reflect a general political outlook or ideology that falls somewhere on a continuum ranging from "liberal" to "conservative." While the meanings of these terms have evolved historically and are subject to change, they are regularly used in the rhetoric of American politics to distinguish the poles of political debate. Thus, it would seem that if we knew whether a person considered himself or herself a "liberal" or a "conservative" or something in between (e.g., a "moderate" or a "middle-of-the-roader"), we would know a great deal about his or her political world view. However, this is not the case. While most Americans (70% or more) are willing to classify themselves in these terms, there is little agreement on the meaning of the terms. In fact, only about half the population can offer any definition of "liberal" and "conservative." Among those that can, the definitions offered frequently bear little resemblance to the way in which the terms are normally used in more informed political discourse (see RePass, 1976, p. 824).

Consider, for example, Ila Conner, an Indianapolis homemaker, interviewed in a 1978 national survey. Although she calls herself a "conservative," she favors government payments for abortion and thinks that government ought to see that everyone who wants a job gets one. She also thinks that government ought to help people get medical care at low costs and should ensure that safety standards are observed in the work place. Since these are hardly positions considered "conservative" in informed political discourse, her explanation of why she thinks of herself as a "conservative" is both interesting and instructive: "I don't butt into people's business. I don't go out and bar-hop. I dress conservatively" (*New York Times*, January 22, 1978, p. 1).

Even among those who define the terms in politically more sophisticated way, the ideological labels they give themselves tend to correlate poorly with the positions that they take on specific policy issues. As Ladd observes:

> Most people just are not conservatives or liberals in any wide-ranging ideological sense. . . . Within the general public, people who call themselves conservatives are consistently more likely to take conservative stands on various issues—but not that much more likely. . . . There are reasons why some people call themselves conservatives while others prefer the liberal label; the choice of one tag or the other is not random or meaningless. But the reasons are not ideological. . . . Instead they are generally narrow, specific, and individualistic. (Everett Ladd, "Conservatism: A National Review," *Public Opinion*, February/March, 1981, p. 19)

In other words, "liberal" and "conservative" are political symbols that are widely significant but ambiguous in meaning. Even though they may be objects of common affective sentiment, the meanings attributed to them are often idiosyncratic and ill-defined (see Conover and Feldman, 1981, pp. 636–640). As a consequence, self-identification in these terms alone tells us little about a person's political world view. In fact, if issue positions are taken as indicators, the American people are considerably more liberal on economic and social welfare issues and more conservative on morality and life-style issues than their ideological self-identifications would imply (see *Public Opinion*, February/March, 1981, pp. 20–31).

An alternative way in which to characterize political world views is found in Converse's well-known work on mass belief system (1964, 1970). Defining a belief system as a "configuration of ideas and attitudes in which the elements are bound together by some form of constraint or functional interdependence" (1964, p. 207), he found that very few people are politically sophisticated in the sense of possessing a stable and coherent belief system. He suggested that as one moves away from those who are highly knowledgeable and well informed about politics, people's political world views become more disjointed and fragmented, revolving increasingly around more concrete and proximate concerns.

Converse's conclusions regarding the rarity of coherent belief systems in the mass public have been criticized on the grounds that he explores only one possible frame of reference (namely, that of conservatism-liberalism as conventionally defined by political scientists). Implicitly, he seems to assume that the same general principles must govern the organizations of everyone's beliefs, if they are to form a coherent system (see Brown, 1970). Converse's findings have also been challenged on more purely methodological grounds. Achen (1975) suggests that because of the low reliability of some of his measures, Converse may have underestimated the degree of stability and coherence in mass belief systems. Smith (1980) questions the adequacy of the type of measures Converse uses to assess conceptual sophistication. He argues that what is being measured is familiarity with current campaign rhetoric rather than basic characteristics of people's belief systems.

Nonetheless, Converse's basic conception of belief systems and his suggestion of their possible molecular character have done much to clarify that issues involved in understanding differences in the ways people organize their world views. His arguments that the political orientations of most people are not structured by a common, overarching conceptual framework have been supported by a considerable amount of empirical research (see, e.g., RePass, 1976; Stimson, 1975). They help to explain observed inconsistencies and the seeming lack of logic often found in people's symbolic orientations.

People often acquire their political orientations in rather ad hoc ways, reflecting their own peculiar experiences. In the absence of a compelling reason to do so, they may feel little need to rationalize the various elements involved. As Lamb observes:

> Human beings are not so intent upon making their ideas consistent with each other as some social scientists presume them to be. Particularly when a directly felt personal interest is involved, political actions may not be constrained by an ideology which, if logically pursued, would limit such actions. That is, an engineer may continue to believe that welfare recipients are bums, while waiting in line for his welfare check, secure in his feeling that he deserves better from the government than others. (1974, p. 110)

How and to what extent a person's political dispositions are structured is reflected in his or her symbolic orientations and the way they cluster in comparison to those of others. Through such comparisons, it may be possible to discern not only how a person's dispositions are organized but also how they are constrained by reference-group identifications. In exploring the principles that govern people's political orientations, rationality should neither be presumed nor precluded. Rationality is but one of the many "logics" that conceivably can govern individuals' political evaluations and behaviors. To dismiss all others as simply irrational is to explain little. Nonrational or arational politics is probably the norm. While one may despair at the quality of popular political deliberations, it is important to recognize that political responses are neither random nor without a logic of their own. To understand this logic, however, requires an appreciation of how people relate to politics.

The myth of the "responsible citizen" who is directly and continually involved in the political process is perhaps ill-suited to the realities of a large-scale society. It may obscure the fact that for most, politics is necessarily a mediated affair often remote from their daily lives and touching them only indirectly. Symbols provide the vehicle through which people relate and respond to such a politics. They both serve the imperatives of psychic economy and make popular political involvement possible. The motivational bases of popular responses to politics, then, are to be found in the manner in which people relate to these symbols. This requires a perspective that subsumes rationality but does not require it. In drawing heavily upon the belief systems and attitudinal traditions of political and social psychology, the symbolic perspective seeks to identify the "metalogic" underlying political behavior that can give rise to rationality but need not.

Micro-Macro Linkages

The second general type of problem to which the symbolic perspective is applicable involves micro-macro linkages. It is these concerns that most serve to distinguish the symbolic perspective from the belief systems/attitudinal traditions upon which it draws. Part of the puzzle is how individual predispositions are translated into collective action, how diverse motivations are synchronized and aggregated. In other words, the perspective seeks to identify the principles that govern the social patterns of consensus and cleavage that structure the politics of a community. The principles, it suggests, rest on the different points of possible convergence in the symbolic orientations of different people.

As we have seen in previous chapters, these principles are vividly illustrated by patterns of popular convergence around party symbols. About two-thirds of the voting-age population in the United States today identify themselves with one or the other of the two major parties. Among these identifiers, there is great diversity in the meanings they attribute to the terms "Democrat" and "Republican." In fact, many have difficulty in articulating any meanings beyond vague associational ones. Still, through the processes of selective convergence, these party symbols serve to define the structure of American electoral politics. Interestingly, of the one-third or so of the population who profess to be "independents," about two-thirds might more appropriately be regarded as partisans. These are people who admit to leaning toward one party or the other. "Lean" seems an understatement, however, since they tend to be as loyal to the party to which they lean as most of those who openly identify with the party (see Asher, 1980, pp. 56–94). Clearly, these "closet" partisans are full participants in the symbolic consensus that surrounds party labels.

Despite the fact that a vast majority of the American people continue to identify with the major parties, there has been a notable decline in the relative number of party identifiers over the past two decades. This trend must be discounted to some extent because of the phenomenon of "closet" partisans, but the fact remains that there has been a significant increase in the proportion of self-identified "independents." Moreover, there has been a general decline in the relative number of people professing to be "strong," as opposed to "not very strong," partisans. All this suggests that the potency of party symbols is being attenuated. Indeed, the role of the party, while still critically important, has waned over this period as an explanation of political behavior; and short-term factors such as candidate images and issues have assumed new prominence. The systemic implications of this change are potentially profound. Increased reliance on less enduring situational symbols in the form of specific candidates and issues contributes to the fragmentation of politics and militates against overall accountability. It tends to accentuate the "knowledge gap" between activists and the mass public, dampening popular participation and skewing public policy away from the modal preferences of the population (see Verba and Nie, 1972, pp. 341–342).

Beck (1974) argues that the attenuation of the potency of party symbols is almost inevitable and that it helps to account for the major party realignments that have occurred periodically throughout American history. The circumstances surrounding the emergence of a new partisan alignment are likely to leave an indelible impression on the generation experiencing it. For them, party symbols are likely to be the objects of poignant substantive or associational meanings and of strong and enduring affective sentiments. As the meanings and feelings the party symbols index for one generation become blurred in the course of intergeneration transfer and as they acquire new and more diffuse connotations, the salience and potency of these symbols are likely to diminish. By the third generation following a major party realignment, Beck suggests, the electorate is likely to be "ripe for realignment" (1974, p. 212). However, dealignment is likely to continue until the right circumstances and leadership come along to give definition to a new alignment. If and when this occurs, the cycle begins anew.

The demise of party symbols and the attendant rise of situational symbols as vehicles for social aggregation in American electoral politics would seem to support Beck's scenario. The last major party realignment occurred during the 1930s in the wake of the "Great Depression." It was marked by the emergence of the "New Deal" coalition forged by Franklin

Roosevelt. It established the Democrats as the dominant party in American politics and relegated the previously dominant Republicans to minority-party status. Since that time, the Democrats have been the majority party; but for better than a decade, there has been widespread speculation regarding the possibilities of a realignment that might alter this status. This speculation has been fueled by the fact that the potency of party symbols has predictably diminished as each cohort of newly eligible voters has entered the electorate. Party symbols today simply tend not to be as salient to younger people as they are to older members of the electorate or were to them when they were young.

As our party example makes clear, symbols play a vital role in translating individual motives into collective action and in aggregating social diversity. It is also clear that differences or changes in the distribution and character of individual symbolic orientations can have profound effects on macro-level politics, influencing its basic character by redefining the operative patterns of political cleavage.

There is, of course, a reciprocal relationship between micro- and macro-level politics. The motives and behavior of individuals both influence and are influenced by properties of the political system and the processes that characterize it. The second aspect of the problem of micro-macro linkages, then, relates to how macro-level forces shape and constrain individual behavior. The range of symbols available for giving social definition to reality is constrained by the culture and the macropolitical process through which new symbols are generated and old ones redefined. These macro-level influences operate in part through the social identifications that give associational meanings to symbols and define the authorities upon which people rely for informational guidance. Earlier we saw how people can shift their orientations toward symbols in the face of new guidance from accepted authority figures, the shift in popular images of "China" orchestrated by Richard Nixon being but one case in point. We also saw how association with even such broad reference groups as political parties can prompt people to alter their issue orientations.

Macro-level forces also impinge upon the individual through the cultural premises and prescriptions that guide his affective orientations and inform the substantive meanings that he attributes to political symbols. Such cultural lessons are conveyed through the socialization process and tend to be reinforced by both the weight of public opinion and the rituals observed in the political system. Even in those circumstances where the culture offers little guidance and the person is not content to rely on the judgments of others, his orientations and reactions are still likely to be colored by those forces that structure the flow of information available to him. In other words, both an individual's vision and behavior are almost inescapably bound to some extent by the political system of which he is a part. These constraints are realized largely through the symbols he has available for interpreting reality and through the guidance of others upon whom he must rely regarding the circumstances of their usage. The fewer and more remote the sources of guidance he receives, the more vulnerable he is likely to be to manipulation. This is but one way the structure of communication in a society can influence individual behavior. Sorting out such influences and assessing their consequences is another part of the micro-macro linkage problem.

Macropolitical Patterns and Processes

The third major set of problems of interest from a symbolic perspective are macropolitical in nature. They revolve around the problems of system stability, leadership, and change. It is assumed that the stability of any political system is heavily dependent upon its legitimacy in the eyes of its members. The sources of this legitimacy are at least twofold, and symbols play an important role in both. The first arises from the allegiances that derive from identification with the basic symbols of the system. Such allegiances are largely a product of socialization and tend not to be contingent in any immediate sense on system performance. The second source is performance-dependent. Although the criteria used in assessing performance are often not very exacting, manifest and repeated system failures can create a crisis of legitimacy and give rise to instability.

Most people are not very vigilant in monitoring the political process, but they nonetheless look for cues that their expectations of the political system are being vindicated. These expectations are largely a product of the political culture and find expression in popular orientations toward culturally salient symbols. The way these symbols are managed plays an important role in popular assessments of system performance. Ineptness in this regard can lead to both a repudiation of leadership and a loss of confidence in the system. Effective symbol management, on the other hand, while vital to the operation of the polity, raises the possibility of manipulation. Indeed, people's reliance on symbolic cues does make them potentially vulnerable. However, this vulnerability is far from total. It is limited by the presense of multiple sources of information and cues regarding symbol usage and by the experiences that afford people opportunities for independent assessments.

Popular expectations regarding the use of culturally salient symbols afford political leaders broad latitude in defining events and circumstances and in activating those cleavage patterns that dominate the political process at any time. However, they also serve as real constraints on the possibilites for political action. While these cultural constraints can be stretched and modified to some extent through effective leadership, in the absence of compelling circumstances they cannot be ignored. As Deutsch and Merritt observe:

> Even very powerful governments by themselves cannot manufacture major cultural changes. Indeed, insofar as strong governments derive their power

from the habits of conformity and obedience among their subjects, their very strength would make basic culture change more difficult. (1965, p. 170)

While inhibiting the latitude and thus the potential abuses of political leadership, the cultural constraints represented by symbols and realized through popular expectations regarding their usage can also inhibit the polity's ability to cope effectively with its problems and to accommodate changes in its social and environmental circumstances. The burden of leadership is in part to find ways of coping with these challenges that both facilitate cultural adaptation and are sensitive to popular values and beliefs. Lamb speaks to this problem when he suggests:

> An appeal for meaningful political change which involves . . . . voters must be couched in terms of the national values and traditions they accept. Political leaders must be dedicated to the restoration of presumed past grandeurs. These voters will not follow those who tell them they have accepted a misinterpretation of history or claim that the promises of America were always fraudulent. (1974, p. 302)

The symbolic perspective thus alerts us to the multiple dimensions of the problems of leadership and of system maintenance and change. It also helps us to appreciate more fully the multiple and diverse stakes of politics—stakes that are ideational as well as material. How these stakes are and can be promoted and preserved are among the macro-level puzzles it invites us to address.

METHODS OF INQUIRY

In principle, all the theoretical arguments we have posited are amenable to empirical scrutiny. Except for some of those contentions we have identified as axiomatic, all are readily subject to fuller exploration using the more or less standard methodological tools and analytic techniques of modern social science. The distinctive features of a symbolic perspective on politics are to be found not so much in its methodology as in the questions it asks and the framework it offers for interpreting research findings. This is not to say, however, that the perspective is without methodological implications. It tends to require a measurement approach that is distinctly more phenomenological in nature than those commonly used in survey research. At least at the current state of our knowledge, minimal a priori assumptions are warranted regarding the meanings of any particular symbols, the ways people structure their orientations toward them, and the political world views these orientations represent. Many of these questions are likely to yield only to more intensive techniques of observation.

Certainly, responses to the closed-ended, structured questions typically found in survey instruments should be cautiously interpreted and not relied on exclusively. Research has repeatedly shown that the responses elicited by such questions are likely to be contextually dependent and to vary substantially depending on how the question is framed and the symbols used (see, e.g., Sullivan et al., 1978, 1979). From a symbolic perspective, this kind of variability is not surprising, and it need not be a source of consternation. It can readily be turned into a research advantage. As Sullivan and his associates (1978) have shown, through the imaginative use of split samples, it is possible to discern the effects of framing questions in different ways. By consciously manipulating the symbols in which survey questions are couched and the context in which they are presented, both the potency of those symbols and the perceptions of their situational relevance may be assessed. This would also provide us with a better basis for understanding popular reactions to the alternative forms that political appeals are actually likely to take. Professional campaign specialists have already made use of such "loaded"-question techniques for purposes of campaign planning (see Harrison, 1980), and these techniques might well be exploited for purposes of more basic research.

In addition to the novel use of structured questions, there are a variety of other techniques available that are likely to yield useful data regarding how people relate and respond to political symbols. In-depth interviews have obvious advantages but generally cannot be conducted on a sufficient scale to allow confident generalization. Short of this, Q-sort, semantic differentials, feeling thermometers, various sorting procedures, and open-ended questions may be used. All these have the advantage of affording individuals a greater latitude to reveal how they relate to and structure political stimuli than that provided by the presumptive measures more commonly used in survey research.

Minimal assumptions are also warranted regarding the social distribution of symbolic orientations. Categoric groups of a conventional demographic nature may or may not index common patterns of political persuasion. As vividly demonstrated by the party reform efforts of the 1970s, one simply cannot presume a correlation between demographic attributes and people's political orientations. In striving to make their conventions more open and representatives demographically, the Democrats made them less representative ideationally (see Ladd, 1982). How and to what extent political orientations cluster demographically is an empirical question and is appropriately left as such. Meaningful political groupings are defined by political homogeneity and should be identified on that basis. A variety of modern cluster analytic techniques now provide the tools needed to approach the problem in this way.

With respect to observational strategy, the simple random or probability sampling commonly prescribed in survey research is appropriate for descriptive purposes and simple mapping tasks. However, to explore questions of more theoretical interest, some form of quota sampling, disproportionate stratified sampling, or what Willer (1967) calls "scope sampling" is often in order. Such sampling should be aimed at ensuring variance on variables of theoretical interest. In other words, observations should be dictated by the theoretical purposes of the inquiry, even at the expense of the tenets of statistical inference.

SCOPE OF RELEVANCE

The symbolic perspective we have outlined offers a vehicle through which a variety of disparate and disjointed research findings on individual behavior can be integrated and placed in a larger, more systemic context. Moreover, it seems to promise an important theoretical module that meshes well with other theoretical concerns and analytic foci. It speaks to a number of general problems relating to popular involvement in the political process. It is thus of potential relevance to students of public policy, social conflict, and political integration. In fact, the processes that the perspective identifies and seeks to explain seem a critical part of the general dynamics of social continuity and change.

References

Aberbach, Joel, and Walker, Jack.
    1970   "The Meaning of Black Power: A Comparison of White and Black Interpretations of a Symbol," *American Political Science Review*, June, 64: 367–388.

Achen, Christopher.
    1975   "Mass Political Attitudes and the Survey Response," *American Political Science Review*, December, 64: 1199–1219.

Alford, Robert.
    1975   *Health Care Politics*. Chicago: University of Chicago Press.

Almond, Gabriel.
    1956   "Comparative Political Systems," *Journal of Politics*, August, 18: 391–409.
    1960   *The American People and Foreign Policy*. New York: Praeger.

Almond, Gabriel, and Verba, Sidney.
    1963   *The Civic Culture*. Princeton, N.J.: Princeton University Press.

Anton, Thomas.
    1967   "Roles and Symbols in the Determination of State Expenditures," *Midwest Journal of Political Science*, February, 11: 27–43.

Arnold, Thurman.
    1962   *The Symbols of Government*. New York: Harcourt, Brace & Jovanovich.

Asher, Herbert.
    1980   *Presidential Elections and American Politics*. Homewood, Ill.: Dorsey.

Banfield, Edward.
    1968   *The Moral Basis of a Backward Society*. New York: Free Press.
    1974   *The Unheavenly City Revisited*. Boston: Little, Brown.

Beck, Paul Allen.
    1974   "A Socialization Theory of Partisan Realignment," in Richard Niemi (ed.), *The Politics of Future Citizens*. San Francisco: Jossey Bass.

Bell, David.
    1975   *Power, Influence and Authority*. New York: Oxford University Press.

Bem, Daryl.
    1970   *Beliefs, Attitudes and Human Affairs*. Belmont, Cal.: Brooks/Cole.

Bennett, W. Lance.
    1980   *Public Opinion in American Politics*. New York: Harcourt, Brace & Jovanovich.

Berelson, Bernard.
    1952   "Democratic Theory and Public Opinion," *Public Opinion Quarterly*, Fall, 16: 313–330.

Blumenthal, Monica, Kahn, Robert, Andrews, Frank, and Head, Kendra.
　1972　*Justifying Violence: Attitudes of American Men*. Ann Arbor: Institute for
　　　　Social Research.
Blumer, Herbert.
　1954　"The Crowd, the Public and the Mass," in W. Schramm (ed.), *The Pro-
　　　　cess and Effects of Mass Communication*. Urbana: University of Illinois
　　　　Press.
Bogart, Leo.
　1965　"The Mass Media and the Blue-Collar Worker," in Arthur Shostak and
　　　　William Gomberg (eds.), *Blue-Collar World*. Englewood Cliffs, N.J.:
　　　　Prentice-Hall.
Boles, Janet.
　1979　*The Politics of the Equal Rights Amendment*. New York: Longmans.
Boulding, Kenneth.
　1961　*The Image*. Ann Arbor: University of Michigan Press.
Brigham, John (ed.).
　1977　*Studies in American Politics*. Lexington, Mass.: D. C. Heath.
Brown, Steven.
　1970　"Consistency and the Persistence of Ideology: More Experimental Re-
　　　　sults," *Public Opinion Quarterly*, Spring, 34: 60–68.
Brown, Steven, and Ellithorp, John.
　1970　"Emotional Experiences in Political Groups: The Case of the McCarthy
　　　　Phenomenon," *American Political Science Review*, June, 64: 349–366.
Campbell, Bruce.
　1979　*The American Electorate*. New York: Holt.
Caplan, Nathan.
　1970　"The New Ghetto Man," *Journal of Social Issues*, Spring, 26: 59–73.
Citrin, Jack.
　1974　"Comment: The Political Relevance of Trust in Government," *American
　　　　Political Science Review*, September, 68: 973–988.
Cobb, Roger, and Elder, Charles.
　1972　*Participation in American Politics: The Dynamics of Agenda-Building*.
　　　　Baltimore: Johns Hopkins University Press.
　1976　"Symbolic Identification and Political Behavior," *American Politics
　　　　Quarterly*, July, 4: 305–332.
Conover, Pamela Johnston, Coombs, Steve, and Gray, Virginia.
　1980　"The Attitudinal Roots of Single-Issue Politics: The Case of 'Women's
　　　　Issues,'" paper presented at the annual meeting of the American Politi-
　　　　cal Science Association, Washington, D.C., August 28–31, 1980.
Conover, Pamela, Gray, Virginia, and Coombs, Steven.
　1981　"'Pro-Family' vs. 'Pro-Woman': Elite-Mass Linkages on Family Issues,"
　　　　paper presented at the annual meeting of the American Political Science
　　　　Association, New York City, September 3–6, 1981.
Conover, Pamela Johnston, and Feldman, Stanley.
　1981　"The Origins and Meaning of Liberal/Conservative Self-Identifications,"
　　　　American Journal of Political Science, November, 25: 617–645.
Converse, Philip.
　1964　"The Nature of Belief Systems in Mass Publics," in David Apter (ed.),
　　　　Ideology and Discontent. New York: Free Press.

1970 "Attitudes and Non-Attitudes.: A Continuation of a Dialogue," in Edward Tuffe (ed.), *The Quantitative Analysis of Social Problems.* Reading, Mass.: Addison-Wesley.

Converse, Philip, Dotson, Jean, Hoag, Wendy, and McGee III, William.
1980 *American Social Attitudes Data Source, 1947–1978.* Cambridge: Harvard University Press.

Converse, Philip, Miller, Warren, Rusk, Jerrold, and Wolfe, Arthur.
1969 "Continuity and Change in American Politics: Parties and Issues in the 1968 Election," *American Political Science Review*, December, 63: 1083 –1105.

Cronin, Thomas.
1980 *The State of the Presidency.* Boston: Little, Brown.

Dalton, Russell.
1980 "Reassessing Political Socialization: Indicator Unreliability versus Generational Transfer," *American Political Science Review*, June, 74: 421–431.

Dawson, Richard.
1973 *Public Opinion and Contemporary Disarray.* New York: Harper & Row.

Derthick, Martha.
1979 *Policymaking for Social Security.* Washington, D.C.: Brookings.

Deutsch, Karl, and Merritt, Richard.
1965 "Effects of Events on National and International Images," in Herbert Kelman (ed.), *International Behavior.* New York: Holt.

Devine, Donald.
1972 *The Political Culture of the United States.* Boston: Little, Brown.

Easton, David.
1965 *A Systems Analysis of Political Life.* New York: Wiley.
1975 "A Re-Assessment of the Concept of Political Support," *British Journal of Political Science*, October, 5: 435–458.

Easton, David, and Dennis, Jack.
1969 *Children in the Political System.* New York: McGraw-Hill.

Easton, David, and Hess, Arnold.
1962 "The Child's Political World," *Midwest Journal of Political Science*, August, 6: 229–246

Edelman, Murray.
1964 *The Symbolic Uses of Politics.* Urbana: University of Illinois Press.
1971 *Politics as Symbolic Action.* Chicago: Markham.
1975 *Political Language.* New York: Academic.

Elazar, Daniel.
1972 *American Federalism.* New York: Thomas Y. Crowell.

Erikson, Robert, Luttbeg, Norman, and Tedin, Kent.
1980 *American Public Opinion: Its Origins, Content, and Impact.* New York: Wiley.

Fainstein, Norman, and Fainstein, Susan.
1974 *Urban Political Movements.* Englewood Cliffs, N.J.: Prentice-Hall.

Fenton, John.
1966 *Midwest Politics.* New York: Holt.

Firth, Raymond.
1973 *Symbols: Public and Private.* Ithaca: Cornell University Press.

Flanigan, William, and Zingale, Nancy.
1979 *The Political Behavior of the American Electorate*. Boston: Allyn and Bacon.
Form, William, and Huber, Joan.
1969 "Ideological Beliefs on the Distribution of Power in the United States," *American Sociological Review*, February, 34: 19–31.
Friedman, H. P., and Rubin, J.
1967 "Some Invariant Criteria for Grouping Data," *Journal of the American Statistical Association*, December, 62, 1159–1178.
Gamson, William.
1968 *Power and Discontent*. Homewood, Ill.: Dorsey.
Geertz, Clifford.
1964 "Ideology as a Cultural System," in David Apter (ed.), *Ideology and Discontent*. New York: Free Press.
Gilmour, Richard, and Lamb, Richard.
1975 *Political Alienation in Contemporary America*. New York: St Martin's.
Ginsberg, Benjamin, and Weissberg, Robert.
1978 "Elections and the Mobilization of Popular Support," *American Journal of Political Science*, February, 22: 31–55.
Graber, Doris.
1976 *Verbal Behavior and Politics*. Urbana: University of Illinois Press.
1980 *Mass Media and American Politics*. Washington, D.C.: Congressional Quarterly Press.
Greeley, Andrew.
1970 "Turning Off 'The People,'" *The New Republic*, June 27, 174: 14–16.
Greenstein, Fred.
1965 *Children and Politics*. New Haven: Yale University Press.
Gusfield, Joseph.
1963 *Symbolic Crusade*. Urbana: University of Illinois Press.
Hacker, Andrew.
1971 *The End of the American Era*. New York: Atheneum.
Hall, Peter, and Hewitt, John.
1970 "The Quasi-Theory of Communication and the Measurement of Dissent," *Social Problems*, Summer, 18: 17–27.
Handel, Gerald, and Rainwater, Lee.
1965 "Persistence and Change in Working-Class Life Style," in Arthur Shostak and William Gomberg (eds.), *Blue-Collar World*. Englewood Cliffs, N.J.: Prentice-Hall.
Harris, Louis.
1973 *The Anguish of Social Change*. New York: Norton.
1974 *Confidence and Concern: Citizens View American Government*. Cleveland: Regal Books.
Harrison, Tubby.
1980 "Impact Polling: Feedback for a Winning Strategy," *Campaigns and Elections*, Spring, 1: 8–13.
Hartz, Louis.
1955 *The Liberal Tradition in America*. New York: Harcourt, Brace & Jovanovich.

Hess, Robert, and Torney, Judith.
 1967 *The Development of Political Attitudes in Children*. Chicago: Aldine.
Hill, David, and Luttbeg, Norman.
 1980 *Trends in American Electoral Behavior*. Itasca, Ill.: Peacock.
Himmelstrand, Ulf.
 1960 *Social Pressures, Attitudes and Democratic Processes*. Stockholm: Alm-
    quist and Wiksell.
Hofstadter, Richard.
 1958 *American Political Tradition*. New York: Vintage.
 1967 *The Paranoid Style in American Politics*. New York: Vintage.
Holsti, Ole.
 1967 "Cognitive Dynamics and Images of the Enemy: Dulles and Russia," in
    David Finlay et al. (eds.), *Enemies in Politics*. Chicago: Rand McNally.
Inglehart, Ronald.
 1977 *The Silent Revolution: Changing Values and Political Styles among West-
    ern Publics*. Princeton, N.J.: Princeton University Press.
Jackson, Thomas, and Marcus, George.
 1975 "Political Competence and Ideological Restraint," *Social Science Re-
    search*, June 4: 93–111.
James, Dorothy.
 1972 *Poverty, Politics and Change*. Englewood Cliffs, N.J.: Prentice-Hall.
Janis, Irving.
 1972 *Victims of Groupthink*. Boston: Houghton Mifflin.
Jaros, Dean, Hirsch, Herbert, and Fleron, Fred.
 1968 "The Malevolent Leader: Political Socialization in an American Sub-
    culture," *American Political Science Review*, June, 62: 564–575.
Jennings, M. Kent, and Niemi, Richard.
 1968 "The Transmission of Political Values from Parents to Child," *American
    Political Science Review*, March, 62: 169–184.
 1975 "Continuity and Change in Political Orientations: A Longitudinal Study
    of Two Generations," *American Political Science Review*, December, 69:
    1316–1335.
Kahn, Robert, Gutek, Barbara, Barton, Eugenia, and Katz, Daniel.
 1975 "Americans Love Their Bureaucrats," *Psychology Today*, June, 9: 66–71.
Katz, Elihu, and Lazarsfeld, Paul.
 1955 *Personal Influence*. Glencoe Ill.: Free Press.
Kautsky, John.
 1964 "Myth, Self-Fulfilling Prophecy and Symbolic Reassurance in the East-
    West Conflict," *Journal of Conflict Resolution*, March, 9: 1–17.
Kelman, Herbert.
 1969 "Patterns of Personal Involvement in the National System: A Socio-
    Psychological Analysis of Political Legitimacy," in James Rosenau (ed.),
    International Politics and Foreign Policy. New York: Free Press.
Kessel, John.
 1980 *Presidential Campaign Politics*. Homewood, Ill.: Dorsey.
Key, V. O.
 1949 *Southern Politics*. New York: Knopf.
 1961 *Public Opinion in American Democracy*. New York: Knopf.

Knoke, David, and Felson, Richard.
1974 "Ethnic Stratification and Political Cleavage in the United States, 1952–58," *American Journal of Sociology*, May, 80: 630–642.
Knouse, David.
1971 *Language, Labeling, and Attribution*. New York: General Learning Press.
Krasnow, Erwin, and Longley, Lawrence.
1978 *The Politics of Broadcast Regulation*. New York: St. Martin's.
Kuhn, Thomas.
1970 *The Structure of Scientific Revolutions*. Chicago: University of Chicago Press.
Ladd Everett.
1982 *Where Have All the Voters Gone?* New York: Norton.
Lamb, Karl.
1974 *As Orange Goes*. New York: Norton.
Lane, Robert.
1962 *Political Ideology*. New York: Free Press.
1969 *Political Thinking and Consciousness*. Chicago: Markham.
Lasswell, Harold.
1960 *Psychopathology and Politics*. New York: Viking.
1965 *World Politics and Personal Insecurity*. New York: Free Press.
Lasswell, Harold, and Kaplan, Abraham.
1950 *Power and Society*. New Haven: Yale University Press.
Lasswell, Harold, Leites, Nathan, and Associates.
1965 *The Language of Politics*. Cambridge: MIT Press.
Lau, Richard, Brown, Thad, and Sears, David.
1978 "Self-Interest and Civilians' Attitudes toward the Vietnam War," *Public Opinion Quarterly*, 42: 464–483.
Lawrence, David.
1976 "Procedural Norms and Tolerance: A Reassessment," *American Political, Science Review*, March, 70: 80–100.
Lemon, Richard.
1970 *The Troubled American*. New York: Clarion Books.
Lewis, Michael.
1970 "The Negro Protest in Urban America," in Joseph Gusfield (ed.), *Protest, Reform and Revolt*. New York: Wiley.
Lipset, Seymour Martin.
1955 "The Radical Right: A Problem for America Democracy," *British Journal of Sociology*, June, 6: 176–209.
1980 *The First New Nation*. New York: Norton.
1981 *Political Man*. Baltimore: Johns Hopkins University Press.
Lipset, Seymour, and Raab, Earl.
1979 *The Politics of Unreason*. Chicago: University of Chicago Press.
Lipset, Seymour, and Schneider, William.
1977 "America's Schizophrenia in Achieving Equality," *Los Angeles Times*, July 31, 1977, Part IV, pp. 1, 6.
Litt, Edgar.
1970 *Ethnic Politics in America*. Glenview, Ill.: Scott, Foresman.

Lowi, Theodore.
  1979   *The End of Liberalism*. New York: Norton.
Lubell, Samuel.
  1971   *The Hidden Crisis in American Politics*. New York: Norton.
  1973   *The Future While It Happened*. New York: Norton.
Manheim, Jarol.
  1982   *The Politics Within*. Second Edition. New York: Longman.
Mann, Michael.
  1970   "The Social Cohesion of Liberal Democracy," *American Sociological Review*, June, 35: 524–537.
Margolis, Michael.
  1977   "From Confusion to Confusion: Issues and the American Voter (1956–1972)," *American Political Science Review*, March, 71: 31–43.
Mayhew, David.
  1974   *Congress: The Electoral Connection*. New Haven: Yale University Press.
McClosky, Herbert.
  1964   "Consensus and Ideology in American Politics," *American Political Science Review*, June, 58: 361–379.
McClosky, Herbert, Hoffman, Paul, and O'Hara, Rosemary.
  1960   "Issue Conflict and Consensus among Party Leaders and Followers," *American Political Science Review*, June, 65: 406–427.
Mead, George H.
  1934   *Mind, Self and Society*. Chicago: University of Chicago Press.
Merelman, Richard.
  1966   "Learning and Legitimacy," *American Political Science Review*, September, 60: 548–561.
  1969   "The Dramaturgy of Politics," *Sociological Quarterly*, Spring, 10: 216–241.
Merriam, Charles.
  1964   *Political Power*. New York: Collier.
Miller, Arthur.
  1974   "Political Issues and Trust in Government, 1964–1970," *American Political Science Review*, September, 68: 951–972
Miller, S. M., and Riessman, Frank.
  1965   "The Working Class Subculture," in Arthur Shostak and William Gomberg (eds.), *Blue-Collar World*. Englewood Cliffs, N.J.: Prentice-Hall.
Miller, Warren, and Levitin, Teresa.
  1976   *Leadership and Change: The New Politics and the American Electorate*. Cambridge: Winthrop.
Mills, C. Wright.
  1956   *White Collar*. New York: Oxford University Press.
Mitchell, William.
  1962   *The American Polity*. New York: Free Press.
Monroe, Alan.
  1975   *Public Opinion in America*. New York: Dodd, Mead.
Mueller, John.
  1973   *War, Presidents and Public Opinion*. New York: Wiley.

Muller, Edward.
1970 "Correlates and Consequences of Beliefs in the Legitimacy of Regime Structures," *Midwest Journal of Political Science*, August, 14: 392–412.
Murphy, Walter, Tanenhaus, Joseph, and Kastner, Donald.
1973 "Public Evaluations of Constitutional Courts: Alternative Explanations," *Sage Professional Papers in Comparative Politics*, 4, 01–045, Beverly Hills, Cal.: Sage.
Nadel, Mark.
1971 *The Politics of Consumer Protection*. Indianpolis: Bobbs-Merrill.
Newcombe, Theodore, Turner, Ralph, and Converse, Philip.
1965 *Social Psychology*. New York: Holt.
Nie, Norman, and Andersen, Kristi.
1974 "Mass Belief Systems Revisited: Political Change and Attitude Structure," *Journal of Politics*, August, 36: 540–591.
Nie, Norman, Verba, Sidney, and Petrocik, John.
1980 *The Changing American Voter*. Cambridge: Harvard University Press.
Nimmo, Dan.
1974 *Popular Images of Politics*. Englewood Cliffs, N.J.: Prentice-Hall.
1978 *Political Communication and Public Opinion in America*. Santa Monica: Goodyear.
Nimmo, Dan, and Coombs, James.
1980 *Subliminal Politics*. Englewood Cliffs, N.J.: Prentice-Hall.
Olson, Mancur.
1965 *The Logic of Collective Action*. New York: Schocken.
Oskamp, Stuart.
1977 *Attitudes and Opinions*. Englewood Cliffs, N.J.: Prentice-Hall.
Parenti, Michael.
1967 "Ethnic Politics and the Persistence of Ethnic Identifications," *American Political Science Review*, September, 61: 717–726.
Percheron, Annick.
1973 "Political Vocabulary and Ideological Proximity in French Children," in Jack Dennis (ed.), *Socialization to Politics*. New York: Wiley.
Pettigrew, Thomas.
1958 "Personality and Sociocultural Factors in Intergroup Attitudes: A Cross-National Comparison," *Journal of Conflict Resolution*, March, 2: 29–42.
1971 *Racially Separate or Together?* New York: McGraw-Hill.
Pierce, John.
1970 "Party Identification and the Changing Role of Ideology in American Politics," *Midwest Journal of Political Science*, February, 14: 25–42.
1975 "The Relationship between Linkage Salience and Linkage Organization in Mass Belief Systems," *Public Opinion Quarterly*, Spring, 39: 102–110.
Polanyi, Michael.
1958 *Personal Knowledge*. Chicago: University of Chicago Press.
Prothro, James, and Grigg, Charles.
1960 "Fundamental Principles of Democracy: Bases of Agreement and Disagreement," *Journal of Politics*, May, 22: 278–294.
Pye, Lucien.
1962 *Politics, Personality and Nation Building: Burma's Search for Identity*. New Haven: Yale University Press.

RePass, David.
  1971 "Issue Salience and Party Choice," *American Political Science Review*, June, 65: 389–400.
  1976 "Comment: Political Methodologies in Disarray: Some Alternative Interpretations of the 1972 Election," *American Political Science Review*, September, 70: 814–831.
Rokeach, Milton.
  1960 *The Open and Closed Mind*. New York: Basic Books.
  1968 *Beliefs, Attitudes and Values*. San Francisco: Jossey Bass.
  1973 *The Nature of Human Values*. New York: Basic Books.
Rosenbaum, Walter.
  1975 *Political Culture*. New York: Praeger.
Rosenberg, Milton, Verba, Sidney, and Converse, Philip.
  1970 *Vietnam and the Silent Majority: The Dove's Guide*. New York: Harper & Row.
Rotunda, Ronald.
  1968 "The 'Liberal' Label: Roosevelt's Capture of a Symbol," *Public Policy*, 17: 377–408.
Rusk, Jerrold, and Weissberg, Herbert.
  1972 "Perceptions of Presidential Candidates: Implications for Electoral Change," *Midwest Journal of Political Science*, August, 16: 388–410.
Sale, Kirkpatrick.
  1975 *The Power Shift*. New York: Norton.
Sapir, Edward.
  1934 "Symbolism," *Encyclopedia of the Social Sciences*, 14: 492–495.
Sartori, Giovanni.
  1969 "Politics, Ideology and Belief Systems," *American Political Science Review*, June, 63: 398–411.
Scammon, Richard, and Wattenberg, Ben.
  1970 *The Real Majority*. New York: Coward-McCann.
Schmitt, Raymond, and Grupp, Stanley.
  1976 "Resources as a Symbol," *Social Science Quarterly*, September, 57: 324–338.
Scott, James.
  1968 *The Political Ideology in Malaysia*. New Haven: Yale University Press.
Searing, Donald, Schwartz, Joel, and Lind, Alden.
  1973 "The Structuring Principle: Political Socialization and Belief Systems," *American Political Science Review*, June, 67: 415–432.
Sears, David, Hensler, Carl, and Speer, Leslie.
  1979 "Whites' Opposition to 'Busing': Self-Interest or Symbolic Politics," *American Political Science Review*, June, 73: 369–384.
Sears, David, Lau, Richard, Tyler, Tom, and Allen, Harris.
  1980 "Self-Interest vs. Symbolic Politics in Policy Attitudes and Presidential Voting," *American Political Science Review*, September, 74: 670–684.
Sears, David, Tyler, Tom, Citrin, Jack, and Kinder, Donald.
  1978 "Political System Support and Public Response to the Energy Crisis," *American Political Science Review*, February, 22: 56–82.
Sears, David, and Whitney, Richard.
  1973 *Political Persuasion*. Morristown, N.J.: General Learning Press.

Shingles, Richard.
  1981 "Black Consciousness and Political Participation," *American Political Science Review*, March, 75: 76–91.
Shostak, Arthur.
  1969 *Blue Collar Life*. New York: Random House.
Sigel, Roberta, and Hoskin, Marilyn.
  1977 "Affect for Government and Its Relation to Policy Output among Adolescents," *American Journal of Political Science*, February, 21: 111–134.
Skolnick, Eugene.
  1969 *Politics of Protest*. Washington, D.C.: Government Printing Office.
Smith, Don.
  1972 "'Dark Areas of Ignorance' Revisited: Current Knowledge about Asian Affairs," in Dan Nimmo and Charles Bonjean (eds.), *Political Attitudes and Public Opinion*. New York: David McKay.
Smith, Eric.
  1980 "The Levels of Conceptualization: False Measures of Ideological Sophistication," *American Political Science Review*, September, 74: 685–696.
Smith, M. Brewster, Bruner, Jerome, and White, Ralph.
  1964 *Opinions and Personality*. New York: Wiley.
Stimson, James.
  1975 "Belief Systems: Constraint, Complexity, and the 1972 Election," *American Journal of Political Science*, August, 19: 393–417.
Stokes, Donald.
  1966 "Some Dynamic Elements of Contests for the Presidency," *American Political Science Review*, March, 60: 19–28.
Strouse, James.
  1975 *The Mass Media, Public Opinion, and Public Policy Analysis*. Columbus, Ohio: Merrill.
Sullivan, John, Piereson, James, and Marcus, George.
  1978 "Ideological Constraint in the Mass Public: A Methodological Critique and Some New Findings," *American Journal of Political Science*, May, 22: 233–249.
  1979 "An Alternative Conceptualization of Political Tolerance," *American Political Science Review*, September, 73: 781–794.
Tedin, Kent.
  1974 "The Influence of Parents on the Political Attitudes of Adolescents," *American Political Science Review*, December, 68: 1579–1592.
Tichenor, Philip, Donohoe, George, and Olien, Clarice.
  1980 *Community Conflict and the Press*. Beverly Hills, Cal.: Sage.
Tribe, Laurence H.
  1972 "Policy Science: Analysis or Ideology?" *Philosophy and Public Affairs*, Fall, 2: 66–110.
Truman, David.
  1951 *The Governmental Process*. New York: Knopf.
Verba, Sidney, and Nie, Norman.
  1972 *Participation in America*. New York: Harper & Row.
Warner, W. Lloyd.
  1959 *The Living and the Dead*. New Haven: Yale University Press.

Watts, William, and Free, Lloyd, (eds.).
 1973 *State of the Union.* New York: Universe.
Weissberg, Robert.
 1974 *Political Learning, Political Choice and Democratic Citizenship.* Englewood Cliffs, N.J.: Prentice-Hall.
Westie, Frank.
 1965 "The American Dilemma: An Empirical Test," *American Sociological Review*, August, 30: 527–538.
White, Leslie.
 1949 *The Science of Culture.* New York: Grove Press.
Whyte, William.
 1956 *The Organization Man.* Garden City, N.Y.: Doubleday.
Willer, David.
 1967 *Scientific Sociology.* Englewood Cliffs, N. J.: Prentice-Hall.
Williams, Robin.
 1970 *American Society: A Sociological Interpretation.* New York: Knopf.
Wilson, James, and Banfield, Edward.
 1964 "Public Regardingness as a Value Premise in Voting Behavior," *American Political Science Review,* December, 58: 876–887.
 1971 "Political Ethos Revisited," *American Political Science Review,* December, 65: 1048–1062.
Wolin, Sheldon.
 1968 "Paradigms and Political Theories," in P. King and B. C. Parekh (eds.), *Politics and Experience.* Cambridge: Cambridge University Press.
Zald, Meyer, and Ash, Roberta.
 1966 "Social Movement Organizations: Growth, Decay and Change," *Social Forces,* March, 44: 327–340.
Zurcher, Louis, and Kirkpatrick, R. George.
 1976 *Citizens for Decency.* Austin: University of Texas Press.

Index

Feldman, Stanley, 146
Felson, Richard, 126
Fenton, John, 104, 105
Firth, Raymond, 28, 30, 31, 33, 34
Flanigan, William, 128
Ford, Gerald, 75, 87
Form, William, 94
Free, Lloyd, 2, 5, 26
Freedom, 34–35, 39, 61, 76, 91,
   105, 118, 119, 137
See also Liberty
Friedman, H.P., 139

Gallup, George, 6, 7, 8, 19, 20, 92
Gamson, William, 118
Gay rights, 18
Geertz, Clifford, 37
Gilmour, Richard, 11
Ginsburg, Benjamin, 21
Graber, Doris, 12, 61, 83
Gray, Virginia, 17, 61, 115,
   129–130
Great Society, 31, 79
Greeley, Andrew, 126
Greenfield, Meg, 132
Greenstein, Fred, 40
Grigg, Charles, 119
Grupp, Stanley, 47
Gusfield, Joseph, 114, 120,
   121–122

Hacker, Andrew, 89, 91, 93, 94
Hall, Peter, 120
Handel, Gerald, 124
Harris, Louis, 14, 91, 95, 100, 110
Harrison, Tubby, 153
Hartz, Louis, 85
Hess, Robert, 35–36, 39, 40, 52, 53
Hewitt, John, 120
Hill, David, 95
Himmelstrand, Ulf, 59
Hobson, Timothy, 87
Hofstadter, Richard, 34, 114
Holsti, Ole, 131

Honesty in government, 14
Hoover, Herbert, 54, 83
Hoover, J. Edgar, 77
Hortatory language, 66
Hoskin, Marilyn, 15
Huber, Joan, 94
Human nature: conceptions of, 44,
   45, 88–89
Human rights, 69, 132
Humphrey, Hubert, 3, 5

Ideological: as a mode of symbolic
   attachment, 58–60, 62, 64, 65
Independents, 148–150
Individualism, 89, 90, 91, 94, 96,
   97, 106
Individualistic subculture, 104, 106
Inglehart, Ronald, 109, 128
Instrumental behavior, 58, 59, 65,
   69, 145
Interest group liberalism, 114, 117
Iranian crisis, 7–9, 15, 25
Irrationality, 1, 148
Issue publics, 64

Jackson, Thomas, 139
James, Dorothy, 26
Janis, Irving, 131
Jaros, Dean, 107
Jennings, M. Kent, 52, 128
Johnson, Lyndon, 2, 31, 71, 76, 79

Kahn, Robert, 11, 26
Kaplan, Abraham, 1
Katz, Elihu, 12
Kautsky, John, 1
Kelman, Herbert, 113
Kennedy, Edward, 6–9, 66, 77
Kennedy, John F., 2, 20
Kessel, John, 139
Key, V. O., 75, 105, 173
Kirkpatrick, R. George, 89, 114,
   117
Knoke, David, 126
Knouse, David, 70, 71, 73